T0272545

Objects of Love and Regret

Objects of Love and Regret

A BROOKLYN STORY

Richard Rabinowitz

The Belknap Press of
Harvard University Press

Cambridge, Massachusetts
London, England

2022

Copyright © 2022 by Richard Rabinowitz

All rights reserved

Printed in the United States of America

First printing

Library of Congress Cataloging-in-Publication Data

Names: Rabinowitz, Richard, author.

Title: Objects of love and regret : a Brooklyn story / Richard Rabinowitz.

Description: Cambridge, Massachusetts : The Belknap Press
of Harvard University Press, 2022. | Includes bibliographical references. |

Identifiers: LCCN 2022001814 | ISBN 9780674268593 (cloth)

Subjects: LCSH: Rabinowitz family. | Jews—Material culture—
New York (State)—New York. | Jews—New York (State)—New York—
History—20th century. | Jews—New York (State)—New York—Social life and
customs—20th century. | Immigrants—New York (State)—New York—History—
20th century. | Brooklyn (New York, N.Y.)—History—20th century. |
Brooklyn (New York, N.Y.)—Social life and customs—20th century.

Classification: LCC E184.36.M38 R33 2022 |
DDC 974.700492/4—dc23/eng/20220217

LC record available at https://lccn.loc.gov/2022001814

For Beverly

Contents

Rabinowitz Family

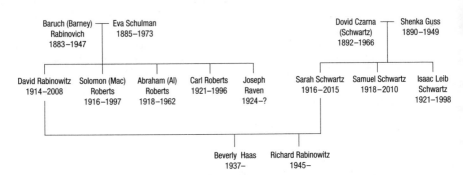

Baruch (Barney) Rabinovich 1883–1947 —— Eva Schulman 1885–1973

Dovid Czarna (Schwartz) 1892–1966 —— Shenka Guss 1890–1949

David Rabinowitz 1914–2008

Solomon (Mac) Roberts 1916–1997

Abraham (Al) Roberts 1918–1962

Carl Roberts 1921–1996

Joseph Raven 1924–?

Sarah Schwartz 1916–2015

Samuel Schwartz 1918–2010

Isaac Leib Schwartz 1921–1998

Beverly Haas 1937–

Richard Rabinowitz 1945–

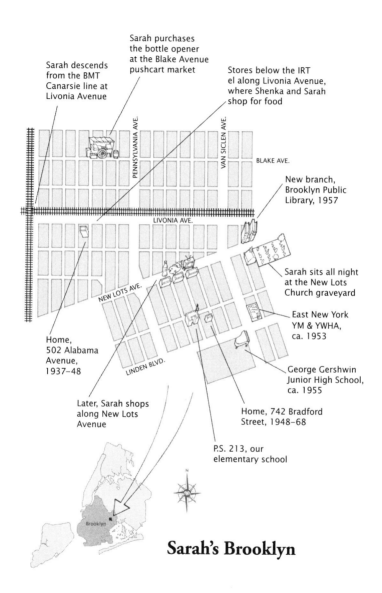

Sarah purchases
the bottle opener
at the Blake Avenue
pushcart market

Sarah descends
from the BMT
Canarsie line at
Livonia Avenue

Stores below the IRT
el along Livonia Avenue,
where Shenka and Sarah
shop for food

PENNSYLVANIA AVE.

VAN SICLEN AVE.

BLAKE AVE.

New branch,
Brooklyn Public
Library, 1957

LIVONIA AVE.

Sarah sits all night
at the New Lots
Church graveyard

NEW LOTS AVE.

East New York
YM & YWHA,
ca. 1953

Home,
502 Alabama
Avenue,
1937–48

LINDEN BLVD.

George Gershwin
Junior High School,
ca. 1955

Later, Sarah shops
along New Lots
Avenue

Home, 742 Bradford
Street, 1948–68

P.S. 213, our
elementary school

N

Brooklyn

Sarah's Brooklyn

Objects of Love and Regret

Objects at Hand, Objects in Memory

Our lives are a dance with history. Most of us dance first as a family, then later as a couple, or as a town or nation. Often we follow the choreography of others, sometimes we add a step or two of our own. History—the experience of those who came before us—is within us and around us, inescapable. Remembered, recorded or not, forgotten, retrieved or not, we rent rooms in History's house for a time, and then we are gone.

When my mother died in November 2015, midway through her 100th year, I was resigned to her loss, but I hated that she was gone. As always, I was the designated family eulogist. It was not a tragic occasion. Sarah Schwartz Rabinowitz's eventful life came to an uncomfortable but not terribly painful final year. She remained in her own home, evading hospital wards and the assisted (which she called "assistant") living places she despised. She was accompanied by round-the-clock attendants (whom she doggedly taught to cook and eat healthier meals) and by the visits of her children and neighbors. Her funeral in Brooklyn gathered grandchildren, nieces and nephews, and the friends of her children. She had outlived almost all of her contemporaries in Florida.

I thought I knew her, and my eulogy began in a relaxed voice. Mom had no great public accomplishments to trumpet. Perhaps her most amazing achievement was to share the matrimonial state with my father for seventy-two years. He was often difficult. I joked that not only had I nominated her for the Nobel Peace Prize several times, but that I had suggested to the committee in Oslo that they rename the award for Sarah Rabinowitz. From the podium, I recounted my mother's various excellences—her talents as a daughter, a sister, a wife, a mother, a friend, and a neighbor. But the longer I spoke the more uncertain I became. Not to doubt her virtues but to wonder whether I was asking the right question. *Who was Sarah for herself? What did she want out of life? How would she have characterized herself?* And where did she find that strength, as a new American, without much schooling or guidance from elders or from peers more experienced in New York, to navigate and then to anchor the transition of her whole family—parents, husband, siblings, and children—in this difficult place, and during some of the worst moments in our nation's history, the Depression and World War II? *Did I really know her, or did I simply take her presence in my life for granted?*

All through the week of sitting *shiva,* the seven-day period of mourning for Jews, our family and friends shared affectionate stories of Sarah. But my questions gnawed at me. As I struggled to find the logic of her long-lived purposefulness, I joined my sister, Beverly, in Florida, where we emptied out Mom's drawers and cabinets over the following week. In her kitchen drawer, I rediscovered a wooden-handled bottle opener, its original green paint worn by many years of use. It felt familiar, as if I was shaking hands with an old friend. My index finger pressed on the prying hook, my thumb under the lifting point, and my other fingers embraced the wood shaft. It was warm in my palm. Holding it in my hand, I recalled the story Mom had told me, thirty-odd years before, of purchasing it on a Friday afternoon at a pushcart in the Blake Avenue outdoor market in Brooklyn. Sarah, just turning eighteen, was coming home from a week of work at a garment factory. She wanted a little something to bring home as a Shabbos-eve present for her mother. "Your *bubbe* [grandmother]," she added, beginning to tear up, "always worked so hard. Twenty cents, it cost me. The man wanted twenty-five."

The story was a puzzle, and I could not stop thinking about it. What kind of a present is a bottle opener? Why was it such a poignant memory in her life? What did it say about these two women? I always knew that Mom was extremely close to her mother. This story was a typical one of hers, inflected with a little pride *(I was a considerate daughter; it was with money I had earned myself; I knew it was the sort of thing that Mama would appreciate)* and a lot of pain and guilt *(I owed everything to her; I couldn't do enough to overcome the difficulties of her making a new home in America, given her frailties; I miss her still).*

After we had closed up Mom's apartment, I took the green-handled opener home with me to Brooklyn. It would be one of the tchotchkes on my desk, along with a Jackie Robinson baseball card, a ceramic whale (I am a devoted Melvillean), and a postcard depicting Michel de Montaigne's tower in southwest France. It sat there for a week or two. One afternoon, when the late winter sun seemed to spotlight the blade of the opener, I noticed that it bore a faint inscription. It read, ".. LUND CO. PAT. NOV. 7 '33. MADE IN U.S.A." I did the newly normal thing and went right to Google. I learned it was a collector's item, with similar ones available on eBay. One blogger described it as the best tool he ever owned.

More important, I discovered that the opener had been made by the Edlund Company of Burlington, Vermont, still in business, and that it was designed by the owner, Henry J. Edlund. In ten minutes, computer searches on Ancestry and the US Patent Office brought to light the arc of Henry Edlund's whole life. A Swedish lad, arriving at age seventeen in New York in 1891, Edlund had chalked up more than a half-dozen patents in his lifetime, become a naturalized citizen, married, joined the business elite of Burlington in his late forties, and died in 1937. I was thrilled to discover that the patent date of the bottle opener, November 7, 1933, dovetailed so closely with my mother's purchase, which must have been in the spring of 1934.

Over the next few weeks, I had what can only be called a "history high." I was intoxicated by discovering more and more about the bottle opener, its particular history, and its place in the history of the country to which my bubbe Shenka and my mother came in 1928. From a table in a study at the 42nd Street research division of the New York Public Library, I learned that Edlund's was only one of dozens of American companies patenting and producing housewares that were transforming the American kitchen and household life. I scoured a whole decade of *House Furnishing Journal,* the trade magazine of the gadgets business. I talked with former owners and engineers to understand the technically innovative manufacturing process employed by Edlund. I discovered that my little bottle opener was perhaps included in a 1938 exhibition at New York's Museum of Modern Art on "Useful Household Objects under $5.00."

A local historian in Vermont helped me identify the individual metalworker on Henry Edlund's shop floor, Adelard Charette, who was most likely responsible for turning out my opener. I traced Charette's family history to a tiny village in Quebec and tracked the emigration of many of its people to New England mill towns like Burlington. I traveled to Vermont and met Charette's grandson at the family home, there to discover that Adelard's woodworking table still occupied a prominent place in the basement almost a century after he acquired it.

Exhilarating as this Vermont excursion was in itself, every discovery also added sound, color, and light to my image of Shenka and Sarah's new American world. Like most of us, I had visualized my family through the narrow lens of domestic life—sitting around the dinner table, doing chores, packed into a car setting out on vacation. My immersion in a Vermont family's story enriched my idea of the Schwartzes and Rabinowitzes as Americans. My family were actors in a much larger story—the transformation of the American economy, social system, politics, and material culture in the 1920s and 1930s. Like the Charettes, my family—my grandparents Dovid and Shenka Schwartz, my mother, Sarah, and my uncles Sam and Isaac—were factory workers and consumers, producing and purchasing in the same national marketplace. They voted in the same presidential elections and for members of the same national legislature. Each family was tightly bound to its immigrant community. Each experienced similar processes of feeling excluded and included by the way America privileged longer-settled elites and marginalized its nonwhite populations.

I kept returning with new thoughts to the tale Mom told about purchasing the bottle opener. Telling the story had brought Mom to tears. It brought her to a painful rendering of the whole arc of my bubbe's "hard" life. This was obviously no trivial event. Why was it so memorable?

Strange as it sounds, Sarah had honored her mother—with a kitchen implement. She could easily have used a moment during lunchtime in the Garment District to buy a scarf, a blouse, or a piece of jewelry to bring as a present. This mother-daughter relationship, it was obvious, was rooted in the kitchen, in their love of that part of their life. And then, she could have brought it home on a Tuesday. Why choose the most sacred moment of the week, when employment and school and play were suspended for the Jewish Sabbath?

And, why, if Shabbos is a *family* event, did Sarah buy a present for her mother? She was just as deeply attached to her father and brothers. And what else was in Sarah's mind? She must already have known that the opener would enable them to buy and use more nationally produced and distributed ingredients, packaged in bottles and cans. Did she feel that she would be even more "American" if her household could own these icons of the new world, these embodiments of the well designed, the modern, and the convenient? And yet, she would not yield her hardheadedness to this enthusiasm. Recall that Sarah had haggled over the price with the pushcart man.

As I examined the many dimensions of this moment, I hoped that it might unlock an understanding of Sarah's singularity. That had become my mission. Hers was a history braided of three strands—the "American story," exploring how she adapted herself and her world to the opportunities and dangers of a new country, the "Schwartz story," explaining how she grew from dependent daughter into the solid foundation for everyone around her, and finally, the third, "Sarah's own story," tracing her inward pilgrimage through a thicket of fears toward the peace, beauty, and order she craved. Parallel to hers, of course, was a similarly multifaceted "Dave Rabinowitz story."

I had prepared for this project by a half-century's professional career inventing new history museums and curating exhibitions in every corner of the United States, most of them focusing on the everyday lives of ordinary people—tenement dwellers on New York's Lower East Side, Chinese-American salmon butchers in Puget Sound, enslaved families on Louisiana cotton plantations, and other dramatic examples of Americans swept up in the tides of history. My quest was the microhistory of these lives, the sensory, immediate, tangible, material, intimate, and local dimensions of their experience. I looked for the marks of history on the most minute textures of everyday life. Others could undertake the biographies of the great and the famous, and especially of those who left voluminous diaries and stacks of correspondence. I sought out personal narratives written with pots and pans in a kitchen, with tools on the shop floor, rather than with pen and ink in a library.

I was always interested in people like my mother and grandmother, who expressed their creativity with skills other than literacy, public leadership, or financial ambition. But I had never examined my own family history so intently. I started hunting for everything I could find about the family and especially about the years before I was born—citizenship papers, ship manifests, census returns, wedding photographs, and family snapshots. I mapped the migrations of family members from Europe to New York and located their places of residence and work in the metropolitan area. In midnight phone calls, I bothered my cousins for memories. Most important, I enlisted the help of my sister, who is eight years older than I. She can vividly recall my maternal grandparents, who lived one floor above my parents in the same apartment building in the East New York section of Brooklyn. Beverly and I shared what we knew about the lives of our parents and grandparents—at work and at home, with family and friends, in the realms of politics and religion.

No standard narrative can satisfactorily account for the diversity of the more than two million Eastern European Jewish immigrants to America. Some, like Barney and Eva Rabinowitz, my father's parents, came from cities like Odesa on the Black Sea, the second-largest port in the Russian Empire. Others, like Dovid and Shenka Schwartz and my mother herself, emigrated from a small *shtetl* (or market town) in rural Poland. The Rabinowitzes arrived around 1905, the Schwartzes some twenty years later—each, therefore, to a radically different America and New York City. Barney Rabinowitz was barely literate and totally dismissive of religion and politics. Shenka and Dovid Schwartz, my maternal grandparents, even without much schooling, read avidly and argued about everything. Barney brought his skills as a cooper and always found work repairing barrels for the herring trade between New York and the North Sea. Dovid Schwartz, however, never stopped struggling to stitch together weeks of employment as a presser in the garment trade. His wife, Shenka, was a superb *balabusta* (homemaker) who cast a cold eye on American capitalism and the exploitation of the working class. Eva Rabinowitz, by contrast, had commerce in her blood and spent decades peddling all sorts of merchandise on city streets and in tenement hallways.

That's a lot of diversity, just in my own family. The search for a *typical* life history is fruitless. But once I had settled on a basic time-line and framework for the family's history, my questions were quite ordinary. What was my parents' childhood like? How did they meet and decide to get married? What kind of work provided the family's livelihood at different moments? How was my family affected by major public events—the passage of immigration restrictions in the 1920s, the Depression, the New Deal, World War II, the postwar economic boom, the urban unrest, civil rights agitation, and countercultural rebellion of the 1960s, the inflation shocks of the 1970s, and so on? You might ask the same questions about your own family.

My answers to these questions, I knew, could only come by researching and imagining, in as much detail as possible, the actualities of their everyday lives, moment by moment. That green-handled bottle opener magically pried open more than a beer bottle. It brought me into the tenement kitchen of my grandparents in the East New York section of Brooklyn in 1934. It invited me to sit down for their Shabbos dinner and encouraged me to eavesdrop on the conversation of family members. I became totally absorbed in the minutiae of that evening. Where did Bubbe obtain the ingredients for the meal? How did five years in the United States alter how and what she prepared? How much of the traditional Jewish ritual did they perform? What else did they talk about? Politics? The weather? School?

Beverly is gifted with our mother's memory for sensory details, for atmospherics as well as actions and attitudes. A witness at many meals like that, she can remember every piece of furniture and every dish on the table. My contribution was to recall each person's turn of phrase and habits of mind—my Uncle Isaac's chuckle and warm sympathy (once he could identify the underdog in the story), my Uncle Sam's darker cynicism and gibes, the warm smile of my *zayde* (grandfather). I set out with a passion to research and document the setting for the story. I tracked down photos of my grandparents' apartment building in the New York City Municipal Archives. From my work at the Lower East Side Tenement Museum I knew how the apartment's rooms were laid out and furnished. From other memoirs and public reports, as well as family stories, I could make educated guesses about my grandfather's and mother's work in the garment industry and my uncles' schoolwork, politics, and social interests. Beverly and I constantly worked back and forth from the stories we had heard, the elements of daily life that we observed during our childhoods, and the gleanings of my library research, in order to construct a narrative true to all the evidence.

As I might have predicted, given my museum work, I realized that it was the "stuff" around them, the concrete, material circumstances of their ordinary lives, that held the key to their personal stories. It was the consistent way they interacted with objects, with time and space, and with one another that illuminated their fundamental characters. Stories attach themselves to objects. Touch something you have known for a lifetime. Hold it in your hand or in front of your eyes for an uncomfortably long moment. Ask some questions: when was it acquired? How was it used, and by whom? What did it replace? Why has it survived so long? Soon the answers will pour out of it, recollections of events and people almost forgotten or intensely remembered.

The object-story of the bottle opener became my model. Nothing in the written record of my family seemed to elucidate the powerful bond between my mother and my grandmother so well as that gift of the kitchen gadget. As I went back and forth over the family's century-long experience in Europe and America, I searched for other objects and places that might cast light on equally important stories. Each chapter of this book is built around an object-story.

My chosen objects, though often less important in themselves, revealed aspects of life that lay beneath the surface of day-to-day existence. The first present that my father bought for my mother, a bottle of French perfume, taught me how fiercely each of them resisted the stigma of poverty during the Depression. The whistle that the mailman blew when delivering a letter from the War Department in World War II laid bare the raw fear of Mom's life on the Home Front. The aluminum and plastic folding chairs that Dad stashed in the car trunk on outings to state parks spoke of how my family detached itself from city life in the prosperous postwar period.

Objects remind us of the centrality of work in our lives: employment outside the home; the labor of keeping house, raising children, and sustaining the well-being of family members; the unpaid and reciprocal efforts we make for others in our community; and our exertions to fulfill our civic responsibilities. Intellectuals like me tend nowadays to focus more on the preoccupations of our fellow citizens than on their occupations. We are always surveying opinions, tracing ideas, and defining identities. We commonly underestimate the deep currents of thought activated in the process of work, thoughts embedded in action and not in argument. We often fail to explore objects as if they are dense continents of skill—of brawn as well as brain, of hand as well as eye, of performance as well as intention and design.

Objects like these are props in a drama. They evoke actions, and actions speak louder than words. Actions recalled to mind become stories, and stories fix the flow of time. They become the building blocks of life histories. Focusing on such objects has allowed me to slow down and capture more precisely the lineaments of my history. Recovering and retelling a story is like projecting a slow-motion film. I am eager to see every element of every scene, who is stage center and who in the background, how long life's moments actually take. I'm less interested in the object in and of itself, as a curator or art historian might be. I want to watch how people pick something up, what they call it, how they handle and use it, how it calls upon skills possessed and still being developed, how it comes to play a role in the habits of home life, and how it is stored or discarded. Here is a bowl for mixing cake batter. It calls to mind the rituals of my return from school to enjoy Mom's baked goodies and a tall glass of milk. That in turn helps me understand much about my relationship with her. Here is a card table covered with green oilcloth, originally a wedding present to my parents fifteen years earlier. I can precisely remember a day in 1950 when I was five and watched my father dexterously wield his tack hammer to fasten that cover for the table and its chairs. The tack hammer is gone, Dad's toolbox is gone, but the table became a repository of memories. I did my homework there for all of my school years. I typed my college senior essay on it. Over fifty years later my grandchildren string beads, draw new subway maps, play board games, and spill milk on it. The oil and sweat of five generations of fingertips now mingle with that ancient table covering. The objects in my family story do not dwell in glass museum cases. They have interacted with the motions and emotions of my family's history and left their residue in the physical world and in memory.

A thousand barely remembered objects once shared our family space. (I've always had a crazy compulsion to imagine them as animate beings.) As I reconstruct their starring moments in this century-long saga, such things bring back to mind the succession of our surroundings over time. Sometimes, as with the bottle opener, the artifact was a fellow emigrant with the family, moved from one closet or drawer to a packing crate and then to a closet or drawer in another residence. At other times, the object was replaced in the new setting by something pristine, using a newfangled material and technology (plastic, aluminum, electronics, pressed concrete). One after another, these objects reveal how we migrated, redefining who were neighbors and who were strangers, what lay close by and what was remote, what was comforting and what was threatening.

We are feeling creatures, and the things around us also become objects of affection and repulsion. Our emotional lives reverberate with and against their surfaces. The subjective world emerges in its encounter with our objective realities. (The two are ultimately one, I believe.) Tell me the story of an acquisition you cherish, and I will plumb the deepest struggles of your heart. Tell me what thing most reminds you of your loved ones, and I will sketch out the geography of your life's journey. Sit with me in a quiet place that has meaning for you, and memories will swarm around us. You will remember stories long unspoken. Objects become touchstones of love, and their loss leaves us with lifelong regret. All I have now of my mother's kitchen, where I found so much love and so much sustenance, is a worn bottle opener. It has to suffice. It has to be passed along to my grandchildren, along with its stories.

The objects I have selected are not precious heirlooms, nor perfect mementoes of the turning points in our family's century-long American journey. Many reflect instances of affection, others moments of pain. But as I learned, affection may be coupled with dependency and pain with liberation. These objects are not unique to my family. At a dinner recently, a friend pulled out his own grandmother's Edlund bottle opener, stamped with the name of a Buffalo, New York, brewery, which evidently distributed it in a promotional campaign. In this book I chose objects that connected me to family stories or to patterns of life that characterized distinct moments in the Schwartz-Rabinowitz family experience. As twentieth-century things, produced in vast multitudes, these objects—and these patterns of life—overlapped with those of many contemporaries. And yet my parents' lives were always particular, singular, distinctive. Their lives were not exactly typical of any group—Jews, immigrants, New Yorkers, or anyone else. Similarly, their experience could not be shoehorned into a psychological or sociological abstraction like "alienation," "trauma," or "gentrification." They did not follow the expected scripts, and their lives cannot be fully explained as an example of some broader phenomenon.

I learned much about my family in this process. I collected lots of facts and lots of stories. But each was not an end in itself. As I worked, I saw the links over time between very disparate objects, experiences, and stories. Slowly I began to see how my mother constructed a whole life with these objects, one after another. I saw the continuity of her skills, of her temperament, of her energy and her fatigue, of the way she confronted and overcame perilous moments. A pattern to her personality had been created. She was the same person as a resourceful eight-year-old, the eldest of three children, as she would be a quarter-century later in nursing her mother, and a decade after that in fighting for a new community library. In a similar way, in Dave Rabinowitz's own story, I could comprehend "the long war" of my father's distrustful life and not just its episodic battles. The zest he mustered in selling newspapers on the street before his seventh birthday could also be found in his fierce drive to find work in his twenties or to capitalize on his quick success in the jewelry business two decades after that. In each case, he had also to deal with an inevitable letdown, admitting failure and moving forward after a necessary surrender.

The life course of each of my parents, I learned, was set in motion by difficult childhoods. By their late teenage years, their characters were well established, their goals and missions set, and their individual purposes propelled them forward. By then, Sarah Schwartz had fixed on a dream of overseeing a clean, quiet home of her own, safe from threats of physical violence (of her Polish youth) and economic want (of Depression-era New York)—a home in which she could cherish and repay her mother's devotion with love for her own children. Dave Rabinowitz, unforgivingly hurt by a father given to gambling and physical abuse, saw himself as a heroic, loyal, but ultimately solitary and wary provider for his family.

If we turned the life stories of Sarah and Dave Rabinowitz into an opera, the first act would feature solo arias depicting their wounds but also their fierce determination to succeed. Inclined to love but prey to fears, they were both strong-willed, thick-skinned people. Their second act, played out on the stage of their early married years, would include a duet of contrasting vocal lines, representing crosscurrents of emotional testing in the face of economic privation and wartime anxiety. Scarred by his failure to clinch a stable income until he latched onto a World War II shipyard job at age 28, Dave simply could not swallow his bad luck or learn from his mistakes. It never occurred to him that he had failed to find an angel, a rabbi, a mentor—whatever you want to call someone who smooths your path forward. Or that he needed to settle into one trade or another, one sphere of business activity, rather than bits of a dozen. He fumed and sputtered, but he never gave up, never stopped working hard every day. By contrast, diminutive Sarah assumed greater and greater responsibility—for her parents, barely able to function in the American context; for her brothers, just coming of age; for her young children's physical needs; and for her husband's unstable temperament. Her omnicompetence met all these demands, but left her exhausted and emotionally fractured when, at age 32, she lost her mother to cancer. Dave denied the possibility of privation, while Sarah's skills during the 1930s and 1940s masked it as sufficiency. By cultivating a sense of style in her personal manner and dress as well as in her frugal housekeeping, she refused to feel sorry for herself. Though ordinary life in a noisy, untidy tenement was discouraging, she embraced her ordinary household labors as if they were holy.

Their third act was happier, and then more painful. Now possessed of a small but comfortable private house in East New York, Brooklyn, they were able to join a peer group of like-minded souls and keep hooligans, creditors, and nosy neighbors away. Public life in the McCarthyite era was repressive and sometimes downright terrifying, but home life, filled with new and shiny acquisitions and leisure-time pleasures, became more peaceful. Sarah and Dave created harmonious duets and humorous *recitatives* with their peers. The duets of this third act, however, never quite harmonized as choral anthems. Friendship was not the same as mutuality. In the end, each neighbor family was singing its own tune. Amicable relationships in a lower-middle-class neighborhood could not constitute an effective communal resistance to the urban turmoil of the 1960s, when corrupt and misguided government and business actors shredded the social fabric of the Rabinowitzes' street. Sarah and Dave were dispossessed of their home, their most cherished possession. They were once again rootless refugees—this time for nearly a decade.

In the fourth act, Beverly and I have grown up and created, in widely separated corners of the country, homes that looked and felt quite different from the East New York we came from. Mom and Dad retired to Florida, to a toothpaste-white condominium village of 8,500 apartments. In a place stripped clean of memories and mementoes, they started to construct a new life—this time without the scaffolding of work and family responsibilities. They thrived, sustained in large measure by government programs like Social Security, Medicare, tax exemptions, and real estate protections. In the healthy Florida sun, they lived remarkably long lives—Dad to age 94, Mom to 99. They shopped, they cooked, they forged new friendships, they welcomed family visits, and they endured, blessedly without much drama. They sang solo arias again, one after another. Oddly enough, Dave now became the hermit, cherishing his domestic quiet, needing no one but the woman he had loved for seventy-two years. In retirement, Sarah was now the roving ambassador, doing her charitable work, dispensing the wisdom of a community elder.

As a history of twentieth-century America, seen through the lens of a single family, and as a history of personal life set within the transformations of an eventful century, *Objects of Love and Regret* demonstrates how public and private lives constantly intersect. Sarah would have laughed at the idea that she was a philosopher, a historian, or even a "domestic engineer." But, in her organization of days and rooms, of ingredients and implements, of loyalties and interdependencies, in her striving to attain a satisfactory product for the labor of a minute or an hour, she enacted almost a full century's worth of philosophical principles and of ways of living and remembering.

As I have untwisted and rewound the strands of my parents' and grandparents' lives, seeing them alone and together, over time and in many places, their tenancy on earth leads me to meditate on the biggest questions—free will and fate, time and space, self and society. Any human life, every human life, is endlessly fascinating.

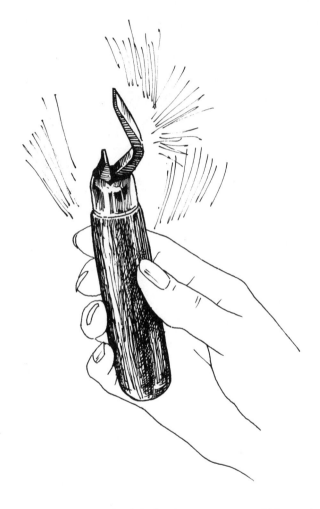

Sarah explained the gift of the bottle opener—it would be good to open Papa's beer bottles, or to break the vacuum seal on a jar, or to reopen a can of Crisco shortening, all three.

1

Sarah Buys a Bottle Opener

I can almost make her out, descending the steel-edged stairs of the Livonia Avenue station on the BMT line, on an April afternoon in 1934. She comes down the right side slowly, carefully. Her sensible Treemark shoes find the middle of each stair. She shies a little to the left, away from the rust-speckled handrails that have been soiled by a hundred thousand fingers since their last repainting. The ruder men speed by, colliding with her and with one another, racing toward the streets below. Others halt at the bottom, where I stand, to light up their cigarettes.

My eyes catch her halfway down, and I want to run up the stairs, against the traffic, and guide her passage down. She is my mother, and I am eleven years away from being born. But in picturing this scene I wish I could protect her, wrap her in the safety of my arms and my comforting words—just as I remember how she comforted me so often. "*Tatele,*" she would say to me, in that lovely and strange way that Yiddish endearments use the term for "little father" to embrace their littlest boys, "*Tatele,* you'll be OK. *Nisht geferlach.* It's not so terrible."

I hear her say, "I'm so tired, I can hardly move myself." She has spent a long workday, maybe ten hours, snipping away the loose threads on the cheap dresses made in a shop on 36th Street, then being called away to the front office to try on this model or that one, so that the boss could make a sale, and finally coming back to arrange the finished stock on the carts for shipping. A dollar or two for ten hours' work. I can't say anything about the job, except that it's barely tolerable and totally necessary. I want to say, "*Mamele*, it's going to be fine. This city, this country, this time." It's pure faith, there's nothing in that Friday afternoon noise and dirt to reassure her.

Nor can I climb the stairs to reach her. Of course not. I am only there as an imagined witness, a historian in waiting. I can only guess at how she clutches her handbag, pulls her spring coat closed, and walks up the street, away from the El. A few blocks away, at Blake Avenue, she is amidst the pushcarts of the street market. A smiling Chesterfield smoker painted on a tenement wall—"It Satisfies"— looms over peddlers eager to get rid of the last *bulbes* (potatoes) and *tsibbele* (onions) before they close up their carts for Shabbos. Sarah— that is her name, Sarah Schwartz, originally Sore Fruma bat Dovid v' Shenka—heads for a pushcart selling implements, useful things— eggbeaters, mousetraps, ladles. She reaches over to a box of wooden handled bottle openers and picks out a green one. The peddler says, "*finef un tvantsik*," or twenty-five cents. Sarah responds, "*tvantsik*, last week it was twenty cents." She's been waiting all week to buy it. He shrugs, she places two dimes in his palm and slips the bottle opener into her handbag.

Sarah turns back to Livonia Avenue and crosses under the elevated subway tracks. She can hardly hear herself think above the rattling of the train overhead. She picks her way against the tide of tired workers coming from both directions, rambunctious children, baby carriages as tall as the weary mothers who push them, and rickety tricycles. The city seems to have disgorged all the detritus of the work week onto these streets—its people and every single thing they have used up since the previous Sunday. Finally, Sarah

turns the corner onto Williams Avenue and sees the endless row of
dirt-gray four-story apartment buildings lining the street—treeless,
shadeless, and windblown. Of the hundreds along the street, three
or four windows display small wooden cottage-cheese boxes with
newly planted zinnias, each probably a project of a fifth-grade pupil.
Sarah skirts the shoulder-slumped pedestrians to walk along the
gutter. There are only a few cars. She has to step gingerly over discarded newspapers, candy wrappers, cigarette butts, bus transfers,
dog waste, and small boys' piss. On the pavement, she tiptoes around
a girls' game of "potsy" (hopscotch), and she maneuvers between
pink and black blotches of ancient chewing gum—so many that it
seems the sidewalk is actually held together by abandoned bits of
Dubble Bubble, Chiclets, and Juicy Fruit.

When she looks up, Sarah sees her mother perched at the window
of the third-floor apartment. They wave to each other. The shake of
her mother's head tells her that her brother Isaac is late again.
Climbing the stairs to arrive at the family apartment, Sarah is eager
to share her purchase of the bottle opener. But at the front door,
she is totally distracted by the smell of the fresh-baked challah. As
she is on every Friday night, Sarah is ambivalent—happy that she
has earned some money for the family, but guilt-ridden for not
having helped her mother prepare the house for Shabbos. For my
bubbe, Shenka Schwartz, it had been such a long day of labor. She
had cleaned the crowded apartment, picked up after the two teenage
boys, and prepared the traditional Shabbos meal, baking two loaves
of challah, roasting a chicken, preparing the chicken soup and the
potatoes and the green beans, and topping it off with *shticklach*
(wedges) of prune cake for dessert. My zayde, Dovid Schwartz, had
spent the day, by contrast, piecing together odd jobs to fill in the
gap left by the slack season in his regular work. He was "a presser
by cloaks," that is, he put the final finishing touches on the making

of women's coats, and his work year was interrupted two or three times by layoffs—after Passover through May, then after the Jewish holidays in the fall, and finally, in the weeks after Thanksgiving. Now he has come home, washed and dressed in a clean white shirt, and treated himself—as he did almost every evening—to a full glass of homemade plum brandy, which was regularly delivered in a ceramic jug by someone my sister remembers as "a wrinkled old lady."

After Sarah has herself washed and changed her blouse, she and my bubbe proceeded to *bentsch licht,* to light the Shabbos candles and cover their eyes as they spoke the customary prayer. By this time, Sarah's brothers, Sam (age 16) and Isaac (age 13), had also gathered. And it's possible that a place is set for my father, Dave Rabinowitz, age 20. My parents had started "keeping company" early in 1934, and a meal at the Schwartzes was soon his very favorite refuge from his often-profitless days as a "custom peddler," buying furniture and appliances on behalf of Yiddish speakers too fearful to negotiate with New York's shopkeepers. Anything to skip dinner with his abusive father, tough-skinned mother, and four really crazy younger brothers. He used to say that even a folding chair at the Schwartz table felt like a throne after that.

According to tradition, the Shabbos meal would then proceed, acknowledging God's provision of the Sabbath as a transformative gift, welcoming the seventh day as a queen, and casting a holy glow over the family table. The rituals embody deeply held assumptions about the family—praise for the wife, hope for the children, and loyalty to the community. Even if the husband is not particularly respectful of his wife, worries that his children are behaving like animals, and thinks that his neighbors are really a bunch of tramps, the ritual prayer speaks of an idealized state that might come true, God willing, someday. For Diaspora Jews, the Hebrew prayers help lift the week's most important meal into a higher sphere. The rest of the week, and even most of the time during this meal, the chatter is exclusively in the mother tongue, in this case Yiddish with a near-Lithuanian accent.

The family knew variations in the way Jews in the Polish shtetl practiced Judaism, but nothing like the amazing diversity they saw every day among their neighbors on the Lower East Side and Brooklyn. The foods my grandmother chose for the table, the accents my zayde used in reading the Hebrew texts, and the actual implements they used to cook, serve, and dine all mirrored the passages of my ancestors through the landscape of Europe, Asia Minor, and America. As the family gathered, the conversation replaced all this by a steady drumbeat of trivial and not-so-trivial comments. Knowing these people so well, I can hear the back-and-forth:

"You should have seen the way this woman was dressed!"
"You know that kid downstairs . . . ?"
"I never saw anyone *handle* (bargain) like that at a
    pushcart—it was amazing!"

That might have led, for a few minutes, to a heated argument about whether the new mayor, Fiorello La Guardia, should shut down the outdoor pushcart markets.

"They're filthy, and they cheat you on the weight."
"OK, big shot, so tell me how these families are going to
    make a living?"
"They're taking jobs away from the storekeepers."
"Not everybody can afford a store rent."
"The city should build them a nice, clean place."
"Where's the city going to get the money?"

Round and round. Strong opinions about President Franklin D. Roosevelt and stronger ones about David Dubinsky, head of the International Ladies' Garment Workers Union. The Schwartzes are noisy people. They love one another, and nothing expresses that love more strongly than interrupting, in agreement or not, but always with emphasis. Dave, the stranger to the family, noticed that everybody was smiling as they argued. Imagining myself there, I am most impressed by each person's strength of purpose. Zayde and Sam are proud of the way they look; Mom and Bubbe are happy to be sharing the table with the people they love most. Isaac is already eager to be a revolutionary, and Dave is buoyantly optimistic about making a good living in the teeth of the Depression. These are not the pitiable poor of the tenements that Jacob Riis described in the 1880s. I know immediately where my sister Beverly and I got our brazenness, our *chutzpah*.

All of the family's Jewish practice, it must be said, had already become detached from the essential text-centeredness of Judaism. The People of the Book, in the travail of their surviving pogroms and migrating to a new land, had transfigured the treasured words of Torah and Mishnah, of commentaries and mystical literature, into a dusty archive of barren, formulaic phrases, devoid of any living meaning. All of that had become, simply enough, proverbs in a forgotten language. The Schwartzes were still Jews to the core of their beings, but their Jewishness was a jumble of customs, with a focus on the everyday, the observance of Shabbos and the holidays, an insistence upon marking life events with family gatherings and Hebrew prayers, all together constituting a map for navigating the cycles of the week, the year, and the journey from cradle to grave.

For the Schwartzes, Shabbos at home had less to do with mirroring God's rest after six days of labor than a way to get everything back to normal. Normal was an aspiration, built of a desire to shut and lock the outside door even more firmly, as if to bar any intrusion. For Dovid, Shenka, and Sarah Schwartz, if not for the two boys, locking out the world secured the calm, safety, and warmth they prized above all else. No longer fearing pogroms from Polish neighbors, they now hoped for protection from the noise and dirt of their American neighbors. The older Schwartzes, including Sarah, assumed that they were always under siege. Somebody was always heard to conclude, "If it's not one thing, it's another thing" as a response to the ills they confronted or feared—anti-Semitism, unemployment, disease, poverty, *schmutz* (dirt), and violence. The rich beauty and goodness of the Shabbos meal, even in the midst of their own cramped apartment, was a symbol of their safety.

But of course, they could not keep the world at bay, and the traditional script for observing Shabbos was irremediably broken. Things did not proceed exactly as the rabbis taught. My grandfather, without much ceremony, mumbled through the *Kiddush* over the wine. The only response may have been a gentle "amen" from Sarah and Sam, but no one joined in singing the prayer. Nor did anyone bother to bless the braided challah before the boys tore off delicious chunks. Bubbe began to bring the food to the table. When times were better, this might have been gefilte fish, made at home from pike or whitefish carried alive from Mrs. Pikoff's fish market around the corner. Often there was just chicken soup as a *forshpeis,* or first course. Bubbe put the soup bowl in front of Zayde, and he began to eat. Then Dave—as a guest—was served, and then the children. To the table came the chicken and the vegetables, one plateful after another. In later years no one could ever remember Bubbe's actually sitting down to enjoy the food she had prepared. Instead she lingered near the stove, tasting, adding some seasoning, and then hovering over the table, carrying bowls back to the stove for more, asking whether it was good, complaining about the difficulty of finding the right ingredients. A hum of delight filled the room. Of course, it was more than good. When the Kabbalah speaks of angels, this was the nectar of angels.

Is it blasphemous to suggest that food, delicious food, had replaced all the other pleasures and rewards of Shabbos in this household? Bubbe had done the hard work and Shabbos was really her moment. Serving the man of the house first and ensuring that the children were satisfied—that may have been more important to Bubbe than the more abstract ideal of participating as God's people in age-old rituals. In the best of circumstances, the conversation returned often to how delicious the food was. No one lingered to say the grace after meals. Sam, the more respectful of the sons, kissed his mother gratefully. Isaac, the rebel, scowled at this Old World nonsense. His parents could not insist on obedience. They felt their dignity had been undermined beyond the apartment walls by their unfamiliarity with local customs, their pitiful dependence on longer-established siblings and fellow immigrants from the old country, and their obvious lack of the aggressiveness needed to succeed in their new country. So they did not have the confidence to place a hand on their children's heads and bless their endeavors in the week ahead— as the prayer book dictated.

In consequence, when the eating stopped, the boys fled. Sam, in a neatly ironed shirt, was off to hang out with his friends at the local candy store, kibitz over pinochle games, and talk about girls. Isaac, in whatever shirt was handy, ran off to join a protest or a picket line. In his busy seasons, Zayde went off to read a little before going to bed and waking early to set off for work on Saturdays, though he was always uncomfortable with having to violate the holy day. For the boys— now that they had satisfied the requirement of having a bar mitzvah— the weekend was pure liberation. Their Shabbos was not going to be a time of study and rest. Dave respectfully expressed his thanks, confirmed that he would see Sarah on Saturday night, and took his leave.

Sarah's constant wish, "to have the family all together," was not to be fulfilled on that Shabbos in the spring of 1934. The menfolk—restless, weary, self-indulgent—left Sarah and Shenka alone, sitting together at the Shabbos table. Like many Jewish women, they took a special pleasure in scavenging the leftover chicken, sucking out the innermost marrow from the bones, breathing in the lingering smell of the garlic, feeling the fat on their fingers—but also sharing stories, drawing out morals, giving and absorbing advice. This lingering over the completed meal was always puzzling to me. As a child, the growing pile of ugly, chewed-up chicken bones was off-putting. But now I sense that there was more than nutrition in this primitive ritual.

At this point in the evening the little bottle opener made its appearance on center stage and began its life as part of the Schwartz family saga. Sarah took it out of her handbag and offered it to her mother. Instead of wrapping paper, it came with an explanation—it would be good to open Papa's beer bottles, or to break the vacuum seal on a jar, or to reopen a can of Crisco shortening, all three. Shenka turned it over in her hand, smiled, and said just one word, *taka,* an endearing Yiddish way of seasoning gratitude with amazement and satisfaction.

It was not a gift in a conventional sense. Coming home to Shabbos dinner was just a regular occurrence, not an occasion for giving presents. This was less about giving than about sharing—what belonged to one assuredly belonged to the other. So the utensil was really about their bond to each other, and to what they both loved—the pleasures of caring for the kitchen, the home, and the family. But, I think, something else was being opened at the same time. The two dimes from Sarah's purse also marked her gradual adoption of the caretaker's role. No longer the dependent daughter, at eighteen she was taking the guiding hand for her mother's progress in America, as well as her own.

Both of them were proud of this moment. Their hands touched, and Sarah put the opener away in the drawer of kitchen things.

On an ill-fated day during the terrible summer of 1920, when
Isaac Guss, Sarah's beloved grandfather, tried to salvage for his
metal shop an artillery shell left behind by one of the armies, it
exploded and shattered his body.

2

Isaac Guss Finds an Artillery Shell

Behind a shed, nearly covered with the unharvested sheaves of wheat in 1920, lay a 122 mm artillery shell. It was made in France, in the Schneider factory near Lyon, to fit a howitzer gun that the Russians might aim at their German foes. But now the Germans have gone, the Russians have gone, and hundreds of the townspeople, too, have gone. The town, a shtetl called Wysokie Mazowieckie, had been racked by war for six years. In the September sun, a local coppersmith, a Jew named Isaac Guss, my great-grandfather, caught the glint of brass on the base of the shell. In wartime, he had been hard-pressed to find material for his pots and pans, for the *fendlach* and *shisselach* in which the ingredients of his neighbors' meals will be mixed, seasoned, and cooked. Having survived the invasion and bivouacking in his village by one army after another, he was eager to get back to work. Guss had seen other shells here and there around the shtetl, spent, half-shattered, twisted, hard to reuse. This one was shiny and clean, a perfectly conical, gleaming projectile. Finding a smooth, unmarked shell was God's gift, he thought. Guss could imagine a pair of beautiful candlesticks from the brass.

Without a cannon to fire it, it could not be dangerous, right? Guss sat, smoked, thought it over. It weighed over fifty pounds, not something he could toss over his shoulder and trot back to his work-shop. Retracing his steps to Moritz's shop, he asked if he could borrow the bakery wheelbarrow. Moritz waved his assent and Guss returned to the shed. On that terrible day during that terrible summer, when he tried to lift the artillery shell, it fell from his arms, exploded, and shattered his body. It was a further punishment, yet another test for the poor Jews of this place.

Isaac Guss had read in the book of Jeremiah, "The harvest is past, the summer is ended, and we are not saved." But like some offended Greek god or like the explosive powder inside the shell, the past was inescapable.

Mom's story about buying a bottle opener for her mother in 1934 was not really about kitchen work at all. It was a story about the bond she had with Bubbe. Mom loved her children and her hus-band, no doubt about that, but her attachment to my grandmother was the visceral center of her being.

Why? What had produced this closeness? The answer, I was sure, lay in Mom's earliest years as a child in Poland, and in the way Shenka and Sarah Schwartz shared that "hard life." But through all my youth, Mom was close-mouthed about her Polish childhood. Each time our conversation veered near the subject of those years, and espe-cially when it touched on the fate of cousins or friends from the shtetl, Mom would interject, "Hitler took care of them!" My curi-osity would be snapped shut. Even though many in her immediate family had left before 1939, the whole idea of Europe was distasteful to her. While many Jews of her generation shunned German-made products and would never set foot in postwar Germany, Mom boy-cotted the whole continent. It took enormous persuasion in 1972 to get her to debark from a Swissair flight in Zurich in order to catch her flight to Tel Aviv. "She didn't want her feet to touch the ground of Europe," my father reported afterward.

By the end of the 1970s, though, Mom had relented. Finally, when she was in her sixties and I in my thirties, I pressed her to start her life story at the beginning and proceed straightforwardly from her Polish childhood to her immigration to America. In doing so, she kept returning to a story that seemed, frankly, a bit improbable to me, at least at first. Her father, my zayde, she said, had spent a whole year living in the back room of the family's cottage in their Polish shtetl, Wysokie Mazowieckie, in northeastern Poland. I asked, how had that happened? She told me that he had been carried away by "Cossacks," and had escaped, walked a hundred miles, and arrived home as a skeletal figure, his beard torn off, stricken with dysentery and typhus. He was kept away from his three children, all under four years of age, for fear that he might bring them an infectious disease. He subsisted on chicken broth occasionally enriched with warm rolls, for month after month—"it must have been a whole year." Sarah often stayed at a friend's house, afraid that she would not find her father alive when she arrived home.

"Cossacks"? I wondered. What were the Cossacks, a term for warriors originating in southern Russia, doing in northeastern Poland? And then, some years later, I discovered the *yizkor buch,* the memorial volume for the shtetl of Wysokie Mazowieckie, in the library of the YIVO Institute in New York. Along with the black-bordered pages listing community members lost in the Shoah, the book included a history, both in Yiddish and English, of the centuries-long experience of Jews in this place. It cited an article in a 1920 Warsaw newspaper describing a pitched battle in which Jews and Poles had fought together against an invasion of the village by Soviet troops. Thirteen Jews died in that battle, and the retreating

Bolsheviks reportedly took 230 Jews and two Poles with them as hostages. When the Polish Army "liberated" the captives, however, its soldiers turned on the Jews and beat them ferociously, and then launched a pogrom against the Jews remaining in the village, despite the evidence of their devotion to Polish independence. In other places in Poland and Belarus, violence was directed against Jews as Bolshevik sympathizers. The "excesses" against the Jews in Wysokie Mazowieckie came out of a longstanding anti-Semitism endemic to the community.

In other words, my mother's memory was far from fanciful. It fit very closely into events described in the history books. Like the date of the bottle opener patent, it proved that my mother had lived both in memory and in history, and that the two were connected. And further, that this memory of Zayde in the back room was in some way an opening both into Sarah's life story and to a much larger narrative. I set to work exploring the Polish background of Mom's family. It was like a jigsaw puzzle. Many pieces came from my mother's large stock of memories (which could, however, not go further back than her grandparents). She was astonishingly accurate, so far as I could tell, about the names and characters of people and places, but dates were another matter. And I was less interested in filling out a family tree than in reconstructing the experiences of the family members. Some of those experiences I could discover through public records, like the United States Census returns, and others through shipping records, citizenship applications, and my grandfather's Polish passport. Maps and gazetteers oriented me to places and modes of travel. I relied upon scholarly histories of Jewish lives during the First World War and the establishment of a Polish republic after the war. I discovered the accounts of Isaac Babel, the noted Russian Jewish writer who accompanied the Soviet troops during the Polish-Soviet War of 1919–1920 (about which I knew nothing before I began this project). I read the English sections and had translated for me the Yiddish parts of the *yizkor buch* for Wysokie. And, perhaps as important as anything else, I traveled to the village in May 2016 with my friend Dale Rosengarten while on a study tour of Shoah-related historical sites in Germany, Ukraine, and Poland.

My grandfather, Dovid Schwartz, the youngest of seven sons, was born in 1890 in the village of Sokoly, about forty kilometers southwest of the city of Bialystok in what is now northeastern Poland. Since the final partition of Poland by the Austrian, Prussian, and Russian Empires in 1795, this area had been under the thumb of tsarist Russia. Dovid's family name in Poland was Czarna, or black. When four of his older brothers emigrated to New York before World War I, they adopted the German equivalent, Schwartz. One of the other brothers died in youth, and the eldest, Avrumka, a ropemaker, remained in Poland until his death. Austere and pious, he wore a long black coat, shiny with age, mended more than once, and he had a beard almost as long. I have a photo of him. His sad eyes are looking down, as if this visit to the photographer's studio was not his idea at all. Most revealing is that both index fingers are buried deep in the pages of a book. Perhaps it was a tractate of the Talmud, and he was sorry to be interrupted in his study. The sight of him and his abrupt manner frightened my mother as a little girl. She thought he looked like one of the prophets in the Bible. Later in life she would laugh to think that he was probably younger than fifty at the time. He would likely have been in his sixties or seventies at the outbreak of World War II, so we do not know whether he was lost in the Shoah or before. The sweet-tempered mother of this brood of boys, Chaya Beyele, my great-grandmother, lived on a farm with Avrumka and his family. (My sister Beverly was named in Yiddish for her.) She would have loved to follow her five sons to

America, but she could not leave her eldest behind. Sarah, my mother, shuddered at the memory of the way her grandmother and uncle lived, "sleeping on straw."

Dovid was a handsome fellow, and his passport picture shows his Slavic features, a squarish head, dark blonde hair and mustache, and notes his medium height and build. Beyond the local *cheder* in Sokoly, where he learned to read Hebrew, to follow the prescribed *mitzvot* (commandments), and to *daven* (pray), he had no schooling. On his passport, he signed his name awkwardly in Yiddish, his native tongue.

World War I had closed the door to any opportunity to join his brothers in America. As a sturdy young man, he found work as a lumberman and then as a leatherworker. Physically strong but something of a mama's boy, Dovid was not exactly a great catch. At some point, a matchmaker had arranged for him to meet and marry Shayna or Shenka Simme Guss. She was two years older than Dovid. Shenka was the third or fourth child of her mother, Sarah Fruma Guss, after whom my mother was named. (Mom was always called "Fruma" until she entered school in the United States.) Sarah Fruma died in bearing Shenka or soon after, and the girl became the unloved stepdaughter of her father's second wife. By all accounts, Shenka was an exceptionally bright woman, an avid reader of Yiddish books and newspapers, many sent to her by her half-brothers in Berlin, Warsaw, Vienna, and Bialystok. In early 1914, at the age of 24, without a dowry, and probably fearful of being a spinster, she and Dovid were married in her hometown, Wysokie Mazowieckie, about sixteen kilometers from Sokoly. It must have been a small wedding, given the absence of so many of their siblings. Here they settled, living in a small house along the street that leads still to the town's largest Catholic church. Wysokie was a little bigger than Sokoly, with 3,214 inhabitants in the 1921 national census, of whom

1,898, or 55 percent, were Jews. The rest were Catholic. The town dates to 1203, with the earliest records of Jews appearing in the mid-eighteenth century. Wysokie Mazowieckie was, variously, the property of the Radziwill family and other "pans" (*porets* in Yiddish), or grandees, and under the domain of one regional power after another. It was an administrative district town, though it was bypassed by the railroad from Warsaw to Bialystok. In the 1920s it was almost entirely composed of wooden buildings.

Whatever *simcha,* or joy, followed in the wake of my grandparents' marriage was extinguished by the outbreak of the Great War of 1914–1918. The Russian tsar's ministers and generals had only the vaguest objectives as they stumbled into war: to aid their Slavic brethren in Serbia against the Dual Monarchy of Austria and Hungary and to assist their French allies by diverting the attention of the German kaiser. Though it was by far the largest army in the world, with almost a million and a half troops mobilized for battle, the Russians had poorly developed supply lines. Their first offensive of the war, in August 1914, was to strike to the northwest against the Germans in East Prussia. This led them directly through the area of Wysokie Mazowieckie. The gentle green landscape of this Podlaskie region was ripped open by violence. The Cossacks, Russia's fearsome cavalrymen, billeted themselves wherever they wished, seized whatever they wanted of foodstuffs and supplies, and taught the Polish peasants how to execute their anti-Semitic frenzies. They tortured and murdered Jews on suspicion of spying for the Germans. Word arrived in Wysokie Mazowieckie of synagogues and *mikvahs* (ritual bathhouses) burned to the ground, whole villages emptied of their Jewish residents, and many, many women raped. The fury of the Cossacks—at least those not among the many thousands taken prisoner by the Germans—was redoubled after their disastrous defeat by the Germans at Tannenberg, just 195 kilometers from

Wysokie, in late August 1914. For the next year, the Russians tried to defend a front that extended from the Baltic to the Black Sea, over 1,900 kilometers in length (three times as long as the Western Front from Belgium to Switzerland). As they gave way to the German advance, they resorted to a scorched-earth policy, destroying rail lines, roads, and bridges. By the end of 1915, the Germans occupied all of Russian Poland.

I've tried to imagine how the townspeople followed the progress of the war. The tsarist regime shut down all Yiddish newspapers in July 1915. There were fewer travelers to bring news and, of course, no radio. Dovid, like all his Jewish friends, was desperate to hide from recruiters for the contending armies or for forced exile in the German *Arbeiterbataillone,* or workers' battalions. Every belt, boot, and harness that came off Dovid's leatherworking bench was instantly confiscated by occupying troops. This formerly rich agricultural region descended into famine. Kosher meat became unavailable. Families that had consumed over 2,500 calories per person before the war were now forced to subsist on one-third that amount. Smuggling, black marketeering, robbery, and arbitrary justice for such crimes became the rule. Leaders of the Jewish community found themselves paralyzed, facing the starvation of their children, outbreaks of cholera and typhus, and random, relentless assaults by their Polish neighbors.

But all this still somehow feels abstract to me. I try to fire up my sensory imagination. The cold and wet of the winter leads to an impression of mud everywhere, of sodden boots and rotting stockings, of splintering door frames and shattered tabletops. I am grateful to writers like Isaac Babel and Vasily Grossman. They have created characters whose skin rubs against these soaked blankets, who breathe in these smells, whose fingers tighten in this cold, whose eyes strain in scarce winter light to locate what they have misplaced a moment before. I know that my sources for the military and political history, those splendidly footnoted monographs I have been trained to read, annotate, and emulate, have been written in warm university libraries by scholars who want to know what was *generally* true. But I need to get down to the specifics of Wysokie Mazowieckie, to the hours, days, weeks, months, and seasons of Dovid's and Shenka's life, to the world in which my mother was born in the spring of 1916. I try to slow down the flow of events to gain a perch on how they encountered the harsh, frightening, endlessly vulnerable conditions of the shtetl in wartime.

Under this strain, my mother once told me, Shenka had already had a miscarriage. But the military situation in 1915 provided an auspicious change in her family's circumstances, at least momentarily. Warsaw, the capital of the Russian provinces, fell to the Germans in August. With the rail lines open between Warsaw and Lomza, near to Wysokie Mazowieckie, Shenka could take the advice of her prosperous half-siblings in Warsaw and come to the metropolis to have her child in a local hospital. My grandmother remembered that the German soldiers were unfailingly polite to her during the train journey. She remained in her relatives' home for a month or more while awaiting the birth. My mother was born, the family story went, with a "strawberry" birthmark on her head and presented to my bubbe, who was still dazed by the ether she had been given. The following day, it is said, the nurses brought a baby boy to Shenka. She cried out that she had had *"eine madel"* (a girl child). Finally, such a day-old female baby, with the recognizable birthmark, was discovered and retrieved from the hospital's communicable diseases ward. Thus were mother and child united, and the little girl was called Sore Fruma. They were almost inseparable thereafter.

My mother's birth was not registered in Warsaw, evidently, or in Wysokie Mazowieckie. Civil authority hardly existed in wartime

Poland, and she grew up celebrating her birthday as "the last day of Passover." Only after consulting rabbis in New York did she settle on April 25, 1916, as her "American" birthday. For the first four and a half years of her life, she would be stateless, as the military and political convulsions of the Great War played themselves out. But Sarah has the clearest evidence of the German and other military occupations of Wysokie Mazowieckie on her arms. When she finally told me her life story, she began by rolling up her sleeve. "Can you see how many smallpox shots I have?" she asked, showing us an arm covered with six or seven marks. "Every time a new army marched into town, it vaccinated the whole population." Tsarist Russians, Red Russians, White Russians, Polish nationalists, Austrians, Germans, Lithuanians, all were equally fearsome. Only the Jews had no army of their own.

For Wysokie's Jews, German occupation meant the relaxation of tsarist repression. Under Russian rule, Jewish organizations and political activity had been strictly forbidden. The Germans, glad that they could communicate relatively easily with locals who spoke Yiddish, which is linguistically close to German, allowed the Jews to establish communal aid associations, orphanages, and medical facilities. Almost immediately, Jews created the first non-Orthodox schools and cultural groups in the shtetl. Perhaps because of the virulence of Russian and Polish anti-Semitism, the Zionist cause—seeking to create a Jewish national homeland—dominated the political talk in Wysokie Mazowieckie for the next two decades. Every Jew appears to have been a Zionist, either leaning left or leaning right.

The Paris Peace Conference in 1919 vowed to put an independent Poland back on the map, but no one was sure where its eastern borders would be. In March 1918, a few months after the October Revolution, the newly triumphant Russian Bolsheviks had been so eager to get out of the war that they surrendered enormous territories to the Germans in the treaty of Brest-Litovsk. A year later Lenin wanted to retrieve the Ukrainian, Belorussian, Baltic, and perhaps Polish lands that had long belonged to tsarist Russia. He hoped, in fact, that revolutions would "Sovietize" everything to the west of Russia, including Poland and even Germany. In that case, national boundaries would no longer be necessary, as a dictatorship of the proletariat would extend from Asian Siberia to the Rhine. But the defeat of the Communist uprising in Germany, the establishment of the Weimar Republic, and the strong support of the Great Powers for a sovereign Poland, destroyed that notion.

Newly independent Poland also had dreams, in its case the re-establishment of the Polish-Lithuanian Commonwealth that had dominated Eastern Europe in the fourteenth to eighteenth centuries. General Jozef Pilsudski, the nation's leading figure, envisaged a coalition of states in Ukraine, Belarus, and Lithuania—allied to Poland—that might shield the new republic from the Russian behemoth. In the Polish-Soviet War of 1919–1920, Pilsudski's Polish army succeeded in capturing Kiev, but they were almost immediately driven all the way back. They stood in August 1920 on the verge of losing Warsaw. And then, in what the Poles call the "miracle on the Vistula," Pilsudski's attack on the middle of the Soviet force turned it almost instantly into a horde of panicky refugees. The Poles swept north and east in pursuit. In the final treaty, Bialystok, Vilna, and Lwow became the major eastern outposts of the new Polish state.

What sort of war was this? The battles on the Eastern Front, and especially those that followed the November 11, 1918, armistice between Germany and the Allies, are not nearly so familiar to us as the trench warfare in Belgium and northeastern France. Other than Pilsudski's militiamen, trained and controlled by Austrian generals

Poland, 1914

GERMAN
EMPIRE

RUSSIAN
EMPIRE

Congress
Poland

AUSTRO-HUNGARIAN
EMPIRE

ESTONIA

LATVIA

LITHUANIA

Baltic Sea

• Vilna

Danzig

East
Prussia

USSR

Lomza • Bialystok

• Sokoly

Wysokie
Mazowieckie

• Pinsk

Poznan

Warsaw •

• Brest-Litovsk

• Lodz

P O L A N D

• Lublin

GERMANY

• Cracow

• Lwow

C Z E C H O S L O V A K I A

Sarah's Poland
1923

The Warsaw –
Lomza – Bialystok
rail line

HUNGARY   R O M A N I A

N

0   100 km

0   100 miles

during the Great War, the soldiers in the conflicts after 1918 were poorly trained, poorly coordinated, and minimally equipped. They were more like roving bands than the well-drilled forces conscripted in the industrial societies of central and western Europe. Temptations to violence undermined military discipline. The landscape left behind was not a burned- or bombed-out ruin like Ypres or Verdun, but rather a scattering of naked corpses of people and their animals, smashed wagon wheels, collapsed chimneys, and fire-scarred barns—a land widowed of its humanity. Added to this was the death toll of the 1918 flu pandemic, which may have taken between two and three hundred thousand Polish lives. (We have no evidence of its prevalence in the Bialystok area; outbreaks were recorded especially in Lwow and Krakow, at first, and then in Warsaw.)

And worse was still to come. The crowning blow of my grandparents' painful first decade of marriage was my zayde's abduction by the retreating Cossacks in August 1920, as a part of the Polish-Soviet War, and then by the violent outburst of the local Poles. Shenka, now barely two months pregnant with her third child, must have been even more vulnerable. Her beloved father, Isaac Lieb Guss, was severely injured when a stray artillery shell left behind by one of the armies exploded in his arms. He lingered at the spot, near death, long enough for his granddaughter Sarah to witness his pain. Sixty years later, she recalled, "I was holding his hand, and I remember someone saying, *'Mamele, kum de,'* come away, and then taking my hand away from him." It was her earliest memory, and one of the most painful.

At age four, Sarah may have been just old enough to remember her grandfather's death. Her mother's grief she would never forget. Seventy-seven years later, when I phoned her with the news of her brother Isaac's death, she began a howling—"Isaac-el, Isaac-el, *o mein bubbeleh.*" It went on and on, seeming to mimic her mother's pain on that August day in 1920. I had never heard such keening, except perhaps in documentary films of war and child murder. It could have erupted from behind an actor's mask on the stage of an ancient Greek theater. The depths of this anguish brought me as close as I have ever been to that even more ancient horror, the fear that the first matriarch of the Jewish people, also named Sarah, had in watching her husband Abraham take their boy, also named Isaac, to the "Akedah," the sacrifice on Mount Moriah.

And then Shenka spent weeks, perhaps months, uncertain about Dovid's fate. Many other husbands and sons were also gone, and many women in Wysokie shared that pain with Shenka, which may have lightened it, or perhaps made it worse. Her father was dead, her husband disappeared, her siblings dispersed, and now she was left with only her mother-in-law and other almost-widows for companionship. What a capstone to six years of marriage! And the first stirrings of a new child within her. The shtetl must have felt like the verge of a collapsed mineshaft or a volcanic eruption, or a fishing village after a giant storm. Who was to blame? Who could take responsibility?

Today, a full century later, this cascade of catastrophes would be deemed traumatic, and the family's response marked by the common diagnosis of post-traumatic stress disorder. Was Shenka traumatized? Did family members evidence PTSD? Public health doctors now attribute a host of lifelong medical and psychological ailments to the number of a subject's "adverse childhood experiences." Nothing in this family's plentiful stock of memories and stories indicates that they suffered in this way—no compulsive behavior, no domestic abuse, no repeated nightmares, no addiction to alcohol or drugs. By all accounts Shenka appears to have maintained her resourceful self-control through these crises. She had nowhere to turn. Her parents had died. All but one of her half-siblings had moved away. Help from the local *kehillah,* the organized Jewish community in the shtetl, was obviously limited by the numbers of needy. On her own, my bubbe found the strength to buffer and support her children through these many horrible months. Her resilience astonishes me.

Finally, after several months of captivity, Dovid staggered home to Wysokie Mazowieckie, probably in the late winter of 1920–1921. As soon as Dovid was able to walk about the village, he could recognize and stare at the *goyim* (Gentiles) who had joined in the pogrom. His first thought was to start anew. Where? Shenka had half-brothers in Bialystok and Warsaw, but Dovid had not grown up among them, and the war had kept them apart. Many emigrants from the shtetl first tried life in Eastern and Central European cities, moving to Warsaw or Vienna. But the most obvious choice was New York. That was where his own brothers lived, and they could help him settle. I don't know if he had news of the tightening immigration laws in the United States, which began to take effect in 1922. The other obstacle was financial. Where would the passage money, remembered as about a hundred dollars for the whole trip, come from? Though Jewish women thought it was unacceptable to clean other families' houses to earn *zlotys,* Dovid's mother did just that to raise the funds for her son's ship-passage. Someone, probably Shenka, wrote to the New York brothers, and they contributed fifty dollars. Soon he had enough for one person's transit. He could never raise enough money to take all of them. Necessity dictated that the family would be separated. Only by going on his own to America would Dovid be able to earn enough for his wife and children to join him.

All this Sarah, bright and observant Sarah, noted. Her acute memories of these days, when she was only four or five years old, is further evidence both of the epochal nature of the crises and Sarah's closeness to her mother. But my hunch is that Shenka did not allow herself to be smothered with her children's needy clinging. Sarah had no memories of her parents' discussion about the decision to emigrate, but she knew that there were differences between them. Shenka thought Poland was increasingly perilous, but she did not want to leave her brothers and cousins behind in Bialystok and Warsaw. If she had her own way, as a left-leaning Zionist, she would have chosen to go to Palestine. But news had recently arrived that a group of several dozen young people who had left Wysokie Mazowieckie for Palestine had fallen prey to malaria and to Arab violence. So her husband's choice became her own. In mid-August 1922, almost two years to the day after the violence that triggered his emigration, Dovid rode by wagon to the closest rail station at Lomza and boarded a train for Warsaw. On August 22, he received a visa at the American consulate in Warsaw, bought a Red Star Line package ticket for travel through Antwerp in Belgium, and arrived in New York Harbor on October 14 on the SS *Zeeland*.

He left behind Shenka, age thirty-one, and three children—Sarah (still called Fruma), age six, Szmul (Samuel), age four, and Isaac, just over a year old. "I had such a horrible feeling that I was never going to see my father again," Sarah remembered many years later. She was wise enough, even at six, to sense the uncertainty, to catch the fear in her mother's reassurances. "Papa was not one of the big earners," Sarah knew. Would he ever be able to bring them together? "He went to better our lives, everybody said, but what could be better than to have him with us?" Shenka, too, must have had a bit of worry, however small, that her husband—like other men who had emigrated from the village—might disappear into the wilds of America and forget about his Polish family. She vowed to keep writing to Dovid through his brothers and sisters-in-law, expecting that they would hold him to his promise.

The children experienced the separation differently. In their father's absence, all three became extremely attached to their mother. Family lore has it that Sam never crossed the domestic threshold without calling out "Mama," even into his late twenties. Isaac, who must have inherited his easy laugh from a distant relative, was the treasured baby, the last testament—in a sense—of the family's intact life before the horrors of the hostage taking. But the two boys soon almost forgot their father entirely.

For Sarah, her father's departure and her parents' separation were the most powerfully formative experiences of her life. Temperamentally more like Dovid than like her mother, she painfully missed his sweetness for six long years. Now she clung to her mother, but Shenka offered fewer warm hugs or cuddles than her husband. Shenka's pain, hunger, fear, and exhaustion were ineradicable. *Tsuris,* misfortune, never seemed to take a holiday. Soon after Dovid departed, Isaac was first diagnosed with rheumatic fever, requiring frequent overnight trips for treatment in Bialystok. Before she was ten years old, Sarah was adept at applying a healing salve to her brother's rash and comforting the aches in his joints. Dovid sent remittances from time to time. Shenka sometimes insisted that Sarah be indulged with a nice sweater or with ribbons for her hair, but it was often hard to make ends meet. Occasionally, she could turn, with some embarrassment, to a half-sister, Malke, whose husband made a good living dealing in black-market goods and forged papers. And even though she recognized the necessity of Dovid's absence, Shenka could not entirely avoid feeling abandoned, feeling angry and jealous that he was already in the *goldene medina,* the New World. The village had, Sarah remembered, six or seven other "Americanskas," wives awaiting the passage-money for reunions in the United States. Even though some of them were better off than their neighbors, they were an "out-caste" in the Jewish community, dwelling in that ambiguous zone where pity could easily slide into envy and disparagement. My mother never forgot the haughtiness of the rich Jews in the shtetl and was always quick to pronounce a triple spit, "pooh, pooh, pooh," recalling how much she hated their air of superiority in the synagogue or on the street.

Life in Wysokie Mazowieckie felt dangerous to the mother and her fatherless children. The local Poles were a constant worry. Representatives of the Polish Republic had fought hard against the requirement by the Great Powers in Versailles that it sign a "Minorities Treaty," promising to grant religious freedom and civil equality to the Jews, Ukrainians, Germans, Lithuanians, and others included in the demographically heterogeneous new nation. Although they acceded to this condition, the Warsaw authorities scarcely concealed their disdain for these non-Poles in a Polish state. After more than a century and a quarter without sovereignty, the new nation did everything it could to isolate, denigrate, and encourage the demise of the Jewish tenth of its population. Jews might, for example, organize a strong socialist party, but the Polish Socialist Party would have nothing to do with it. Jews like Bubbe's half-brothers had no official papers as they sought their fortune in Berlin as illegal immigrants. Germany was no more welcoming, of course, and they made their way to Palestine early in the 1930s, and thus saved themselves from the Shoah.

For my mother, anti-Semitism was local and personal. Relations with the local Catholic peasantry were never easy. Verbal abuse was constant, even over trivial matters, and often led to physical violence. Except for the constant economic interactions, especially at the Monday and Thursday markets in the center of the shtetl, the Jews steered clear of the *goyim* much of the time. Sarah remembered watching with her playmates as the local priest and rabbi, in an alliance unusual in this region, walked up and down the main street plotting to create a new public school that would be open to all children. Each strutted about, hands clasped and fingers interlaced behind his back, or waving his hands to and fro (so the children thought) to dispel the fumes of flatulence he produced. But as there was no other schooling for girls, Sarah was sent to the new school, where she excelled. She was also tortured, day in and day out. In later life, she could still feel where a Polish classmate had yanked a braid out of her scalp. Once, when her mother was with Isaac in Bialystok, Sarah was seized with a toothache. She visited the only dentist in Wysokie Mazowieckie, a Polish woman, who—without a word of comfort, much less anesthetic—pulled the tooth and left the small child bleeding. As she returned to the street, with a blood-stained rag stuck in her mouth, she was attacked by a band of young toughs and their dogs, and barely escaped into a neighbor's front room and welcoming arms. At moments like that, Dovid's absence felt especially painful.

Even today, the geography of the town, though much changed, suggests the division of life. The greensward in the center, once the site of the twice-weekly market, is now the refuge of early morning and late afternoon dog walkers and gossiping pensioners. A kiosk selling cigarettes, lottery tickets, and chewing gum stands at either end. The square is marked with a memorial to the eight or ten local men who died in World War I, so far as I could make out. None of the names sounded Jewish. There is no memorial to the pogrom of 1920.

Two or three low-scaled streets surround the square, with ground-floor shops offering discounts for mobile phones and work boots. This had obviously once been the heart of the shtetl, when the center of Wysokie Mazowieckie consisted of little else. I could imaginatively repopulate the shops with women selling fabrics or ceramic jars of pickles, or men (like Dovid Schwartz) cutting leather for belts and boots. Around the square townspeople could patronize "colonial shops" for canned and bottled goods. One memoirist identified the local Jewish elite as the most prosperous shopkeepers—Brane, Kiwajko, Tomkiewicz, Zakimowicz, Aftel (the pharmacy owner), and Jakobi (the photographer). On market days, the square itself was jammed with stalls—a counter with eggs, pyramids of purple cabbages, and cages of live geese—and customers drawn from the surrounding countryside, where very few Jews dwelled. At the close of those busy days, the Polish farm folk refreshed themselves, inevitably and noisily, at the local Jewish-owned taverns.

Then as now, the shtetl was encircled by beautiful and fertile farm fields. Today Wysokie Mazowieckie looks like a new, bustling town, with hundreds of detached houses and garden apartments on leafy streets radiating in all directions from the seldom-visited town center. Servicing agriculture—equipment sales and repair, supplies of feed and tools, packaging and distribution—is the business of the place. And everything looks fresh and tidy. And, except for an occasional American or Israeli tourist, there are no Jews.

For six long years, from 1922 to 1928, Shenka and Sarah and the boys remained in the shtetl, anticipating letters that seldom came, ready to go, eager to slip off their attachments to this place. They feared what mayhem might destroy their hopes of reunion with Dovid in New York, and they feared what violence lay around the corner every Eastertide when the local peasants were most likely to burn down a Jewish home. Stuck there, stymied.

To compensate, mother and daughter grew even closer. In Dovid's absence, Shenka and the children moved into a new house, with three apartments side by side. In the corner of the front room sat a good, solid stove of stone and brick, with a cooking surface attached to it. The floor was of hard-packed dirt, covered with rugs that needed frequent beating on outdoor clotheslines. There was no running water and no electricity. The latrine out back needed to be washed down with disinfectant. The two large jars of water delivered daily needed to be carefully portioned out for cooking and washing, and the kerosene lamps trimmed and filled with equal economy.

The work was hard, but Shenka reveled in her tasks, cooking to a lip-smacking *tam* or taste, dressing her daughter in crisply ironed blouses. Mother and daughter embraced each other in the warmth of the ceramic stove. Even bathing the children, which entailed lifting buckets of water on and off the stove, was an expression of love. Shenka passed this enthusiasm down to young Sarah "with double interest," as the family would say. The girl inherited her mother's exacting standards. Even the scantiest meal, noodles and a piece of cheese, was herb-seasoned and slowly savored. When Shenka invited the half-dozen "Americanskas," the women waiting to join husbands in the United States, to share their own Passover seder, each was asked to provide one main dish. At the meal, young Sarah exclaimed, "Who made this soup? It's terrible!" Shenka was mortified, and after the guests had gone, she smacked her daughter for her impoliteness. But the next year, Sarah assured each woman beforehand that she needn't cook anything. She and her mother would provide the whole meal themselves.

Fortunately for both mother and daughter, Sarah was not a dreamy child. Over the course of her whole life, she was seldom meditative. Like her grown-up self, she was a keen observer, though with little interest in nature. She never seems to have taken walks along the rural roads leading out of Wysokie, except in the company of the fellow members of a young Zionist "pioneer" group, role-playing their futures as members of a kibbutz in Palestine. But Sarah seems to have noticed everyone and everything along the town streets. Much of her earliest life consisted of watching materials being gathered—food, fabrics, fuel, tools, utensils, containers, and ornaments—and transformed at households and shops into things of value. The Jews of Wysokie Mazowieckie did not live in a self-sufficient economy. They did not grow any of their own food, apart perhaps for a few vegetables and herbs, or fashion their own tools. Other than the children's undergarments, the women didn't make their own clothing. Wysokie was well integrated into the commercial networks wrought by the Industrial Revolution. Mass-produced and commercially distributed goods were everywhere in the market, and one could acquire almost anything available to a sophisticated city dweller, from a jar of caviar to a Model T Ford. And on her trips to Bialystok to visit relatives, Sarah's horizons expanded further. When she arrived on Friday afternoons, her freethinking uncle, a school principal, would whisk her off from the railroad station to an ice-cream parlor and a movie theater. She had fond memories of Cecil B. DeMille's first (silent) version of *The Ten Commandments* (1926). No, she didn't learn a lot in school about the verses of Adam Mickiewicz, the poet of Polish nationalism, or about the life cycle of the butterfly. When she left Wysokie Mazowieckie for America in 1928, she shut the door on any knowledge she had gained of Polish history or folklore. In later life, her Polish consisted only of a few lullabies and nursery rhymes. But the shtetl itself had provided a fine education for such a curious child.

Sarah became her mother's eyes and ears in the community, doing the daily shopping with clear instructions about what to choose and how much to pay. Hers was a hardheaded intelligence, wary of *narishkeit,* or foolishness. She knew exactly when the seasons brought in new fruits and vegetables, and when they were no longer worth buying. Sixty years later, when she visited me in Brooklyn, she would spend her first day scouting the local supermarkets and food shops, then returning home with reports that the price for Bumble

Bee tuna was better at Key Food, but the berries at Dagostino looked fresher. Her purse was still unopened, her battle plan for shopping still being formed. That is what she learned in the shtetl during those six years of Zayde's absence.

Sarah was a playful child, but she had to grow up quickly. She was gradually pressed into service as another parent, expected to assume responsibilities and to exercise skills far beyond her age. The longer they spent together in that little cottage in Poland, waiting impatiently for Dovid to send them passage money, the more dependent they became on one another. Shenka's vulnerabilities—her ailments, her loneliness, her apprehension about Isaac's health, and her anticipation of an explosion of anti-Semitism in the village—rang like alarm bells in Sarah's ears. Later she remembered feeling anxious about her mother, continually on alert for every change of mood.

Late in life, Sarah complained ruefully that "I never had a doll of my own." She had her playmates and school friends, but anecdotes about older girls dominated most of her memories of childhood. Perhaps they had been asked to keep an eye on her and on the house while her mother was away or busy or ill. Shenka attracted a coterie of young women similarly frustrated by the rigid piety of their parents and the absolute authority of their fathers. In that little cottage, where adult men were totally absent, there was lots of lively talk. Many in Shenka's generation were part of what we might call "the Jewish revolution," in which young men and women cast off the authority of local rabbis, modified their adherence to ritual practice, embraced elements of secular culture, and joined in one among a spectrum of political groups, including Communists, Bundists, and diverse Zionists. Fierce arguments among them raged, even within tiny Wysokie Mazowieckie, but most of them recognized that their place in interwar Poland was tenuous, and that a better life lay elsewhere.

My mother recalled many years later that these women would often come to Shenka for advice. First, they would lay out their story: one girl's father had rejected a suitor, or someone's husband wanted to go away to learn a trade. They would ask, *Was zogs du?* What do you say? Shenka was not a bomb-thrower. She usually advised women to make an explicit compromise with the unreasonable men in their households, in the process establishing a principle that they would get part of what they wanted. I have the impression that Sarah was both pleased and frustrated by her mother's attention to all these other people, as a bright, voluble preadolescent might be. They brought life into the cottage but also competed for her mother's affection and time. Sarah missed her father and the "ordinary" family life that she could barely recollect of the days before he left. From time to time, she probably blamed her mother in part, consciously or not, for the separation. But gradually Shenka's wisdom sank in. I smile at the thought that eighty years later Sarah Rabinowitz recreated this role of community sage with the elderly ladies gathered at a swimming pool in Deerfield Beach, Florida.

Sarah watched as adults performed the rituals of worship and life events—circumcising infant boys, celebrating weddings, burying and mourning the dead. But her Judaism was always a religion of action. She left the words to others. The boundary between piety and ordinary life was breached constantly. Everything she did felt like the performance of a ritual. At home, therefore, she became another pair of hands, learning how to keep the cottage spotless, how to keep the stove supplied with coal, how to clean and store every utensil immediately, how to clean and dress her brothers, how, in sum, to make a tidy and quiet home out of the dirt and danger of the world outside. Shenka's *practical* tutelage in the arts of domesticity was a perfect gateway to the *moral* education of her daughter.

Shenka's management of the household, and especially of the kitchen, conveyed a lot more than technical knowledge. Every peeling of an apple, every sip of a simmering soup, and every decision about leftovers also taught Sarah about patience, frugality, and *tzedakah,* righteousness toward others.

Sarah's religion did not come out of a book, not from the Torah and not from a cookbook. It emerged instead from her embrace of everyday tasks, performed with forethought and thoroughness. Hovering over them, perhaps lying in wait around every corner, was something like another artillery shell. After those six years together in Poland, the more that Shenka and Sarah became reliant upon each other, the more they distrusted others. Their loving bond was their security but also their fragility. No parent and no child, we know, are assured of a lifelong tie. What made them strong and special also made them vulnerable to the risks of growing older, weaker, and increasingly challenged by life in a new country.

"Papa, you know, over there, on Scammel Street, in the other candy
store we get a napkin, and they thank us and they give us extra,
and they have all different flavors, and the lady here only
has one kind of ice cream."

3

Papa Doesn't Know from Ice Cream

For the Schwartz family, as for most immigrants, arriving in New York both tightened and loosened the family bonds. Adjusting to the new country required everyone to collude, to play a role in a conspiracy to succeed in America. Even the most confident and adept parent could suddenly turn out to be a bumbler, a *schlemiel,* at some of the operations of ordinary life—spelling his name or getting the correct change at the store. For months, the mother and father were only semiliterate in the language of the streets. The unprecedented happened daily. Parents had to depend on the accelerated adaptability of their children. Each child was tacitly deputized as a scout, discovering and reporting on what was different here. The dinner table, then, became a sort of think tank for assimilation strategies, as family members argued over alternative ways of mastering the challenges of a new homeland. But even the most trustworthy children could not divulge all they learned. Something within each of them was becoming distinctive, secret, American.

One of the first battlefields for the clash of old and new cultures was street food, and particularly ice cream. From the early nineteenth century, New Yorkers—often living in cramped rooms and without the rudiments of cooking equipment—fed themselves with food and drink from wagons, carts, stands, or peddler's packs. The menu has changed over time: hot corn, strawberries, peanuts and chestnuts, baked potatoes, apples and hard cider, hot dogs, soft pretzels, coffee, Danish pastry, Coke, knishes, shaved ice cones, focaccia, gyros, souvlaki, halal chicken, momos, empanadas, pupusas, Poland Spring Water. Many of these were first seen in America on the streets of New York. But ice cream cones, immigrants to the city, have been the all-time champions.

In every generation, city street food threatens parental control. It "spoils your appetite" for family mealtimes. It expands the palate and the nose and may menace the entire digestive tract. It forces open competition among foods, dethroning treasured treats that had held sway for centuries.

Twelve-year-old Sarah Schwartz had her first ice cream cone on New York's Lower East Side a few days after arriving there in August 1928, and she bought them for her brothers as well. Three cents each. For a few days, she remembered, ice cream was their secret. But soon it became a challenge to the family's way of becoming American.

Landings: New York, 1928

Even seventy and eighty years later Sarah Schwartz Rabinowitz beamed with pleasure in remembering her arrival, alongside her mother and brothers, in New York on Sunday, August 26, 1928. After a nine-day passage from Antwerp, she thought the Statue of Liberty looked "so gorgeous in that morning light." At least that's how she remembered it. In fact, August 26 was a cool and rainy day, a relief to New Yorkers, who had suffered through a brutally hot

August, during which twenty-six people had died of sunstroke. With the closing of Ellis Island's immigration station in 1924, ships like the SS *Belgenland* of the Red Star Line carried its passengers, including those in third class, right past the Statue to dock at a pier on Manhattan's West Side. Even before they disembarked, some passengers started to sing, "My Country, 'Tis of Thee."

For Sarah, this was the moment she had long awaited. "The minute the boat came in I recognized my father, even after six years apart." After her father, Dovid Schwartz, showed his naturalization papers to the United States officials and her mother, Shenka, brought forward the visas, issued in Warsaw, for herself and the three children. "It was not hard to get away from the boats," she said. The family sheltered under two umbrellas that Dovid had brought. A porter helped them to a taxi stand, where a newsboy called out the headlines of a terrible subway crash at Times Square two days earlier: "DEATH TOLL REACHES 18, DOZENS AT HOSPITALS." Even without understanding the English words, Sarah knew immediately that New York was a far cry from bucolic Wysokie Mazowieckie.

They crowded into a car, "my first taxi ride," and they were off to their first American home on Manhattan's Lower East Side. Dovid had rented the apartment because it was near Beyeleh Dimnick, a former neighbor in Poland. "I'd rather live near her," Sarah remembers her mother's instructions to Dovid, "than by my sisters-in-law." On the way downtown, Sarah's mind couldn't stop racing. Questions and more questions. What kind of place was this? She had been to visit Bialystok and Warsaw, but New York was so much larger and busier. What would her life here be like? Could she learn to speak English? How about school? Would she find friends? How about the cousins she had never met? What was her Papa like? Did he know a lot about New York life? What would life be like, with the five of us all together again? How would Mama and Papa get along? How would Mama's health be, after all the turmoil of her years alone in Poland?

Sarah couldn't focus. Her brothers kept sliding off the jump seats, giggling, making Papa nervous. Still wearing their overcoats, the newcomers were hot and sticky in the cab, and Dovid opened the window until the rain began to come in. Discomfort competed with excitement. The sky seemed to disappear. Even on a Sunday afternoon, the streets were more crowded than anything she had ever seen. Her head swung left and right, barely catching a glimpse of this and that. Stalled by a traffic jam on the Bowery, Sarah was nauseated at the smell of rotting and stinking garbage on the streets. Later in life, Sarah wondered whether there had been a sanitation workers' strike, but there's no evidence of that. Like many newcomers to the city then and now, she may simply have been overwhelmed by the ordinary piles of uncollected trash. The wooden houses and unpaved, hard-packed dirt streets of the shtetl had been much cleaner than this filthy place, so full of litter and broken things.

The taxi pulled up in front of the dilapidated tenement at 350 Madison Street. Papa paid the fare and led the way out. He prevailed upon the taxi driver to help him bring the family's trunk, plastered over with travel stickers, through the front door into the hallway and up the steep and narrow steps to their second-floor apartment. The children followed, Sam joyfully stamping his boots on the steel front steps, Isaac hauling a little bag that kept banging against his knees. Sarah held her mother's hand. The dark day got darker when they passed through the front door. The cave-like hallway was lit only by a single dim bulb. As they ascended the creaky wooden stairs, they could see cracks of light from doorways opening on either side of them—neighbors checking to see who was moving in.

The front door of their apartment led into a tiny, windowless kitchen, with a single faucet, a large washtub, and a small enameled-top worktable. They walked through to the larger front room, where their trunk had been deposited. They could hardly turn around in the space. Sarah remembered that her father had assembled "such a mishmash of chairs and tables and beds, you would think that a hurricane had dropped all of this into the rooms." Dovid had spent a fortune, hundreds of dollars, as Sarah recalls, to furnish that front room. He bought an ornate dining room set with a mirror over the "breakfront," and a full set of six chairs. "God Almighty," Sarah recalled later with a shrug of the shoulders, "it took me a year to clean the thing." Sarah wondered what they would do with all this furniture. They had little by way of clothing to fill the drawers and the armoire, but Papa told her not to worry. Friends would come with "nice American clothes" for the children. (Sarah wondered what that said about what she was wearing.) Already Dovid's sister-in-law Minnie had brought over a dinnerware service for twelve that she bought on Grand Street. "My mother," Sarah said, "wasn't very happy with it, but we accepted. And we started to use that."

Dovid had bought a porcelain platter and a galvanized white pitcher for milk, and a smaller matching bowl for sour cream. On the dining table he placed bowls of salad. It was my mother's first view of tuna salad, and nearly her last, she would recall seven decades later. She also remembered that a "horrible cake thing" sat in the middle of the table, the icing proclaiming "Welcome to America" in English script. The newcomers, still queasy from the ocean voyage, could stomach little of this. Though they yearned for a bed on terra firma, Dovid insisted on having each of them first drink a bottle of citrate of magnesia, a powerful laxative, to "get all of Europe out of their system." Shenka refused, already in nearly constant discomfort from ulcers. The three children therefore took turns, over the course of the next twelve hours, in trekking to the filthy toilet in the tenement hallway. Sarah could recall mice or rats running across her feet. Nothing in Wysokie Mazowieckie was this disgusting.

The next morning Sarah, characteristically, took matters into her own hands. With a few nickels from her father she went to a nearby hardware store, purchased a heavy brush and cleaning liquid, scrubbed down the toilet walls and floors, put a lock (costing two cents, she recalled) on the door, and gave a key to each of the residents of the floor. Mrs. Katzman, the landlady, was not so thrilled at my mother's brash "*greeneh tuchas*" (immigrant posterior), but she finally stopped screaming long enough to recognize that this was a good idea. Though she lived on the fourth floor, the landlady began to use the much nicer toilets on the second floor, where Sarah kept things spic and span. The twelve-year-old girl had inherited this fastidiousness from her mother. "Mama was spotless," Sarah remembers. "She wore two aprons. If someone dropped in to visit, she took off the top apron. Everyone in the building laughed at how careful she was."

Sarah was certainly Shenka's daughter. But slowly she began to recognize her deep affinity for her father. She was a lot like him. Shenka had little patience for foolishness, even from a child. Dovid was more indulgent. Among her memories of her first American year, Sarah still would smile at her initiation into the American enthusiasm for ice cream. Here's a story she told me in 1988, while we were touring the building that would become the site of the Lower East Side Tenement Museum:

The lady who ran a grocery store on the ground floor of their tenement complained that Dovid's children did not buy ice cream from her. "Schwartzke," she asked, "What's with the kids? Why don't they eat ice cream?"

So my father says, "I don't know from ice cream." My father came upstairs and he said, "Look, she's a nice person, I buy my cigarettes from her. She's a poor widow with three children—three poor children—well, you know, the children are three times as big as you, and she needs to make a living."

So we said, "Papa, she's dirty, her hands are terrible. You know, over there, on Scammel Street, in the other candy store, we get a napkin, and they thank us and they give us extra, because we say, 'we want this color [flavor], this color, this color.'" And they had all different flavors; she only had one kind of ice cream.

I love this story. It's obvious that Sarah was Shenka's daughter, fastidious to a fault, expecting to be treated well. But she was also Dovid's daughter, like him in always aiming to avoid conflict and accommodate others, even at the sacrifice of her convenience or pleasure. My hunch is that Sarah made sure that she and her brothers finished their ice cream on Scammel Street, out of the grocery lady's view.

It's also a story about money. In all her dozens of anecdotes about Wysokie Mazowieckie, Sarah never mentions the price of anything, or buying it, or not being able to afford its purchase. In New York, money comes up all the time. It was an essential ingredient of becoming American. It represented freedom and independence. Thus, when their parents went to gatherings of the Wysokie *landsmanshaft,* the association of their townspeople, Sarah recalls, she and her brothers pried ten cents from her parents so that all three could go to the local movie house at Clinton and Delancey Streets.

But, digging deeper, the ice cream story is also about Dovid's cluelessness—his ignorance about his children and about ice cream, and the quickness with which *they* were mastering the landscape of streets, shops, theaters, schools, and play spaces in the American city. Among the most familiar Yiddish expressions in my family was *"mish dikh nisht areyn"* (mind your own business), most often said to children and others who definitely had no business of their own. Dovid kept his head down, minding his own affairs, missing much of the detail of everyday life that his daughter took in every single day.

Sarah's relationship with her father was inextricably linked to the family's financial struggles. Even in Poland, the legendary success of Jewish immigrants in America had become a popular theme, one which continues to thrive today in those 500-page paperback epics that make perfect beach reading. Did Sarah imagine that her Papa would have come to America with no English and only a few kopecks, and turn himself into a triumphant hero, an industrial giant, a tycoon?

That never happened in my family. We don't come from titans. Our American saga is much more pedestrian. Sarah had no such illusions and she knew, intuitively, that she would have to be the resolute leader of the family's assimilation into American habits of mind, as the hallway toilet story shows. Some steel had obviously gone out of Dovid Czarna's spine after the terrible events of his hostage-taking by the Cossacks in 1920. Coming to America transformed him into a dependent of his older siblings. His Polish passport carries the address of his brother Samuel Schwartz at 216 Henry Street on Manhattan's Lower East Side, perhaps penciled in by the Warsaw travel agent or an American consular clerk. The names of two of his brothers, called Schlemchah and Sachar, were both En-glished into Samuel, so we can't be sure which was the one who welcomed him. Dovid had two other brothers in New York, Elyah (Elijah) and Erschel (Herschel). All of them had switched their Polish surname, which means black, for its German-Jewish equivalent, Schwartz, and Dovid followed suit immediately. Dovid was also dependent on his brothers' recommendations for finding a place to live and take meals. It appears that he had remained in this Manhattan neighborhood for the next six years, though his brothers moved to Brooklyn or the Bronx.

Through his brother Sachar, Dovid also found work as "a presser by women's cloaks," that is, the last workman to put a coat into shape as a garment ready for shipping. In the needle trade, pressers were "low men on the totem pole," compared to the highly skilled cutters and sewing-machine operators (like Sachar). Dovid often showed up at the "*hazzar* (pig) market" in Seward Park, where bosses and contractors rounded up day laborers each morning. And after a day's work with the heavy and dangerously hot coat presses, he couldn't count the blisters they had left on the backs of his arms and hands. Dovid lived in a widow's boarding house on East Broadway with four or five other men during most of the six-year period when his family was left in Wysokie Mazowieckie. In the slack seasons, when the coat factories shifted their seasonal models, he was out of work and forced to look for day jobs in construction. In 1929 and 1930, he spent quite a few days carrying sand for the bricklayers at the Empire State Building project on 34th Street. Every time I walk by that building, I envision a plaque that would commemorate the vital contribution of my zayde to its construction.

Not only was he not an industrial titan, then, but he barely earned the title of breadwinner. On his arrival he was, I hate to say it, already an "old" thirty-two-year-old. Immigrants typically build American lives by relying on relatives and Old Country connections, but Dovid was more passive than most. He never attained much proficiency in reading or speaking English, and he remained eternally baffled by people with New York street smarts.

Dovid had taken six years, an eternity, to raise the money needed to bring his wife and children to America. Other than cigarette smoking, he did not develop bad habits—he did not gamble or take more than one shot of *slivovitz* (plum brandy) a day. And despite the smirks of Shenka's neighbors in Poland, he stayed away from alluring ladies. He was just grateful that his landlady made a hearty borscht, a hefty beef stew, lip-smacking *lokshen* noodles, and a strong cup of morning coffee. With his two breakfast rolls, he could last a whole day of work on his feet. Whatever skills Dovid had acquired in cutting wood, stripping hides, and tanning leathers in Wysokie Mazowieckie were useless in New York. A Polish acquaintance, or someone he met on the ship, apparently advised him to consider settling in Beverly, Massachusetts, in the heart of the shoe-manufacturing district, but nothing ever came of it. He would have been lost without a tether to his brothers. Over the next dozen years he was periodically forced to borrow a few dollars from them to tide his own family over until the slack season ended and he resumed regular employment. Each loan was a humiliation, compounded by a sister-in-law's snide comment, "I don't think we'll ever see that fifty-dollar-bill again!" In other Jewish immigrant families, a self-help association, akin to a credit union, pooled resources that allowed individuals to borrow, sometimes to get ahead, sometimes to meet emergencies. Not among the Schwartzes. Each loan was a separate negotiation. To Dovid (and to Shenka) the behavior of his brothers—whom, after all, he had not seen for a decade until he arrived in New York—

disappointed him. America seemed to have coarsened them. He hated being obligated to them. Once she had come to America, Sarah also overheard the sneers: "He had no business bringing them over if he couldn't afford to make a good living for them!"

Dovid Schwartz was a sweet and gentle man, a lovable person. Later in life, during his slack seasons and in retirement, his greatest joy was to take his granddaughter Beverly for long walks and treat her to delicacies at the bakery or candy store. Even if his arms were tired and scarred from workdays, his hands were soft, warm, and loving. Decades later, I fondly remember his hugs and kisses, his tender touch on my cheeks and shoulders. He knew fabrics so intimately that he could judge the quality of woolens and worsteds with the brush of a finger, and he seemed to have transferred that sensitivity to the way he embraced his *ayniklakh* (grandchildren). Once, when I was marching with my classmates into the auditorium at the start of my graduation ceremony from elementary school, he leapt out of his seat, pulled me out of the line for a moment, kissed me on both cheeks, and then guided me gently back into the procession. Others might have been embarrassed by this impulsive display, but all I recall is how much he loved me. The Yiddish verb for his affection is to *kvell,* to hug oneself with joy over one's dearest ones. I wish I knew the term for what it feels like to be *kvelled* over.

Dovid and Shenka Schwartz lived in an almost completely Yiddish-speaking world. But he was not an old-fashioned, backward-looking, religiously devout Polish Jew. I find it difficult to understand the religiosity of my grandparents. Theirs was a religion of shared practice, not of law or debatable propositions. Their observance of Jewish rituals was rooted in a deep attachment to their community of origin, to the opinions of others like them, and perhaps to some folk proverbs. I don't recall their ever criticizing someone for being lax about the dietary laws or about Shabbos.

Like nine in ten of the immigrant Jewish men in East New York and Brownsville, Dovid did not attend synagogue every week, even when he did not have to *schlep* into the Garment District for work on Saturdays. When he did go, he was like many attendees at these Orthodox services, who pronounced the prayers rapidly, unreflectively, as an exercise of muscle memory familiar to them from early childhood. Dovid was not a *macher,* a big shot. He did not have the money to bid for an *aliyah,* in which he would be called to the Torah, and the congregation did not think to honor him for his community service. He raced through the morning, Torah, and additional worship services with his companions, standing for the core prayer, the *Amidah* and its "eighteen blessings," *shuckling* forward and back in his pew and paying little heed to the rabbi's complaints in a Yiddish sermon about the declension of piety in America. He had no patience, and no intellectual preparation, for commentaries on the Aramaic and Hebrew texts in the Torah and Talmud. At the end of Shabbos services, he joined the other men at the Kiddush for a shot of whisky and maybe a piece of herring and black bread.

Then he strolled the block home, dug into a nice veal sandwich on a slice of challah left over from the night before, drained a big bottle of Trommer's beer (opened with the Edlund utensil that his daughter had brought home as a gift), and lay down for a Shabbos snooze. He did not return to the synagogue for the *havdalah* services concluding the Sabbath, or indeed, until some future Saturday morning. He abstained from smoking on Shabbos, and, if possible, from carrying money. But he was not strictly observant. At Rosh Hashanah and Yom Kippur, he wanted his granddaughter Beverly to sit with him, despite the frowns of congregants who wanted all women and girls firmly confined behind the *mechitzah,* or partition.

He was a member of the International Ladies' Garment Workers Union, a hotbed of union organizing in 1930s New York. And he joined the Workmen's Circle, a lodge for pro-socialist, Yiddish-speaking Jewish workers—through which he gained access to life insurance, free loans, and a network of doctors and clinics. The union sponsored cultural programs in Manhattan but also in Browns-ville, and these afforded members their best opportunities to see live theater. Dovid and Shenka also joined the Wysokie Mazow-ieckie *landsmanshaft,* the association of immigrants from his shtetl, and they attended its annual dinner at the Hotel Diplomat in Man-hattan. Some historians distinguish among those immigrants who leaned left politically, those who were religiously observant, and those whose identity was rooted in Old Country attachments. Dovid was all three, like many other men. But he was not an active member of any of these groups. He did not attend regular meetings, and he certainly never stood for office. He liked sitting in the back row. He enjoyed his several friends and family connections, mostly when he met them in Shenka's company. (She was the social magnet.) They were good for jokes about Poland but not much for jobs in New York. None of them, it turned out, ever opened a store, bought a truck, owned a piece of an apartment building, or leased a ma-chine that produced anything. All of them were, like him, wage workers. Consequently, in the parlance of our own day, he had no network to give him a step up.

He was much less political than his wife and he periodically fought with his younger son, Isaac, who joined the Communist Party, but he shared with them—and with thousands of his generation of men and women in leftist or Zionist groups in Eastern Europe, Palestine, and America—the conviction that he lived for the future, for his children's and grandchildren's future success, and not for his own. Shenka and Dovid became American citizens and voted regularly, but they seldom ventured out of their own social worlds. They knew that their children would not be so confined, although they were always cautious about the promise of assimilation.

So when it came to observing the public world of New York City, they were often agog. During her first year there, Shenka returned home one day and exclaimed, "What an amazing country this is—they built a park right down the middle of Delancey Street!" She meant the median strip on the newly widened access street to the Williamsburg Bridge. But the outside world mostly meant unwelcome intrusions into their newly reunited household. In the 1920s, with many fewer cars and trucks than today, the streets—not just the sidewalks—were filled with children playing, men and women repairing shoes and sewing artificial flowers, and everyone buying and selling something. From April to October, whenever it wasn't raining, every front window opened onto the street, and older people leaned over pillows to survey the scene below. The noise was unending. Trash was everywhere—banana peels, shards of broken crates, discarded cigarettes and cigarette packs. Shenka was horrified. Walking along Madison Street on one of her first days as a New Yorker, she saw a nicely dressed young woman pelted with wads of filth by neighborhood boys.

Still, Shenka was the hardier character of the two. With Sarah's assistance, Shenka gradually took over the reins of the family. Her handsome husband was by no means a pitiful character, but Dovid's authority was undercut by his basic shyness, his precarious hold on a livelihood, and his unfamiliarity with his two sons. Over the years, this once young and gutsy lumberman and leatherworker had shrunk within himself. He became more and more self-effacing. His fears flourished. He worried about everything, and his worries became a greater cause of concern in the house than what worried him. He would from time to time, however, reassert his authority—forbidding his children to go somewhere or to spend money on something, or pressing them to "be nice" to his neighbors.

Shenka did her best to give Dovid respect. "She never criticized him," my mother remembered, "she never pushed him." Unlike other wives in the building who called their husbands by their surnames—"Adler," "Feldstein," and so on—she always called him Dovid, his name in Yiddish. Everyone consulted him before buying a wool suit or coat. He insisted on the finest material. And in turn Dovid reciprocated with real respect for his wife's intelligence. Jewish husbands, a commentator notes, commonly called their wives *"Hersdu?"* (Do you hear this?), as if the wife was the ultimate reality tester. He washed the dishes when she was busy with other tasks, and even scrubbed the floors when she was ill. In the end, they had a keen sense of each other's strengths and weaknesses.

But they could do little for their children. Though she had only been in the country a few weeks, Sarah had to take the responsibility for enrolling herself and her brothers in school. At registration, she was asked by the local school clerk, an African American woman, what she wanted as her "American" given name. She mumbled something about "Shirley," but the clerk told her that "Sarah, with an h" was much nicer—and that became her name for the rest of her life. "Fruma," her shtetl name, vanished. Sam and Isaac went directly into the third and first grade classes, but Sarah joined an "Absorption School" class, sharing a classroom and English lessons with other immigrant children aged six to eighteen. She loved school, but it was hard to make friends in a classroom without girls of her age.

Sarah did not easily overcome her disappointment in America. She felt betrayed when she returned on a school trip to the Statue of Liberty on a drizzly afternoon to discover it garbed in a dreary grey-green. Her world was tightly bounded by the Lower East Side neighborhood. For two or three years, Times Square was only a rumor to her. "I felt that I knew Bialystok much better than New York!" she recalled. On the other hand, she loved the movies and especially the vaudeville acts that followed the films. She tried to get her brothers to hide under the seats so that they could see the shows again, but they were invariably discovered and routed by the "matrons." The Educational Alliance, a settlement house on East Broadway, introduced her to basketball, handcraft classes, and dance lessons.

Sam, the older of Sarah's two brothers, felt trapped in New York. A shy boy, he had already been tested in Poland during his years as the oldest male in the family. Sam wanted to protect his mother from every injury and problem, but he was always a bit daunted by Sarah's superior competence and self-confidence. Arriving in America at age nine, he never quite took to his father after their long period of separation. Dovid's efforts to exercise authority invariably sparked Sam's resistance.

Though he was the best-looking of the Schwartzes, carefully dressed and a fine student in high school, Sam internalized all of the family's worst anxieties. He dropped out of school, captivated by the allure of a job offer of $20 a week in a milliner's shop. But after a while, as might be expected, that job vaporized, and Sam followed his father as a presser in the shops making women's coats. He could barely snag a place from week to week. Instead, he relied upon the "shape up" in the Garment District every morning. When he failed to get a job that day, he passed his time, fruitlessly, hanging out with his cronies—most of whom Sarah considered "nothings"— at a candy store on Livonia Avenue. "Schmuggy," as he was called, was self-deprecating to a fault and cynical about all of his brother-in-law Dave's schemes and his brother Isaac's political causes. He was torn in half by his parents' expectations. Faced with the draft in early 1942, he tried desperately to figure out how to avoid serving. Shenka was clear: *Daf gehen,* you have to go. His mother encouraged, but his father was the negative one, and he crippled Sam's initiative. Dovid was horrified when Sam was selected for the paratroopers, and Sam's sons believe that he deliberately flunked out of trooper training to avoid upsetting his old man.

The outlier in all of this was Isaac Leib Schwartz, the youngest sibling. He was a sickly child, his heart weakened by chronic disease, and as a young man he was wounded during his World War II service. He was nonetheless the cheeriest member of the Schwartz clan. He was my favorite, and his GI photo sits right next to my computer screen as I write this. Only seven years old when he arrived in New York City, Zeke was already a radical in his early teens. His complete indifference to religion vexed his father. But Shenka, to whom he was fiercely attached, was a more powerful influence. She was an ardent *linke,* a leftist, who read the communist *Di Freiheit* [Freedom] while her husband read the liberal *Der Tog* [The Day]. (Almost every one of the ten Yiddish dailies in New York leaned to the left. The most popular paper, the socialist *Der Forverts* [The Forward], with a circulation of a quarter-million, found no takers in the Schwartz household.) Unhappy from her first days in the United States, Shenka distrusted American politicians and had little faith that her children would prosper here. Zeke did not derive his politics from reading the classics of Marxism. He was not an intellectual. Nor was he an alienated assembly-line worker, a member of the industrial proletariat on whom Marxists depended as the vanguard of revolution.

Before he left school, before he began work in earnest, Zeke was convinced of the injustice of capitalism in two ways—first in the

misery he could see all around him in Brooklyn, but more important in the frustration he saw in his own family. His father's, his
brother's, and, later, his brother-in-law Dave's desperation for the
dollar registered its humiliation on him, the baby of the family, perhaps more than on his elders themselves. The oft-repeated motto
of the impoverished immigrant community, *Gelt is de welt* (money
is the world), repelled him, as it would me a generation later. Shenka's clear-eyed perspective on her new home—glad that she was safe
here and still intensely critical of the injustices in a capitalist system—
empowered Zeke's own politics. She was never hearty enough to
join other leftist women on neighborhood picket lines, but she respected her youngest child's willingness to help carry an evicted
family's belongings back into their apartment. Her caustic views
opened Zeke's eyes to the poverty and violence of America and allowed him to become his own man. In turn, his radicalism unshackled the political opinions of the next generation, of my sister
and me, and of his own children.

Zeke was more than a casual sympathizer for the communist
cause. He begged his mother to allow him to join the Abraham Lincoln Brigade fighting the fascists in Spain in 1936 or 1937—he was
only fifteen when the civil war started. She refused. He was a stal-
wart of the Young Communist League at Thomas Jefferson High
School. His daughter Jeanne preserved this mock diploma, distributed as a leaflet,

**Board of Education
of the City of N.Y.
John Student
has completed satisfactorily a four year course
at the Thomas Jefferson H.S. and is here-
by authorized to graduate into the 7th year**

of the Depression with the degree of Bachelor of
the "Lost Generation"
He now merits the study of unemployment, war
fascism, hunger, crime and prison
In testimony whereof we have affixed our
signatures hereto this 24 day of June 1937
(signed) Pres. of Industry Pres. of Board of Ed.
To blot out the mentioned prospects, join the
YOUNG COMMUNIST LEAGUE
for a life with a purpose
You can become part of our educational,
social, and athletic life at the
following places:
397 New Jersey Avenue, 558 Warwick Street,
105 Thatford Avenue
[all in East New York or Brownsville]
Issued by the Thomas Jefferson H.S. branch
YOUNG COMMUNIST LEAGUE
[printed by Rotary Process, 799 Broadway,
and union label]

Zeke found work as a housepainter and paperhanger, and he loved regaling us with stories of his attendance at Communist Party events on New York's Upper West Side, when well-coiffed fellow travelers would ask him about his work. "I'm a painter," he would reply, and they would press him further, "and what's your medium?" "Latex on walls," he responded, always to be met with a stunned silence. "You can see my work in the best apartments and hotels in the city!"

He was irrepressibly good-humored, though dead serious and consistent in his politics. He never entirely gave up the party line and the cause, even unto his death in 1998, not even after the pact with Hitler in 1939, the Khrushchev speech revealing Stalin's crimes in 1956, the Prague Spring of 1968, or the collapse of the Warsaw Pact and the Berlin Wall in 1989. He always believed that Stalin had saved millions of Jews from the advancing Nazi troops by transporting them to the eastern edges of the Soviet Union in 1941–42. Even when elected a county committeeman for the Democratic Party in Brooklyn, he held to his ideological positions. He never talked about party meetings or political actions with other family members, and this reticence created a zone of anxiety for Sarah. Did he have a double life? I doubt it. He retained all of his boyhood friends, though none of them signed on as party comrades. When he was demobilized from the service in October 1945, he raced home in the middle of the night and burst into my parents' apartment. Everyone rushed to hug and kiss him. But his first thought, Mom remembered, was to reach into my crib and lift and toss me up in the air—I was three months old—and shout his joy at his new nephew. I have never known a sweeter person.

Best of all, he was an ardent anti-racist, in a place and time where vicious stereotypes were common. While Brooklyn's Black population was growing in the 1940s, our family and our neighbors had few contacts with Black people. In the work world, they encountered Black domestic workers, delivery men, and "stock boys" at larger shops. As consumers, East New York's Jews confined their patronage to butcher shops, bakeries, and fish stores catering almost entirely to a Jewish clientele. To be sure, there was no apartheid in the public sphere. Jews sat next to Blacks on buses and subways, at public offices and medical facilities, and took their leisure alongside Blacks at parks, playgrounds, ballfields, and swimming pools. At the movies and on the radio, Blacks were often represented as subservient but also as more sensible than their white bosses or "superiors": think of Eddie "Rochester" Anderson on the Jack Benny Show. A half-joking but still toxic racism persisted around gin rummy tables and backyard barbecues. Parental directions about travel in the city often included not-so-subtle instructions about avoiding predominantly Black neighborhoods. Over coffee and donuts, or Canadian Club and soda, card players dealt out plenty of anecdotes illustrating the supposed inferiority of Black people, without any objection. A shared history of violent European pogroms and more casual American anti-Semitism made most of the Jews we knew more wary of strangers, not more sympathetic to others who also suffered stigmatization. Racial prejudice could serve as a basic social bond among our neighbors and, most tragically, an easy gateway into becoming an American.

But our Uncle Zeke, temperamentally mild and constantly smiling, laid down the law. He forbade Beverly and me from expressing fears about a "bogeyman" hiding in the backyard. Zeke viewed that as an anti-Black slur. No one was allowed to make dialect jokes in his company, whether Yiddish or those mimicking southern Blacks—although these had been my father's stock-in-trade as a part-time comic in his youth. We never got to see *Gone with the Wind* or Disney's *Song of the South* because they presented an insulting view of Black Americans, nor could anyone order in Chinese food if they called it "Chinks." Zeke, who had many Black friends in the movement, traveled to Peekskill, New York, to defend Paul Robeson from racist rioters in 1949. Other kids got bicycles when they graduated from junior high, but my Uncle Zeke and Aunt Luba bought me a beautiful set of Frederick Douglass's writings at the Jefferson Bookstore near Union Square in Manhattan, a shop owned by the Communist Party. I returned there often in high school to get books about Black history. There was no other place in New York to find them.

Zeke followed the party line when the Soviet Union voted in 1947 at the United Nations to end the British Mandate for Palestine, endorsing partition and the creation of the State of Israel (and a Palestinian state as well). But when the Soviets turned against Israel in the 1950s, Zeke loyally opposed Zionism as antagonistic to the shared interests of all working people. This sparked a decades-long cold war with his older sister. Sarah had been affiliated with Zionist youth groups even in childhood, and she retained a deep commitment to Israel for her whole life. One of my fondest childhood memories was Zeke's arrival at our house at 9:30 or 10 PM, after a long day of work. He was always ready for a fresh cup of coffee, and his sister was equally ready to offer him a sandwich, some homemade cookies, and a chat. They would sit across from each other at our dinette table, sometimes for hours, and share stories, complaining about the corruption of Brooklyn politicians and policemen, until they came to Mideast politics. Then they would ping-pong vehemently opposed opinions, my mother a little more shrill, Zeke always calm and self-assured. They bartered anecdotes. She would invariably start, "Let me tell you something," and he would counter, "I'll tell you one thing," as if they had learned debating from the same coach. I marveled that they could do this week after week, never reconciling their positions but always expressing such deep devotion to each other. That you could disagree politically and still love each other—that was a great lesson.

The long economic depression of the 1930s hollowed out the economic prospects of my grandfather and my Uncle Sam, and to a large extent, my father, Dave Rabinowitz. You would never have known it from their physical appearance. Growing up, I was always aware of how "sharp," how well dressed they were. They could not count on a better tomorrow, but they were always ready for today, always dressed for the show, somewhere between dapper and dandyish. They adopted carefully chosen men's clothing and accoutrements—silk ties knotted perfectly, well-shined shoes, polished cufflinks, leather gloves, carefully coiffed hair, and aftershave lotion. They invariably displayed an image of mastery, an easy elegance without stiff formality. Beverly thought her Uncle Sam "looked like a movie star." They aimed to glide through life, floating above the raw streets of the immigrant neighborhood. They loved the weddings and bar mitzvahs, even with the dowdy cousins, and the other celebratory dinners, where they could show themselves to the best advantage.

But, though dressed to the nines, these hollow men actually felt like twos or threes on the inside. Under their gloves, their hands were less calloused than they would have liked, for that would have represented more time at work. As the Depression deepened, the material of their lives moved farther and farther away from the world of making things. They were surrounded by stuff that was worrisomely either bureaucratic or trivial. Many days, their passage led through a blizzard of threatening signs—posted notifications of factory closings, induction notices, leaflets about upcoming meetings, examinations, regulations, and qualifications for positions they could not get. Or they devoted their time to objects of pleasure rather than the tools of work—cigarettes and sodas, pool cues and racks, overdue notices from the library. Movie tickets were no substitutes for pay slips, cue chalk not a satisfactory substitute for muscle liniment. Unworthiness assaulted them on all sides. On the line on the form where it asked, "Occupation?" they had nothing to write.

I can't judge them harshly. Quite the contrary. Each of them loved me and loved my sister unfailingly, decade after decade. Our zayde Dovid Schwartz, our uncles Sam and Zeke, and our father, Dave Rabinowitz, were each capable of extremely tender love and generosity. But the pain of their lives, apart from us, is unmistakable. They were dedicated to providing for their families and expected to succeed in this role, but they simply could not score a success in worldly terms. Fortunately for all of us, they did not become self-destructive or abusive. They were saved, I believe, by the strength and love of Shenka and Sarah. Our family could barely have survived the crisis of immigration from pogrom-torn Poland into Depression-era America without the tenacity of these two women. They doggedly maintained a vision of a stable, well-managed household as a polestar for the future, and they figured out how to bring comfort to every single day.

But nothing comes without a cost. Sarah's bond with Shenka showed in her impassioned sensitivity about any insult or injury—real or imagined—directed at her mother. Beverly and I developed a similar defensiveness about our father, grandfather, and Uncle Sam. We came to mix our love with sadness, almost pity, and maybe a bit of condescension. Our generation, especially the male members of it, knew that we were much luckier than our parents, and a thousand times more secure than our grandparents. Our scores on school tests and our career successes were, I'm convinced, accidents of history rather than accurate measures of our abilities. It's likely that we overcompensated for the failures of the men who came before us.

My mother's sympathy for the underdog, exemplified in daily acts of *tzedakah,* most powerfully shaped Beverly's and my politics. But witnessing the pain, the wasted talents, of the men in our family proved the urgency of our commitment to social good. Their heartache and disappointment still tear at me. Frankly, it embitters me toward those who are more privileged and escape this pain. Yes, there are many others in my American world who suffer needlessly, but whatever sympathy I have for them, especially for the immigrants among them, was born in the hurt of my zayde, my Dad, and my Uncle Sam.

*These repurposed cigar boxes housed the housewife's spools of thread,
the half-broken pieces of the children's Crayola crayons, and the
handyman's drill bits. They were, paradoxically, emblems of
abundance, of having more than you needed right now, in a
metropolis of scarcity.*

4

Shenka Puts Pencils
Away in a Cigar Box

Immigrants like the Schwartzes who arrived in steerage with a family trunk did not often need (or find!) closets in their tenement apartments. After all, dressers, armoires, and kitchen cabinets would take up precious floor space in dwellings that measured less than 500 square feet. Eventually, though, the newcomers had no choice. They needed to separate special things—dress shoes, seasonal clothes, and precious keepsakes—from the objects of workaday use. A winter coat had to be put aside in March, as did the goose-feather quilt. Offsite storage units did not exist. So heavy, carved pieces of furniture, often bought used, were recruited to serve as storage.

There were few purpose-made containers for smaller items in most households, apart from those used in remunerative work. Adolfo Baldizzi, the carpenter whose family lived at 97 Orchard Street and whose story is interpreted by the Lower East Side Tenement Museum, fabricated his own tool box. Tenement denizens rarely had the time or the resources to pursue hobbies and crafts. So there were not many well-designed holders for a hobbyist's collections, supplies, or ongoing projects, like a camera case or a fisherman's tackle box. Jewelry boxes were the exception. They had proliferated in aristocratic and bourgeois boudoirs over the centuries, but it was Coco

Chanel's notorious popularization of costume jewelry in the 1920s that opened the floodgates for such ornaments among all classes. F. W. Woolworth & Co. probably was selling plenty of jewelry and jewelry boxes by the time Sarah arrived in Manhattan.

It was the plastics boom of the 1940s that spurred the availability of empty, closeable containers of every shape and size, suitable for holding bulk (flour, sugar), bits and pieces (nuts, pasta), or liquids (pancake syrup, vanilla extract). Earl Tupper did not patent his "burping seal" Tupperware storage containers until 1946. Rubbermaid did not get into the plastics business until 1956. The Container Store retail chain did not exist until the 1970s. When a film of the 1930s and 1940s showed a character getting a piece of pie or a sandwich from the icebox, it was usually sitting right there, on a plate. For most households, including my family's, reuse of commercial packaging came to the rescue. Cigar boxes, originally of wood and then of cardboard (introduced ca. 1840), shoeboxes (ca. 1890), and snap-lid tin boxes for Sucrets cough drops (1931) could store a thousand different items, often with identification labels fastened on with Scotch tape (1930). Coffee cans, dating back to the mid-nineteenth century, became excellent catchalls for brushes and small tools. Wooden cheese boxes placed on warm-weather windowsills became perfect sites for displaying small flowers. No one ever threw one away.

Outdoors, in the world of the street, the wooden orange crate (1892) ruled supreme, until it was replaced by cardboard in the 1950s. Today the brightly colored label has become important to collectors, but the wooden crate itself, measuring 12″ by 12″ by 27″, was the fundamental building block of Brooklyn street life for over six decades. Orange crates were stacked side by side on pushcarts and in market stalls, one kind of fruit or vegetable to each crate. Set on end, proprietors used them as stepladders to reach high shelves or the tops of awnings. On nice days, crates provided seats and tables for matches of dominoes, checkers, chess, or craps. Orange crates were the thrones of kibitzers, the onlookers and bystanders who let nothing on the street go unnoticed. In an era of widespread under-employment, sitting on a wooden box was pretty good work for a day, bumming cigarettes, sharing a bottle, "waiting for one's ship to come in." For boys, even into my generation during the 1950s, orange crates supplied the bodies of our "scooters." They rested on a wooden board to which roller-skate wheels were attached—vehicles for competing in our version of the all-American Soap Box Derby.

All these boxes lacked what our glass or plastic containers now give us—those smooth and sanitary surfaces and made-to-measure capacity. They kept the women of the house in touch with the rough industrial processes of mass production. Both in their feel and in their utility, all of these repurposed trade containers were, para-doxically, emblems of *abundance,* of having more than you needed at the moment, in a metropolis of *scarcity.* These containers stored the housewife's spools of thread, left over from darning the children's socks. They housed the half-broken pieces of the children's Crayola crayons. They sheltered the handyman's drill bits. For all of these, a commercial box with a handsome pictorial label was just the ticket. Stacked neatly on a shelf in the bedroom armoire, they represented a defense against destitution.

The overabundance of unusable men and women during the De-pression was a greater malady that storage boxes could not cure.

Housekeeping Women: Brooklyn in the 1930s

In 1929, Shenka decided that she could more easily put up with her husband's family than with the filth of Manhattan, and they moved to East New York in Brooklyn. Once it had been a settlement of

Dutch farmers, and then of Yankee industrialists and German and Irish laborers. Now this part of East New York was a half-step up from the adjoining neighborhood of Brownsville—which had replaced the old Lower East Side ghetto as the largest and densest Jewish community in the world—and rivaled it as the poorest. The Schwartz family occupied a three-room cold-water flat at 458 Alabama Avenue, heated erratically by a coal stove. Dovid saved Shenka the trouble of filling the coal scuttle every morning and carrying it up to the fourth-floor apartment. A year later, in 1930, economic conditions worsened after the market crash. Rents fell, and they moved around the corner to an apartment on Williams Avenue with hot and cold running water and steam heat, all for $28 per month, with a new paint job thrown in. Families preferred to move just before Passover, so that they could cleanse the apartment of dirt and *hametz* (or traces of leavened bread) at the same time.

Sarah was a good student, and she sped through two years and summer sessions at Junior High School 109. By age fourteen, she had caught up to her American-born age cohort. Her favorite teacher, Mrs. Sherman, pressed her to go on to high school, and Sarah actually registered at Thomas Jefferson High School in the fall of 1930. As always, she felt the sting of poverty and the indignity of unemployment as a terrible insult to her parents, and so she abandoned her plans for more schooling. Sarah, hard-headed Sarah, never had fantasies of a working life outside the home. "I knew the situation we were in." She enjoyed a part-time job with some local lawyers, but they paid her a pittance. Instead she traveled daily to the Garment District in the West 30s of Manhattan, seeking out signs with the golden words, "Girl Wanted for the Day." Some evenings she brought home three or four dollars, some none at all, but every penny was needed. She was eager to relieve her parents of the responsibility of caring for her.

On one occasion, she was paid only a dollar for the day. As she was preparing to leave, the owner asked her to lend him ten cents for his own carfare. She entrusted him with two nickels from her little purse, asking in return whether he would have work for her tomorrow. "Tomorrow?" he replied, "no, not tomorrow, but Thursday, come in Thursday." So when Thursday came around, Sarah was right there, first thing. And on the door, she saw the note, "Shop closed." And through the glass she saw that everything in the shop, every sewing machine and mannequin, every pair of scissors and spool of thread, was gone.

She often roamed the Garment District with her friend Tessie, also an immigrant and not so haughty as Sarah's American-born cousins. Tessie was an orphan, dwelling with a stingy aunt in Brooklyn, her upkeep paid by an uncle in Philadelphia. Once, having failed to find work, the two fifteen-year-olds passed by Macy's in Herald Square, "the world's largest store," and decided to peek inside. Half-expecting to be evicted by a security guard, they instead found their way to the sparkling and colorful housewares department. For Sarah, this was a glimpse of heaven. Wall-mounted can openers, nickel-plated potato mashers, a dozen kinds of slotted spoons, gravy strainers, milk strainers, wine strainers—gadgets whose uses were as mysterious and unfamiliar as the American cities where they were manufactured. A new cookbook, Sarah remembers, was being introduced. Years later she thought it might have been Irma Rombauer's *Joy of Cooking,* but that did not find a national publisher until years afterward. A lady in a starched apron was preparing samples of dishes made from the recipes in the book, cooking them right in the store. The two girls gawked. They each held the other back from reaching out to try the delicacies arrayed before them. An older gentleman behind them said, in Yiddish, *"nemst du a bisl,"* take a little bit, and they did. Delicious! Feeling as though they had just robbed the First National Bank, they giggled their way delightedly out to the subway and the trip back to Brooklyn.

Sarah rushed upstairs to tell her mother all about her discoveries. But Shenka had no patience for such foolishness. Sarah felt her mother's disapproval like a slap in the face. "What business is it of yours to go looking at things like that? Your eyes should not waste your money." Sarah's pain, she confessed, was palpable. But she was hooked, forever, on kitchen gadgets, and she loved bringing them home, waiting until she was alone, and trying them out for herself.

Each of the many apartments in the four-story buildings along the streets of East New York opened into a kitchen. In warm weather, or on weekends, when residents and visitors kept streaming in and out, cooking smells permeated the hallways and stairwells. Garlicky tomato sauce signaled an Italian family. Boiled cabbage smells migrated from an Irish family's doorway. At 502 Alabama Avenue, the wife of the Polish "super" was said to make a soup with duck blood, or at least that's how neighbors explained the weird odor, my sister remembers, that came from their ground floor apartment. But the prevailing aroma of 502's halls emanated from the pans frying *schmaltz* or chicken fat in all those Jewish kitchens. *Gribbenes,* or chicken skin fried with onions, perfumed the air for days after its last greasy bits were consumed. Fried potato pancakes, or *latkes,* not reserved for Hanukkah as they often are today, offered a more pleasant smell. Fried fish, broiled liver, and roasted chicken told the whole world that paychecks were good. *Lokshen* (noodles) with farmer cheese and stewed vegetables quietly hinted at hard times. Rolled up in dough and fried gently, farmer cheese and fruit preserves served as the filling for *blintzes,* the Ashkenazic version of crepes. From the Schwartz apartment the nicest smells were of baking—bialys and challah. Sarah was already a more ambitious baker than her mother, turning out cakes, pies, and a dozen kinds of cookies—twice-baked *mandelbrot* (almond-flavored cookies with a hint of vanilla, sometimes with raisins, resembling biscotti), vanilla and chocolate cookies curled like snails, *rugelach* (dough rolled around a filling of *lekvar* or prune butter and walnut bits), chocolate chip, and oatmeal raisin cookies. In later years, when Mom was baking, a line would form in the second-floor hallway—the building's children waiting patiently to get one of Sarah's wonderful treats.

After Sarah was married in 1935, and especially after Shenka and Dovid moved into an apartment at 502 themselves, mother and daughter were frequently in and out of each other's kitchens. The kitchen was where they spent most of their lives and felt most at home. It was their workplace but also their sanctuary, in effect the laboratory in which they reinvented themselves as Americans. Though they had crossed an ocean a decade earlier, Sarah and Shenka shared kitchen talk much as they had before emigrating. The men of the household came and went, taking their meals, delivering their news and opinions, and exhaling cigarette smoke and shoulder-weary complaints into the close air of the tiny rooms. If they lingered for more than a minute, the men were sure to be accused of wasting time, and were rapidly shooed out. How else could work get done? The room was small. Its workspace was limited by the doorways to the middle room, to the toilet, and to the exterior. The stained white walls, needing to be repainted every year or so, were covered with shelves and piles of implements. Counter space was still decades away, so after the dishes for one meal were cleaned up, the dining table was pushed up against the wall, and the labor of preparing the next few meals resumed.

The Brooklyn kitchen was better outfitted than the cottage in Wysokie Mazowieckie. Here steam heat blasted out of radiators, hot and cold water flowed from the faucets, and for a few extra dollars each month, the landlord supplied an electric refrigerator, which eliminated the stains and the strains of leaking iceboxes. But the city soot was on every sill and shelf, and the linoleum floor was harder to keep clean than the hard-packed dirt of the shtetl cottage. The noise could be deafening. The IRT elevated train clattered half a block away. Delivery trucks growled along the narrow streets, honking horns to express the drivers' frustration. Up the stairs and down the halls of 502, Shenka and Sarah could hear every extreme of human voice from bawling babies and the screaming of spouses to the incessant weeping of the abandoned. "You could hardly hear yourself think."

They concentrated their attention on the tasks at hand. Cooking deserved it. In the flux of American life, when jobs were scarce and often intermittent, and the prospects for the young very uncertain, Shenka and Sarah used food to secure their menfolk in a comfortable and stable home life. The more familiar the flavors, the less precarious America would feel. The women made a point of not complaining about sparse funds, and the men ate gratefully what they were served. They were never asked what they preferred, and pickiness about particular foods was not allowed. There was enough *tsuris* in the world, everyone acknowledged, and no one wanted to add another drop to the family's portion.

Shenka and Sarah did not adopt American foodways. They did not want to abandon their Polish-born cuisine. So only those ingredients and tools that helped them make a *familiarly* tasty meal were important to them. White bread, Silvercup or Wonder Bread, as we will see, was not. "It tasted like air," Mom complained. Canned soups were too salty. Better to buy spices from Moishe's little shop on Livonia Avenue—he was a nice man, with "a family to feed." Crisco was a genuinely valuable innovation. It was *parve,* that is, neither meat nor dairy, and consequently could be used as shortening with meals of either type. For Procter and Gamble, its maker, the

Jewish market was significant, as the company demonstrated by issuing a Yiddish-language cookbook in 1935. But, my sister assures me, Bubbe and Mom would never have made any of the dishes in the Crisco cookbook—they were too fancy, too *goyish,* altogether too much trouble. Later, when Mom became an expert pie baker, she loved using Crisco, and pried open the pressed lid cover with the Edlund bottle opener. Sarah began to write down recipes on scraps of paper and eventually on index cards, sometimes after tasting something really unusual at the table of a cousin, a friend, her daughter, or a daughter-in-law, but she never owned a cookbook. She always thought in terms of meals, not dishes.

Brooklyn offered a much greater variety of ingredients than had Wysokie Mazowieckie. The shtetl was still largely a world of unmixed ingredients. True enough, canned goods filled the shelves of the "colonial" store in the village center. But basic foodstuffs still had a local genealogy. Flour came from a nearby grist mill, water from neighboring wells, butter, milk, and cheese from cows given names by the dairyman, potatoes and onions from so-and-so's garden patch. The kitchen was a place where the ingredients of dishes were combined.

In the American metropolis, year by year, the women witnessed the arrival of a huge variety of packaged and processed foods to the market. Condensed milk, granulated sugar, bleached flour, hydrogenated vegetable oil shortening, double-acting baking powder, condensed soups, canned vegetables, spices in tin boxes, and packaged noodles and cereals conveniently allowed homemakers to skip onerous steps in preparing meals. (They also dotted the Yiddish-speaking kitchen with its first English words—names like McCormick, Heinz, Carnation, Domino, Crisco, and Campbell's.) The Schwartz women made meals of these ingredients that were refined or processed in the factory before reaching store shelves.

On the other hand, fresh ingredients were highly inconsistent and often unreliable in the city. Some were sold by weight, others by volume. Fruits and vegetables were seasonally available and of uncertain origin and freshness. The heat source on the gas range and oven was only barely more precise than the coal stove that preceded it in Poland and America. The marketplace—pushcarts, street peddlers, and housewares counters in hardware and department stores—sold lots of pots and pans and utensils. Made of cast iron (heavy), copper (expensive), or newly available aluminum, they were of vastly different grades. Some were clad in porcelain enamel, some not. But in almost all cases they transmitted heat imperfectly and unpredictably. A cookbook writer might specify ten minutes of cooking over a high flame, but no one outside her kitchen knew exactly what she meant. Cooks like Shenka and Sarah, distrustful of recipes in cookbooks and newspapers, instead learned to be extra watchful— on the alert for how mixed ingredients changed color in the pan, or how they became more transparent or darker or more golden when cooked, how they separated or combined, or for how they responded to temperature or humidity in the kitchen.

Cooking was highly ritualized in the Schwartz household. For Shenka and Sarah, it was really the center of their religious ritual, too, reconceived. They seldom ventured to Beth Sholom Tomchei Halav, "the Alabama Avenue shul," where Dovid Schwartz went to pray and to schmooze with his Old Country friends. My grandmother and mother obligingly went to disavow their too-casual oaths and promises at the annual Kol Nidre services, and they gathered at the end of Yom Kippur to hear the *shofar* blown before rushing home to prepare the (relatively) sumptuous meal to "break the fast." Sometimes Shenka came to the synagogue to murmur *Yizkor,* the prayer memorializing her parents and the age-old martyrs of the people. At other times she said the prayer at home. That was mostly it, so far as their synagogue life was concerned. In any case, they had a lifelong distrust of rabbis, born of a close familiarity with the domestic lives of the religious authorities in the shtetl. They were always wary of what Mom called "big shots," loudmouths, hypocrites.

From childhood, Mom had imbibed a fundamental fact of Jewish history, that after the destruction of the Temple by the Romans in 70 CE, the major responsibility for ritual performance had passed to the family table. She knew, without fancy explanations, that Jewish worship was now mostly transmuted into blessings pronounced over examples of God's bounty, even in the modest Schwartz home—glasses of wine, trays of braided challah bread, lamps of oil or candles, and at the Passover seder, a rich assemblage of foods symbolic of chapters of the Exodus story, all of it happening around the family table, her table.

At home, therefore, Shenka and Sarah strode about the kitchen like priest and acolyte—planning, preparing, and presenting meals as though they were fulfilling divinely ordained destinies. If pious men attended shul thrice daily, these women produced three good meals on the same schedule. Their week, too, centered on the Shabbos, especially on the Friday night meal, which had a sequence of heavy and lighter dishes. Chicken soup and chicken were often preceded by gefilte fish and accompanied by vegetables and potatoes. The meal concluded with fruit compote and prune cake. The rest of the week pulled these elements apart and focused on a single main dish—milk or meat, but never the two mixed. As in many immigrant families, the week would rhythmically reflect the royalty of Shabbos. Because Friday night dinner featured meat dishes, it meant that Thursday's and Saturday's meals would be dairy dishes—broiled flounder, salmon croquettes, noodles and farmer cheese, kugel, potato pancakes served with sour cream.

As in the Temple of old, annual festivals brought with them special opportunities—baking *hamantaschen* (triangular pastries filled with *mohn,* or poppy seeds) at Purim, making honey cake at Rosh Hashanah "for a sweet new year," frying *latkes* in oil at Hanukkah to recognize the oil miraculously preserved in the Maccabean triumph, commemorating the speed with which the Israelites departed from Egypt by eating *matzo* (unleavened bread), matzo pancakes, and *matzobrei* (matzos and eggs fried together) at Passover, and so on. *Borscht* (beet soup) and *schav* (sorrel soup) marked the autumnal and spring equinoxes.

Shenka and Sarah were observant but not particularly pious. They did not experience *kashrut* (the Jewish dietary laws) as a limitation or a burden. They were not attracted by *treyf*—nonkosher pork products or shellfish. And they had developed an aversion to forbidden combinations—drinking milk or putting whipped cream on dessert during a meat meal. Still, they marched steadily, fearlessly, and even happily through a landscape of obligations. They did not cook this way because they revered tradition and certainly not out of loyalty to the old life in Europe. They were delighted to be away from the officious surveillance of the pious Jews in Wysokie Mazowieckie, and they enjoyed the freedom and relative anonymity of the big city.

They loved being *balabustas,* highly competent homemakers—but in their own eyes, not by the praise of rabbinic authority. They found such pleasure in lip-smacking and deeply fragrant meals, in *geshmakte* (delicious) food. These were not people who arrived home at 5 PM and puzzled about what to make for dinner that evening. Instead, they contemplated the three or four days in front of them as if they were a series of rooms—how could they be palatially furnished with well-prepared and economical meals? How could the green beans served with (kosher) hamburgers on Tuesday night become an ingredient in mock chopped liver for Thursday lunch? How could the last hard pieces of salami get saved for a luxurious Sunday breakfast of salami and eggs?

Shenka had packed just a few things for the voyage to America. Ours was never a family devoted to sentimental remembrance (despite excellent genes for remembering places and objects). The only "heirlooms" carried across the ocean were a seldom-used Kiddush cup and a service for twelve of silver-plated flatware produced by the Fraget company in Warsaw, a gift from Shenka's half-sister. The treasured down-filled duvets occupied the larger share of the trunks carried in steerage. Sarah remembered that she brought few clothes and no playthings.

So the New York kitchen had to be equipped from scratch. The Edlund bottle opener was a recruit, therefore, to an expanding army of utensils. Sarah had glimpsed the future at Macy's a few years earlier, and slowly she introduced new implements to the kitchen. Some were newly invented and patented devices—Edlund also made an eggbeater and several kinds of can openers—there were many competitors in the marketplace. A grater, potato and apple peelers, egg poachers, and stovetop potato bakers slowly took their place in the kitchen on Alabama Avenue.

Sarah loved to poke through the boxes of gadgets on the pushcarts, and she was glad to live a half-block from Fortunoff's housewares emporium, which she watched grow over the decades into a retail empire stretching from the Jersey and Long Island suburbs to Fifth Avenue in Manhattan. Now she also found smaller versions of the Macy's kitchenwares department at the five-and-dime on New Lots Avenue, just a few blocks away, where enthusiastic salesmen demonstrated the miracles of "labor-saving" devices to slice, dice, chop, and squeeze vegetables, performances which gave rise later to television infomercials.

The two kitchens at 502 Alabama Avenue—the mother's and the daughter's—became brighter, more electrified, more convenient over the years. Even in hard times, and with strained budgets, consumerism marched on, slowly. Toasters and vacuum cleaners, aluminum pans, scouring pads and dishwashing detergents, more brand-name food products (many now carrying the kosher label), more fragrant soaps and creams—month after month the parade continued, turning even these tiny apartments into habitations for the things that the advertisements on the radio promised. The Ekco "Miracle" can opener joined the green wooden-handled bottle opener in the Schwartz kitchen drawer. As one twisted the butterfly handle, a sharp, serrated wheel cut against a fixed wheel and moved along the top inner edge of the can. Such inexpensive kitchen equipment was the cutting edge, so to speak, of the modernizing impulse for families like this one. They did not have the space or the money to furnish a living room in the most up-to-date style, or to purchase a bedroom suite with matching bedsteads, chests, and dressing tables. They were two decades away from owning cars. Aside from electric lamps and the rented refrigerator, they still had no other electric appliances or devices. Kitchen utensils were for these two women a humble but very real way to assimilate to the "American way of life."

Almost a century later, ingredients have been standardized, regulated, and packaged. Kitchen equipment has become more precise. Cooking is ever more mechanically and electronically monitored. For the experienced eye, nose, tongue, and touch of the cook, twentieth-century cookery substituted appliances and monitoring instruments like timers, thermometers, scales, and measuring bowls, cups, and spoons. As early as the mid-1920s, West Bend Aluminum Ware advertised that its Waterless Cooker "needs no watching. . . . While the meal cooks, you can shop, make a call, go to church or a movie—when you come home you will find the whole meal temptingly done." Tempting perhaps, but not the Schwartz way. Sarah, an observant child in Europe, never wandered very far from her stovetop while she cooked. Periodically, mother and daughter would check on the progress of each other's stewpots—adding water, salt, a squeeze of a lemon. Watchfulness became their watchword. They were not so much obsessive as driven, as an artist is, by the challenge of getting the meal done "just right."

In those early years, the Schwartzes never ventured into restaurants. If they hosted relatives or *landslayt,* fellow immigrants from Wysokie Mazowieckie, they offered coffee and homemade cakes or cookies. Only if one went all the way up to the Bronx to visit a brother and sister-in-law, say, could one expect a real meal, and then it was usually a "spread," a sumptuous display of breads, cheeses, smoked fish, and pickled and savory delicacies, capped by coffee and sweets. So home cooking provided almost all of one's diet, and for Sarah this was exactly the way she liked it. "Who knows what they put in it?" she would ask of the soup or stew at the finest restaurants, even when her children tried to fête her for a ninetieth or ninety-fifth birthday.

Of course, there were no takeout restaurants (aside from delicatessens), ready-to-eat meals on supermarket shelves, toaster ovens, or microwave ovens in Brooklyn, circa 1935. What the family did have were, literally, dozens of small food shops within their ambit. With a tiny refrigerator and very little storage space, it was necessary to shop three or four times a week, buying just a little at a time. The proximity of all these food stores was a blessing.

Beverly and Richard Go Shopping, Eighty Years Later

I can recall shopping at my mother's side in the early 1950s, and a few blocks away from Livonia Avenue, but my sister Beverly's much keener memories stretch back to the war years at 502 Alabama. She can still conjure up many of the food shops on Livonia—their locations, their specialties, and the characters of their countermen and women. They were more than shops. Almost all were "mom and pop" establishments, only rarely employing anyone outside the family. They lived above the store, or even behind the business space, often isolating the domestic realm with a thin curtain. The children of the proprietors, and sometimes their elderly parents, contributed to the hubbub. Patronizing these businesses meant paying a family visit. All the stores, but most especially the candy stores, also had their hangers-on, people with too little to do, from whom a continuous kibitzing issued forth. They sat in judgment, like members of a privy council, but on orange crates—which could be taken outside in fair weather and used as the seats of contestants and referees at card games and dominoes. Salesmanship was not in great demand in food stores. The customers knew what they wanted. The art of the deal was to get them to see what they wanted in the stock the shopkeeper had on hand.

Nothing of these small stores remains eighty years later. Those along Livonia are all gone, together with the Supreme movie theater and the pool hall, replaced by a community health and drug treatment center. But memories still cling to the street, and so, as a thought experiment, Beverly and I pulled a shopping cart out of our imaginations in November 2016 and traveled to Livonia Avenue to look for good things to buy at good prices. We arrived early in the morning, when the selection would be best. Mom's Tante Minnie famously put off her shopping till late in the day when everything was going at bargain prices—a product of her husband's stinginess. This earned Shenka's and Sarah's pity and scorn. Our inspiration, which could have been embroidered as a motto on Mom's kitchen wall, was *"Az me iz foyl, hot men nisht in moyl."* (If you're lazy, you'll have nothing to eat). We still get up early to shop.

Mother and daughter had dressed neatly, if not formally, to do their shopping. They had an undeniable resemblance, although Sarah's face was fuller and her cheeks rosier than her mother's. Neither would go out into the streets without combing their hair and putting on a little bit of makeup. Even into her 100th year, Mom never left home wearing a housedress or an apron.

On Livonia Avenue west of Williams Avenue, under the elevated IRT train, the city had rented half of the Rubel Brothers coal and ice garage and turned it into a public produce market. The business of coal and ice was disappearing. Here we could find two different greengrocers called "vegetable men," and named, interchangeably, Zack and Zim. One was only minimally less dishonest than the other, but Beverly can't remember which, and we recall Mom warning us to watch the way they put a finger on the hanging scales. She could have bought her fruits and vegetables from the pushcarts on Blake Avenue or from a man with a horse and cart, who stationed himself just outside 502 Alabama Avenue several mornings a week. But she didn't like the way he was dressed; he wasn't clean enough. Instead, she joined the constant battle taking place in the produce market, in which the owners' wives fought off the tendency of the local ladies to pick and squeeze the tomatoes and to dig like rescuers at an earthquake to discover the perfect apples at the bottom of the pyramid.

Bubbe taught Mom to pick out the nicest turnips, and how to grate them and fry them with salt and chicken fat. Even standing on a frosty day, out in the middle of Williams Avenue, they would begin to savor the warmth of the pan on the gas range. It was as much an expression of affection as of physics. Bananas, string beans (never called green beans), iceberg lettuce, cucumbers, potatoes (available all year), and peas and carrots (usually cooked and served together) were the most common purchases. On the other hand, broccoli,

Brussels sprouts, and cauliflower might have been exotic specimens at the Brooklyn Botanical Garden for all that Bubbe and Mom considered them fit for human consumption.

Across the street, Mrs. Pikoff's fish store sparkled. I had never seen a woman with such large hands, fire engine red from the cold water. As a child, I loved peering over the side of the cold-water tank in the middle of the shop, where carp and other freshwater fish vigorously swam in aimless circles. But the fish store was always scary—the sounds of killing were inescapable. Mrs. Pikoff cleaned and fileted a fish so fast she could have been hired as a killer by our local mobsters. She was a hulking presence, dressed in men's jackets and shoes, a woman who obviously did not need men to help run her business. But she was clean.

The butcher, George Kostitisky, on Livonia between Alabama and Georgia, never gave Mom the very best cuts. She suspected that he was saving them for others. The butcher shop was quieter than the fish store, and Kostitisky incurred greater responsibilities, because of the strict laws about kosher meat. The animal, free of blemishes, had to be slaughtered by a rabbinically certified *shochet,* and the rules about knives and cutting techniques were very strict. One butcher later told me that everything had to be "one hundred per cent no monkey business." But Mom called Kostitisky, and anyone else she disliked, an anti-Semite, "un ahn-ta-se-**mit,**" though all his customers were Jews. Mom preferred the butcher on Hinsdale and Riverdale, two blocks away. She never bought ground meat—to the end of her long life, she ground her meat for meatloaf and hamburgers in her own grinder, with onions and peppers. We loved watching the meat and onions and peppers descend into the maw of the Universal meat grinder and pour out its mix in a rich cascade of "worms" at the other end.

Lou and Sally Sheeber sold freshly killed chickens at a storefront next to the movie house on the south side of Livonia. They also lived at 502 Alabama and became family friends. As a preschooler Beverly was awestruck when Louie cut open the chicken, took out the eggs, threw the guts in the can, and hacked off the feet. Sally Sheeber's instructions in how to "flick" chickens (removing the feathers) was for a while Beverly's "A–Number 1" career choice. One of my most revealing insights from Mom came when I asked her how she prepared to cook the chicken in those early years in America. In turn, she asked me, "What time of year are we talking about?" In those days, before the world ever heard of Frank Perdue or industrially produced poultry, chickens varied in color, fatness, density, and texture according to what they had been fed, and their feed varied widely through the year. Later in life, when Mom could buy supermarket chickens, she consoled herself for the diminished taste by the reassurance that the world had finally seen the last of the lice in the Sheebers' store. As with many other aspects of the consumer culture among immigrants in the 1930s, who had not yet become susceptible to advertising in newspapers or radio programs, the shopkeeper was the best source of information about products. The process of cooking, then, began in the chicken store.

Fox's dairy, selling milk, butter, eggs, cheese, and oatmeal—all in bulk—sat squarely at the southwest corner of Alabama and Livonia, where Miller's drugstore had been earlier. We also got canned goods and toilet paper there. Fox occasionally allowed Beverly to fish for a sour pickle in the barrel near the door. (Most of the time Mom made her own sour pickles from the kirbys she bought at Zack's.) But Mom was joyful when Breakstone's began to market butter in sealed half-pound packages. Now eight ounces was certifiably eight ounces. "He never gave you the weight," Mom complained rancorously about old man Fox.

Shenka and Sarah would generally skip the numerous candy stores on these blocks, except to drag Sam and Isaac, for whom they were important hangouts, home for meals. The candy stores, sometimes advertised as "luncheonettes," had a big soda cooler in the middle of their front room, with six- and ten-ounce bottles swimming in frosty water. At the counter, four or five stools faced the owner's array of fountains (for Coca-Cola syrup, seltzer, chocolate, and sometimes other soft drinks and flavored syrups). The front end of the counter displayed packages and packages of candy and gum—Hershey's, Tootsie Rolls, Wrigley's Juicy Fruit, Chiclets, LifeSavers, O'Henry's, Baby Ruth, Necco Wafers, Snickers, Three Musketeers (with a strawberry flavor!), and Red Hots. Penny candies sat in tall fat jars—colored dots on narrow sheets of paper, cinnamon balls, and dozens of others. For most children, brand-name candy was our first initiation into the pleasures and puzzlements of consumer choice.

The counter faced what could be called a galley kitchen. Behind the owner, there was a cooking surface for toasting bread and frying eggs (no bacon crossed these thresholds, though the observance of kashrut was minimal), a small refrigerator, and a Hamilton Beach mixer that spun ingredients into milkshakes and "malteds," which became my favorites. Between the owner and his customers on the red plastic-topped stools and below the fountains, there sat a sink and three or four tubs of ice cream—usually just vanilla, strawberry, and chocolate. The water in the sink ran continuously. Ice cream was only a store-bought treat—no one had freezers at home, even in a corner of their refrigerators. On the opposite wall of the room there were often two or three booths, sometimes a jukebox, and racks of reading material, none of it likely to be assigned in the high schools where the clientele should have been instead of the candy store.

Candy stores also served as the communications hubs of the neighborhood. Each of them had its own coterie, a reliable source of income to the proprietor but also a deterrent to other patrons. I counted nineteen such stores in the phone book listings of the eight blocks surrounding 502 Alabama Avenue in 1939 and 1945, plus another three "cigar stores." They were each listed as "stationery stores," although I suspect that most of the shop's paper was actually used for recording bets with local bookmakers. That business was surely one of the reasons that every candy store had a pay phone.

The phones also served as lifelines for local residents. Not a single person at 502 Alabama Avenue in 1939 or 1945 had residential telephone service. To make a call, one ambled down to Gerson Lerner's candy store at 563 Livonia and used his pay phone. And you gave out Lerner's number to your landsman Broderson living in Brighton Beach or your cousin Celia in Los Angeles. If either of them called you, there was sure to be some enterprising lad, often called "Butch," who would sprint the half-block to the door of your apartment house, race up to the second or third floor and summon you by name. Hastily pulling on a coat and shoes, you would run down to get the waiting call, often pursued by other family members and a few interested neighbors, so that the candy store was transformed into a theater, with a dozen spectators gathered around the proscenium of the phone booth. "Who is it?" "Is she all right?" "Why is he calling?" After all this drama, someone would remember to give Butch his nickel's reward, just about the price of an egg cream, Brooklyn's favorite concoction of U-Bet chocolate syrup, milk, and seltzer.

Next, Beverly followed Bubbe into Moshe's tiny but aromatic store on Livonia, where she haggled with the aged proprietor for *bebelach* (small beans), dry vegetables, lima beans, lentils, and walnuts. Everything was packed in brown paper bags as diminutively scaled as the store itself.

I went with Mom to Miller's bakery on Livonia. Oddly enough, you served yourself here, picking out the rolls and bread you wanted, and bringing them to the ladies enthroned at the cash register in the front—those old registers which had tabs in the window that popped up to read "$1," "50¢," "5¢," "2¢." Mom was always uncomfortable with this arrangement—who knew who had touched the baked goods before you got there? And the city health department shared her concern and shut the place down. Though she early on disdained the empty nutritional value of mass-marketed Silvercup and Wonder white breads, she knew why one could talk about "the greatest thing since sliced bread." In addition to convenience, those packaged breads were sanitary in a way that bakery products could never be. For a half-century the city authorities constantly worried about the damp, mold-infested conditions of bakeries, often located in cellars. Bakery workers, the city discovered, came down with respiratory ailments at alarming rates.

Mom didn't get her bread from Chobotkin's, a fancier place two blocks west. Chobotkin's was where my grandfather took Beverly for an afternoon treat of a *charlotte russe,* a sponge cake confection with whipped cream and cherries. My mother, warned by her pediatrician to restrict Beverly's diet, tried in vain to curb her father's indulgence of his only grandchild. With his limited income, though, Zayde wanted to bring delight to the little girl. Food, forbidden food, made him very special in her eyes.

Finally, Mom went to the small A&P grocery, hardly big enough to warrant the title of supermarket, on New Lots and Georgia Avenues. There she bought sugar, flour, Velveeta, some canned vegetables like Heinz baked beans (the first mass-marketed product to carry the Orthodox Union, or OU, certification of kashrut), canned sardines and tuna fish, Postum for Bubbe, and coffee for herself. (Mom loved the A&P's own dark blend of Bokar Coffee.) The A&P, the first and only national chain with a store in the neighborhood, proved a more hospitable place for Sarah than the local merchants, especially during the war years when the store manager paid more honest attention to ration cards, coupons, and tokens.

There were other food vendors as well. The delicatessen on Pennsylvania and Livonia, under the IRT station, was a hub of local gossip and "making book" on the ponies. "Deli," as its offerings (corned beef, pastrami, knishes, cole slaw, and potato salad) were called, was a rare treat in our family. Beverly saw the Sheebers indulging themselves with deli every week, evidently sick of eating chicken, and begged Mom, but it was beyond our means. My zayde got his bottle of Trommer's beer from the delicatessen shelves. And, once in a blue moon (that is, almost never), the family had its only restaurant meals at the deli.

Smoked fish (lox, sable, sturgeon, herring, and whitefish)—all cut by hand—came from "appetizing" stores, like that of Feldstein at 560 Livonia Avenue, across the street from Fortunoff's, or Kornfeld's a few blocks west. They also sold bagels and bialys, which were then only seldom part of our family's diet.

The chain store posed a threat to the community of storekeepers. Its windows advertised weekly specials, sales of three cans for a quarter, two pounds for a half-dollar, and so on—the independent stores and stalls could never match that. The "mom and pops" tried everything to compete—new and bigger refrigerators, fancier counters, new paint jobs, brighter lighting, preparing food for takeout. But in the Depression, extra capital was usually unobtainable. The small businessman was a tightrope walker. A bout of pneumonia could put you out of business. If you argued too many times with your brother-in-law over who would take Mama to her cousin in Yonkers, it could lead to the demise of your partnership. And what happened when the credit offered by the cousins' club ran out? At eleven o'clock in the morning, on many Depression days, it was a good bet that one of the doors along the shopping street was not going to be open for business. At eleven o'clock that very evening, every neighboring proprietor feared that the empty space would be occupied by a seller of the same merchandise as his own, in a fancier setting, for lower prices. And sure enough, such was the inextinguishable hope for success in the neighborhood that soon a new shoe store, another barber shop, or another merchant in handles and hinges would occupy the abandoned store.

If selling was an adventure, shopping in the neighborhood was inherently a rich social experience. Gossip, inside dope, crucial information about vacant apartments or jobs, sympathy, harsh judgments, and endless advice were dispensed along with the kraft paper bags and the string-tied bundles. Bubbe and Mom knew each of the countermen and women, knew their *tsuris und nachas* (troubles and joy), and in turn they were expected to share their own news. But the Schwartz women steered away from most of the *bubbe meises* (old wives' tales) they heard. They must have seemed standoffish to the storekeepers and fellow shoppers.

That the A&P was impersonal was both a plus and a minus for Mom. You could not get up-to-date information on the freshness of produce, the meats were not kosher, and there was a fixed price for everything. But she also loved the anonymity of buying there. No one knew your story or wanted to know what your kid brother was doing with those Communist Party leaflets. Friendly to a fault in public, Mom had an instinct for suspicion in private. She had learned wariness in Poland, and it never left her.

For Beverly and me, this long shopping trip into the early 1940s had loaded our imaginary granny cart to the breaking point, and we were glad that it had been spread over several days. We put away our snap-lock purses, shaking our heads at being able to buy anything substantial for coins. We turned back to 502 Alabama Avenue, following Mom and Bubbe as they schlepped their bundles up to the second floor. It was as though they were crossing into a different country. As frenetic as the streets were, nothing exceeded in craziness the scene inside the apartment building. Coming up the front stoop, Beverly and I would first encounter Sara Kaufman, just awakening as the clock struck twelve noon. Clad only in a nightgown, she stood in the doorway of her apartment, the middle of the back row on the first floor, a cigarette dangling eternally from her discolored lips. Sara was the ringleader of the building's endless poker game.

Married late, Mrs. Kaufman paid little attention to her husband, and neither one took much care of her daughter Marjorie. Beverly remembered that Marjorie never had a clean middy, a blouse modeled on a sailor's shirt. (Beverly's was washed and ironed daily.) Sara Kaufman was not a gifted poker player, but she had enough cash to ante up for each hand. During an especially bad run, she would customarily undertake a run to her own bathroom. On five or six occasions she was known to rush back to her comrades, shrieking, "My fox, my fox, it's been stolen, I've been robbed." The game would halt, and one of the more sober (and successful) players would retrace Sara's steps to the windows that faced the courtyard behind 502. And there amid the trash cans, Sara's fox wrap—with those tiny fox faces that scared little kids—would once again be located, apparently left behind by the "thieves." More than once, returning to the cards, Sara's debts had somehow been forgotten in the tumult. Sara had no poker face, but she sure had a poker ploy.

Her companions in the card game seem never to have cooked or cleaned. The players dressed as shabbily as Mrs. Kaufman, usually in housedresses, without bras, their hair undone, reeking of smoke. Beverly picks out Fat Lily, who crossed the street to join the game, as the ugliest one. The apartment door remained open all day, sometimes until three in the morning. In the apartment, the ashtrays were always filled and the coffee cups empty, and Yiddish curse-words periodically exploding into the hallways. Every so often a neglected husband or a "poker-orphan" child would wander in, seeking out a mother, sparking an argument that resounded through the whole building. Bubbe called them *vilda chayas* (wild beasts).

Every apartment at 502 had a story, most of them frightening or sad. Childhood diseases—mumps, measles, and chicken pox—made their rounds to almost every apartment, and so did noisome af-flictions like lice, nits, and ringworm. On the ground floor, a lady named Betty had a husband who was in jail. The building's super and his wife, responsible for the coal furnace and the garbage cans, were Polish people whose Christmas celebrations scared the Jewish children. On the next floor lived Mike the barber. As the most ac-tive bookmaker in the neighborhood, he shaved the odds of boxing matches and horse races more often than facial stubble. Most of the cops in the 75th Precinct, it was said, were on his payroll. Down the hall, a widow whose name Beverly has forgotten lost her only son in the USS *Arizona* at Pearl Harbor. The police arrived one day to escort a third-floor tenant, wrapped in a straitjacket, to a mental hospital.

Lou and Sally Sheeber lived in the front apartment on the second floor, facing the street. They were good friends of Shenka and Sarah, and Beverly found an excellent playmate in their son Eddie. Eddie called our grandmother "Bubbe Smortz." Louie the chicken man was dark-skinned, and he was thus called "Niggy." His lighter-skinned brother—whose real name is lost to history—was always "Whitey." Racial epithets were probably even more common than four-letter vulgarities among the residents of 502. Louie Sheeber was a high-stakes poker player, and the game around his dining table was a more serious affair than that of the crazy ladies upstairs. Beyond attracting more serious gamblers, it once drew the at-

tention of gun-toting robbers, who took away the proceeds from
a whole week's brood of Louie's chickens. The gamblers would
chuck aside decks of cards after just a few hands, and Beverly and
Eddie seized the discards for lots of games. Older kids would
gamble by tossing whole packs of playing cards in a game of "closest
to the wall."

Beverly's best friend in the building, Francine Adler, was also nine
years old. She had been given a Blue Willow patterned toy tea set,
made of real china. Beverly played with it every time she could
wangle her way into Francine's house, and desperately envied her
friend. She begged her parents a thousand times for her own set, and
a thousand times the answer was no. Beverly's nemesis, by contrast,
was the next-door neighbors' daughter, Ilene Failand. Ilene's jeal-
ousy of Beverly's cozy home life led to constant bullying. She played
horrifying pranks, once dipping Beverly's braids in a classroom ink-
well. In their three-room apartment, Ilene's family had a real living
room, which meant that the girl had to share a bedroom with her
parents. Still, as early as 1942 or 1943, Beverly came over to listen
to radio shows in this living room. *Inner Sanctum,* a thriller full of
terror and suspense, was a favorite. After an hour or so of radio,
however, Ilene's behavior scared Beverly back to her own apartment. Ilene was a troubled child, prone to wetting her bed and
soiling herself, and perhaps already trapped in confusions about her
sexuality, as we later learned after her suicide attempts.

In sum, the Brooklyn apartment building was like a shtetl—in its
intimacy, its disrespect for boundaries, and worst of all, in the
cacophony of other people. For Shenka and Sarah, it blessedly
lacked a hierarchy of socially, economically, and religiously "superior"
people. Everyone here was nearly equally poor, and the Depression
made them equally desperate. Bad news about a particular family's
troubles spread quickly, and neighbors gave them a wide berth,

commiserating in silence. By the beginning of World War II, Eastern European Jews elsewhere in New York and around the country had already completed high school and even college, established and expanded businesses, and become politically powerful. Not here. These immigrants and children of immigrants had barely grasped the lowest rung of the economic ladder. Every small-business proprietor on Alabama Avenue was a step away from bankruptcy, every union member a week away from a layoff, a lockout, or a strike, every student just one discouraging teacher away from dropping out, every cop on the take. One week at a time, that was the building's mantra. The semi-religious hoped that "God would be good to us." Class-conscious union members might hate their boss, but they said a *brucha* for him, a blessing, hoping that he would stay in business even in hard times. Whether one called it a rat race or a carousel, each family felt all alone in aiming for the brass ring of American success.

The building teemed with stories—comedies, tragedies, melodramas, adventure tales, fantasies, nightmares. Every corner gathered heartache as much as it gathered dust. Every surface was smudged with disappointment as much as with the grease and grime of long work days. What the building lacked was space, air, a pause in the rush of human lives. Shenka and Sarah found this calm for themselves and cultivated it in their close bond. They soldiered on, depending on their skills in the kitchen and their *balabatishe* orderliness and frugality to distinguish them from the madness of the building and the city around them. They had no safety net other than their dependence on each other. That they jealously guarded. The little green bottle opener and its companions in the kitchen drawer were apt symbols of and modest contributors to their mutuality.

The Gospel of Sufficiency

The members of my family never described themselves as poor. They had no unmet desires for material objects, and they lived in a time before expensive experiences like evenings at nightclubs or travel for vacations were plausible. Instead, the abundance of pleasures emanating from the kitchens of Shenka and Sarah, and the orderliness of their housekeeping, continually obscured the difficult circumstances of their bank accounts. It was yet another talent of these two skillful women.

Up to my seventeenth birthday, when I went away to Harvard College, I had never spent much time in a household that displayed more finery in its architecture or furnishings than mine. The two or three that stood out as different, in my memory, were those with lots of hardbound books on their living room shelves. That seemed amazing to me. In Cambridge, of course, my few visits to the homes of senior professors—often in my capacity as a bartender at faculty parties—introduced me to the understated elegance of the New England social elite. But during my early professional life in Massachusetts, my peers, even those who had "private resources" that obviated living off their incomes, seemed to live no more luxuriously than I did. Later, when I was nearing forty, as some of those friends began to inherit and spend the wealth of their parents, I realized how rare it was to have emerged—as my sister and I did—from the fragile economic status of an East New York tenement.

Like magicians, Shenka and Sarah had made poverty disappear and plenitude appear in its place. They were devotees of sufficiency. They learned the genius of "enoughness." If you savored the details of a meal, or of a happy family's time together, and stretched it out to the edges of your attention, it would leave no room for emptiness.

The saleslady at Abraham & Straus advised Dave to buy Evening in Paris, the perfume in that beautiful blue bottle. "A perfect gift," she said. "You'll have her eating out of your hand."

5

Dave Splurges on
a Bottle of Perfume

My father's first gift for my mother, five or six months after they met, was a fancy bottle of Evening in Paris perfume. The idea strikes me as crazy. Where did this nineteen-year-old boy, barely surviving as a peddler and a delivery man on New York's Lower East Side, get the idea? Who did he think he was? Who did he think Sarah Schwartz was?

Bourjois, a French perfume company, introduced Evening in Paris to the American market in 1928, even before it was launched in France. Perhaps aware of the perfume's exotic appeal, the company set the US price higher than the European one. Following the brilliantly successful innovation of parfumier François Coty, the Bourjois firm also created a distinctive bottle for the new scent, in a striking cobalt blue glass. Evening in Paris soon became the bestselling perfume in the nation, peaking in popularity during World War II, when it was a favorite gift of GIs returning home on leave.

I found a 1930s advertisement for Evening in Paris featuring an image of a beautiful woman in the style of Salvador Dali, with cooing birds forming her eyes and a cloche of pink and white flowers covering her head. Dave's local candy stores and newsstands did not hawk fashion magazines, and I don't believe Dave Rabinowitz ever saw this sophisticated piece of advertising art. So how and where did the world of costly fragrance intersect with that of a poor, unsophisticated son of an unhappy immigrant family? He hated his father. He had no uncles, teachers, or neighborhood wise guys to give him advice. He didn't have an older sister or a knowledgeable aunt. Did he pick up tips from the fellows with whom he shared a "cellar club" in East Flatbush, listening to phonograph records and inviting nice girls to come and dance with them? Comedians like Eddie Cantor never pitched for "poi-fyoom" on the radio.

After striking out on all these alternatives, I'm left with just two possible influences. One is the movies. Dave was addicted to moving pictures. He mimicked the way debonair actors in Hollywood movies—John Gilbert, James Cagney, Fred Astaire, and George Raft—dressed, spoke, and danced. If Dave knew anything of Paris, he got it from a series of grade-B noirish features like *While Paris Sleeps, Phantoms of Paris,* or *The Hunchback of Notre Dame.* Maybe that gave him the idea of treating his girl to something glitzy.

Young, urban, underemployed Jews often spent their Depression-era afternoons and evenings engrossed in screen comedies and dramas featuring women in strapless gowns and men in snap-brim fedoras. Nobody they knew ever languished on one of those elongated sectional sofas or popped the cork on bottles of champagne. Nor did they know anyone who aspired to live like that, or made the decisions those characters made, like investigating a murder or informally adopting an orphan as one's own ward. But movie actors expanded the audience's awareness of verbal expressions and bodily gestures—an outraged "Hmph," a raised eyebrow, or a quick retort like "Whaddya askin' me for?" Movie people could carry a telephone like a treasured pet into their bedrooms at a time when no one in your apartment building even had a private phone. They could shoot someone dead without spilling a drop of blood. In sum, the movies invited Sarah and Dave into another world, one without rent to pay, washing up to finish, or children to discipline. A fake world. But pieces of it—a perfume bottle, the right sort of hairdo, shoes with a dazzling shine—could be like stamps on a passport, even if you didn't have a passport. These hallmarks of an imaginary journey could prove that you'd been there, or at least that you could talk about it.

If Dave didn't see that perfume bottle on a stylish dressing table in a moving picture, perhaps inspiration for the gift might have come from the sales lady on the first floor of a department store, right off the street entrance. Well into the 1930s, especially in working-class settings, the retailer had the first and the last word on merchandise choices—whether it was the freshness of the fish or the appropriateness of a birthday gift. Perhaps Dave strolled into a store like Abraham & Straus on Fulton Street in downtown Brooklyn and was advised to spend a dollar or more on this blue bottle, which contained a fragrance he found glamorous and alluring. A perfect offering, the lady said. "You'll have her eating out of your hand." On this my sister Beverly disagrees, believing that Dad would more likely have picked up the idea—and maybe the smelly stuff itself—from one of his cronies in the peddling business. Maybe "it fell offa truck," as the local lingo phrased the "accidental" acquisition of valuable commodities. After all, we can't recall that Dad ever "bought retail." But did he know anyone who might have peddled perfume and would have been willing to swap for Dave's merchandise—watch straps, alarm clocks, cheese graters? We will never know for sure.

The proximity of elegance and poverty was an essential part of Dave and Sarah's courtship. Poor as they might have been, the tenement dwellers in East New York did not feel themselves excluded from the better things in life. In addition to celebrating wealth and glamour, films showed the destitute, people living in shantytowns on the wrong side of town, slovenly dressed and drunk. Dave and

Sarah did not associate themselves with that. Even in their crowded three-room apartments, they could fantasize about "steppin' out with my baby," as the Irving Berlin song had it.

Getting In Too Deep

Sarah was anything but a dreamer. She could accommodate Dave's aspirations to style, but she was always realistic about what was more important. At work in her kitchen, as a daughter and then later as a wife, Sarah wanted mostly to shut the door and fill the space with deliciousness and harmony. Every morning, she checked to see if everything and everybody were all right. She had had enough of history for one lifetime. No matter how difficult her New York life was, she pinched herself with pleasure in the calm that followed quitting the shtetl, reuniting with her father, and settling in New York.

So it is all the more surprising that she married a man who was anything but a peaceful soul, and then remained happily married to him for seventy-two years. Warm and generous, physically affectionate, Dave Rabinowitz was also unpredictable, harsh, infuriated, and infuriating. Nobody could have predicted the course of their marriage. He was a storm system in the days before meteorology became such an exact science. Sarah did not get an umbrella or a raincoat as a wedding present.

It is hard to get inside the drama of your parents' marriage. Sarah and Dave Rabinowitz were first of all individuals. Beverly and I had quite different, though very intense, relationships with each of them. We seldom thought of them as a couple. At their retirement apartment in Florida, Mom was invariably in the kitchen, and Dad in the sitting room with the television playing. That is not to say that they did not interact with each other. Theirs was an intimate connection, sometimes suffocatingly so, but it was somehow closed to us. But if

I wish to understand my parents' marriage and Sarah's attraction to Dave, of course, I have to begin with learning more about Dave.

My parents' bedroom, which doubled as my childhood playroom, featured furniture they had purchased on the eve of their wedding for their first apartment on Riverdale Avenue in the East New York section of Brooklyn. In addition to the bed, two night tables, and a chest of drawers, there was a "vanity," or a freestanding chest with three small drawers on each side flanking a marble surface in the center. A three-part mirror sat atop the drawers and the stone. A little stool could slide beneath the marble. Except for the inadequate lighting in the bedroom, it was a perfect place for a lady to do her makeup, or for small boys to imagine little plastic Indians ambushing little plastic cowboys carrying gold from California.

Resting permanently on the marble surface was my mother's modest array of perfume bottles. My favorite was a Prince Matchabelli bottle in the form of a royal crown. But even more important to my parents' shared life was the cobalt blue bottle, labeled "Evening in Paris," which my father bought for her a few months after they met in June 1933. They had had one really big date, when he splurged to take her to Radio City Music Hall. Mostly they had met with other couples to dance to records at the cellar club Dave joined, to go to the movies, or to picnic in Prospect Park in fine weather. With Christmas approaching, Dave felt it was time to make a statement. "Evening in Paris" was a megaphone.

Almost immediately afterward, he got worried. "I was getting in too deep. I just couldn't afford to get married, or even to keep taking her to the movies." He telephoned and, with his voice full of regret, broke off their relationship.

"Getting in too deep" was always Dave Rabinowitz's great fear. At other points in my 1977 oral history interview with him, he recalled that he was "not deep into school," and later "not deep into a career or anything long term." Still shy of twenty, he was definitely a skater, darting here and there on the surface of life, at least until he presented Sarah with the perfume bottle. It is not hard to see why.

Baruch "Barney" Rabinovich, Dave's father and my grandfather, was a brute. A native of Odesa, on the Black Sea, he had been drafted into the Russian Army in 1905 in the midst of its war with Japan. Shipped off to Vladivostok, on the Siberian coast, he later told his cronies that he had no argument with the Japanese and promptly deserted. Somehow he made it home to Odesa, scraped together the funds to get across two or three imperial boundaries to reach the North Atlantic ports, and arrived in the United States by the end of that eventful year. I asked my father if Barney had any knowledge of the political turmoil in 1905 Russia. "Not a bit. The man could not be bothered."

Odesa was an important city in Jewish cultural life, a center for Yiddish writers like Sholem Aleichem, the author of *Tevya the Milkman* and other sardonic tales of shtetl life. (Although Sholem Aleichem's real name was Solomon Rabinovich, he was no relation.) Isaac Babel, whose account of the Soviet-Polish War of 1920 provides the clearest account of the war's damage to shtetls like Wysokie Mazowieckie, was also a proud Odesan Jew. But Barney came from a different quarter of the town. He could not read or write a word in the Latin, Cyrillic, Yiddish, or Hebrew alphabets. Still he was always a shrewd customer, eavesdropping to get inside information, angling for deals. In the seaside alleys of Odesa, Barney had learned the trade of coopering, and he quickly found work in New York repairing the barrels used to ship and sell herrings, which arrived in New York from Scotland and Ireland. On some days, poor Eastern European Jews like him ate nothing but herring and potatoes.

Dave's mother, Eva Shulman, was born in 1884 in or near Kiev, in Ukraine, which was then part of the Russian Empire. She was the first and only child of her mother, who was named Ruth, and her father, whom she never knew. Ruth, a fish peddler, moved with her daughter to Odesa, remarried, and had three more children, all sons. At age fifteen, just before the turn of the century, Eva left home for Berlin. Here she learned to roll cigars by hand and then to operate a cigarette-rolling machine, one of the first mechanical devices to produce a consumer product. Emigrating to the United States on her own in 1905, Eva's first American domicile was in Schenectady, New York, where she also worked at making cigarettes.

"She was a fantastic saver," Dave remembered, and in two or three years she had earned and put away enough money to buy the passage to New York for her mother and three half-brothers. They all lived in a very primitive tenement apartment on the Lower East Side, with no running water and a toilet out in the backyard, probably in violation of the recent Tenement House Act of 1901.

Barney probably met Eva at a local *landsmanshaft* gathering of these hot-tempered Black Sea Jews. In those days it was pretty easy to recognize someone who spoke Yiddish with your own regional accent—the varieties that had evolved all over the Russian, Austrian, and German Empires were very distinctive. They married at City Hall on June 19, 1909, and thereafter almost nothing in their lives was happy. A first baby girl died in infancy, and a second lived to age three before succumbing to a long bout with polio. Eva, just then pregnant with Dave, was exhausted and devastated.

Barney was worse than no help. I can see him at five o'clock on a late winter evening, traveling by omnibus from the fish packers in Bushwick, Brooklyn, across the Williamsburg Bridge. Rolled up in his sack is his woolen union suit, wet and heavy after a day's immersion in the brine. He reeks of the pickling. His hands, my dad remembered, never lost the herring smell. Barney jumps off the streetcar on Delancey and Essex streets, turns left, and reaches the tenement at 39 Essex. (It is still standing, and bears a date plaque of 1874 in its cornice.) He gives out a huge *schrei,* a scream, to his wife to come down and pick up the bundle, and he heads off to one of the second-floor tearooms on Forsyth or Christie Street to meet his cronies.

These men did not drink alcohol, choosing to slurp tea with sugar cubes firmly planted between their lips. They passed the time of day in kvetching about wives, children, and mothers-in-law, or in listening to whoever was literate read aloud from the Yiddish paper, or most especially, in gambling. Their preferred game was Stuss, a version of Faro that is about as complex as the children's card game of War. The players bet on which two cards will be turned over next by the banker, losing if their choice matches the first, or winning if it matches the second. If the banker turns over two equal cards, he takes the whole pot, a big advantage. The action is fast, the bets and payoffs flow quickly, and the temptation to cheat is contagious. Not infrequently were insults tossed, then glasses of hot tea, and finally fisticuffs.

At least a few times Barney won big. Especially during World War I, when the supply of North Atlantic fish dwindled, he became a vegetable peddler, carrying his produce on a horse and wagon through the East Side streets. He scorned the street peddlers and even the pushcart men. Dave remembered watching him at the end of the day leading the horse up the ramp to the second level of the livery stable, leaving the wagon on the ground floor. Once, the family legend goes, Barney lacked the funds for stabling and tried to squeeze his horse into the tenement itself. Unsuccessfully. And then, as sure as a dog at a hydrant, Barney would eventually make a bad bet and lose his stake in the vegetable business.

He was ill-tempered and often violent. And yet he wasn't above taking pride in his progeny. Once, with three-year-old Dave in tow, Barney picked up a comic book about Christopher Columbus on the street and gave it to the boy. In the tearoom, Dave scoured the pages of the book. The proud father beamed at the boy's precocity until one of the other patrons noticed that the comic book text was in Italian! Sometimes Barney would surprise the family by appropriating and bringing home a plank of the best herrings, or a huge tub of caviar, as dinner for his family. But more often he dished out stinging words and blows.

One can only pity poor Eva. I see her come down the stairs and lift the sodden union suit. Washing it was a herculean task. She had to carry water upstairs from the pump in the backyard, boil it in a huge vat, lift and twist the garment, pull it out and scrub it with harsh soap, dump the wastewater down the drain, and carry it downstairs for a last rinse, wringing, and final hanging on the clothesline— what a job, and six days a week at that!

Her burdens grew with the size of her family, as four sons followed Dave—Solomon (called Mac), Abraham (called Al), Carl, and Joseph. Eva was a fierce protector, but she could not manage the household by herself. Eager to make a success of her boys, Eva would never allow them to speak Yiddish at home. Always on the edge of destitution, Eva used her midday hours to work as a custom peddler, helping other Russian Jews to navigate America's material cornucopia. She had to identify recent immigrants, especially those whose weakness with English made them fearful about negotiating with local retailers. Then she had to convince them to trust her as a personal shopper. A dollar a week in the peddler's pocket would lead, she promised, to a toaster in two months or a child's winter coat by the time of the first frost. It helped if local retailers advanced the peddler some money so that she could win the customer's heart with easy credit. There was, as local argot would have it, "small percentage" in such a business. She did what she could to keep the family intact, moving from one apartment to another each year in order to profit from the landlord's promise of one month's free rent.

Finally, after acquiring a better apartment in Brooklyn in 1926, one with hot and cold running water, this marriage was just too much for Eva, and she threw Barney out. For three years, from 1932 to 1935, she placed her two youngest sons in the Brooklyn Hebrew Orphan Asylum. They were ten and seven, respectively, when they went away. Though it was less than a half-hour walk or bus ride from her home in a Brownsville tenement and she could visit frequently, she must have felt the separation as wrenching. Barney hovered around the family for decades until his death in 1947, but Dave cut off any contact with him. Barney was not allowed to come to my parents' wedding and was never allowed to see his baby granddaughter. That child, my sister Beverly, was shocked to discover that her father's father was still alive when Dave's brothers brought the news of his final illness to the family.

His father's temper had made Dave's home life as a child oppressive, so he roamed all over the "East Side," as he always called it, looking for adventures, pursuing opportunities. His memories of that time are painful—"To get food was a struggle. Nobody really had any decent clothes to wear. Few people lived in decent housing." Devoted to his mother, indebted to her, guilty because he sensed her pain, he tried to help. As the oldest child, Dave often had his brothers in tow. Day in and day out, even as a kid, he carried the coal scuttle up the five flights to feed the stove that served as the apartment's only heating source and bake oven. He remembers that the windows farthest from the kitchen were invariably frozen over in winter. But Dave's relationship with his mother was never easy or comfortable. He admired and emulated her entrepreneurial energy, that dogged search for the extra nickel and dime. She could barely respond. Her struggles made her more *farbisseneh* by the day—embittered, sullen, mean-spirited. Whatever he did was never enough.

Dave knew his own talents. He was a quick study, gutsy or temperamental in the instant, but he could not grow in this garden of failure. He turned to the street world. His earliest memories date from the age of six or seven, in the first grade, when he joined a kid from next door in peddling newspapers at the gates of the R. Hoe printing-press factory on Grand Street. For a fast half-hour every afternoon, the boys sold between fifty and one hundred copies of the *New York Sun,* the *Journal,* the *Telegram,* and the *World* for two cents each to the exodus of workers on the day shift. He and his partner pocketed half a cent for each paper. On the best days, he proudly gave his mother the twenty-five cents he had earned. He loved learning how to handle money, add and subtract, make change—all on the streets, not in the classroom. (Now that I have a bright ten-year-old grandson, who would be completely perplexed by the task of selling newspapers on the street, this is all the more astonishing to me!) When school was out, he zipped over to a lunch joint and hawked dozens of newspapers to the crowd as they waited in line for a sandwich. "I was Johnny on the spot," he said proudly, always one of his favorite expressions. A year or two later, the family moved again, and he couldn't get to the Hoe factory or the restaurant on time. So every Saturday afternoon he and his brother Mac (and about 200 other "newsies," he recalls) took a bundle of Yiddish papers—*Der Forverts* [The Forward), *Der Tog* [The Day], and *Di Freiheit* [Freedom]—and ducked under the turnstiles onto the subway. They sold papers up and down the line, into the Bronx and back down to Lower Manhattan until all of the papers were gone. "I had no idea what the city looked like above ground." By 8:30 PM, the boys had sold out and were ready for a reward. "The biggest treat of my week was to buy a corned beef sandwich for Mac and me, five cents, and a big pickle for two cents. The look on Mac's face when he saw the sandwich! Oh, we enjoyed that so much."

Even at this early age, he was forever looking for ways to earn a few cents. That took precedence over his other activities: playing punchball in the streets with his mates, swimming in the East River during summer afternoons, or flocking to Park Row in October to watch the news of the World Series games as they were posted, play by play, on a gigantic billboard in front of the Pulitzer Building. He loved the movies and haunted the nickelodeons that flourished in this neighborhood. Admission was two for a nickel, so Dave was always hunting for someone with three cents to add to his two. The Yiddish theater was out of reach, with prices upwards of 25 cents. He avidly read the sports section of the newspapers he sold, but never saw a live baseball game until he was in his late teens. Except for the docks that girdled his home island, Dave lived in a world of brick and stone. Except for the weeds that sprang up between the headstones of ancient graveyards, hardly a blade of grass grew, river to river, between the Battery and City Hall Park. Dave never took the ferry to the Statue of Liberty or darkened the doorways of New York's museums. Uptown sites like Times Square or Central Park could have been located in foreign countries, for all he knew of them.

School came last, after work and play and popular amusements. Twice he was "left back," told to repeat a grade because of truancy, and each time his mother got the decision reversed. "My Dave, he's something special," she said. It was hard for his elementary-school teachers, conscientious as they were, to argue with her, since he excelled in school when he did show up. At the end of grade six, he attained the highest marks in the school. Still, he never accepted the idea that education was a way of moving forward in life. His father loved to recite miscellaneous facts, tidbits derived from conversation and eavesdropping. But Dave met no one, other than the Irish women who taught in his school, who had any meaningful education at all. Certainly not the rabbis, who tried unsuccessfully to badger him into learning enough Hebrew at a neighborhood Talmud Torah. Dave avoided organized activity as if it were a snare, almost as bad as being sent to a "reform school." Plenty of East Side boys joined the programs at the Henry Street Settlement or other settlement houses, but not Dave. The playground movement was in full swing, inviting children to romp on fenced rooftops and corner lots, but Dave and his pals steered clear of do-gooders. When the *New York Times* complained in the 1910s that street urchins on the Lower East Side lobbed dirtballs at bow-tied young lads cycling to Wall Street jobs, they were probably talking about kids like Dave Rabinowitz.

He loved his mother, but he believed in no one and nothing. Affable, even a bit of a charmer, he never trusted anyone in authority. I mourn for his lost opportunities. Smart, quick with figures, enormously hard-working, willing to defer gratification to see a job done well, he could have invested his effort in some group of people or some field of work and followed a track to success. But he never parlayed a friendship into a job, and he was still getting leads only from his brothers well into his forties. He had no cousins' club to lend him fifty bucks, no teacher or mentor to take him in hand. Something should have been possible even in the Depression. Beverly and I have both inherited some of his quick temper and recklessness, but we have lived in gentler and more forgiving times. Despite all his calculations, he could never put himself in the other guy's shoes. The question always was, What was in it for him? Afraid of trust, he could never sell himself or his customer on the idea of tomorrow.

Still, Dave was by far the most stable of the sons of Eva and Barney. Mac, the second son, plied a charmer's smile and sported an elegant pencil-thin mustache to gain the confidence of customers for jewelry and furs he acquired from his "contacts." Al, the middle one of the quintet, was a family man like Dave, always scrambling to try a new business venture, until he died in 1962, age 44. Carl, number four, the most sensitive, loved classical music. His father-in-law, notorious among Brooklyn's bookies, got him a job as a pari-mutuel clerk at New York's racetracks until, like his father, he fell prey to gambling. Joe, the fifth and youngest, was a rough customer, "like a cold-blooded murderer," Beverly recalls. For a while he worked alongside Dave in the jewelry business, until he was intolerable. Sometime in the 1950s, he left New York for Los Angeles. Family lore has it that he nearly beat his stepdaughter to death after learning that she was a lesbian.

Only Dave retained his surname, never trying to hide his obviously Jewish ancestry. Al and Carl adopted "Roberts," and Joe became Joseph M. Raven. Mac, ever the showboat, went the furthest. During World War II, he ditched his given name, Solomon Moses Rabinowitz, and became Maxwell Kenneth Roberts. Even more audaciously, he registered his Social Security claim later in life as the son of "William Roberts and Evelyn Cash."

From his earliest days, Dave's best escape from this family maelstrom was reading books. He claimed to have devoured thousands of them in his childhood. He never missed the Friday afternoon story hour at the Chatham Square Library on East Broadway, a beautiful building designed by McKim, Mead & White, New York's greatest architectural firm, with funds from Andrew Carnegie—though getting there required a dangerous passage through the tough Italian neighborhood that surrounded it. He took out six books at a time and raced back for replacements every two or three days. He read all the Andrew Lang fairy books, named for twelve different colors. He graduated to the Alexandre Dumas romances—*The Count of Monte Cristo, The Three Musketeers, Twenty Years After,* and those of Sir Walter Scott—*Ivanhoe, Rob Roy.* The librarians directed him to the classics of American literature—Mark Twain's *Tom Sawyer* and *Huckleberry Finn,* Booth Tarkington's *Penrod and Sam.* I never knew him to read a nonfiction book.

Perhaps no one in American history was more indebted to the public library. From age four, when he got his first library card at Chatham Square, until he died at 94 in Deerfield Beach, Florida, and except for the few days while he was moving from one residence to another, Dave always had books on loan from a public library. In his life he never purchased a single book, not at an airport or train station. He never gave a book as a present or received one. Glancing at the walls and walls of books in my home in Brooklyn, he asked accusingly, "What's the matter? They close the libraries on you?" In retirement, he devoured newspapers and television news programs. But he never allowed his curiosity late in life about politics and current events to draw him to the nonfiction shelves of his local public library.

Sometime in his twelfth or thirteenth year he had arrived at the adventure novel, and there he stopped—for the rest of his life. The adventure novel alone became a cornerstone of his inner life. His sacred scripture was the tale of a hero confronting adversity over the terrain of three hundred pages. I have tried to discover how young Dave found the time, the space, the light, and the solitude to have read as much as he did. I have climbed the stairs of a tenement like the ones he knew. I've imagined the open apartment doors and inhaled the omnipresent smell of cabbage and garlic. In my mind's eye, I have stumbled onto the reminders of five rambunctious boys. I tripped over what could have been Mac's first-baseman's glove, wide as a catcher's mitt is now. I picked up a few pages of a torn Hebrew book, and I was mortified to see that it was a *chumash,* the holy Torah, that should have been treated with more respect. A crutch leaned against the wall, the relic of one son's injury. A net shopping bag was draped over it. Unmatched dirty socks lay on one of the three bedposts in the boys' bedroom. Flimsy wrappers from the crates of oranges were crumpled up, ready for use as toilet tissue, in a pile with shredded up newspapers. Not one of the details of my imagination could help me figure out when and where young Dave did his reading.

Next I turned to the books themselves, most of which I hadn't read for sixty years. Jack London's *Call of the Wild* and *White Fang,* Dad told me, were among his favorites, so I decided to reread them for myself. These exciting stories celebrated the hero's pure physical stamina. Again and again he surmounts terrible life-threatening wounds and soul-deadening exhaustion to defeat his villainous enemies, man or dog. In the face of human cruelty and animal brutality, the canine protagonists of London's novels discover an elemental power in their feral nature. "Not only did he learn by experience," I read in *Call of the Wild,* "but instincts long dead became alive again." While they are shaped by their adventures, the capacities of Buck and White Fang are hardwired. For boys growing up on the tough terrain of the early twentieth-century city, it was useful to acknowledge that they were made the way they were, and couldn't, shouldn't, ever be expected to change to suit somebody else's expectations.

Through defeat and victory, the hero is alone. He can never be harnessed into a team of dogs, never run with a pack of wolves. Though allied with others for a moment now and then, he is responsible for himself. In the center of each London novel, the world of the "wild" becomes a parable of cutthroat capitalism. "EAT OR BE EATEN," White Fang learns. Yet after all his battles, the hero finally encounters one trustworthy soul, a human being generous enough to treat him gently, to bind his wounds, to teach him reciprocity, and to provide food, shelter, and companionship. He is redeemed. This never happened for young Dave.

Like other adolescents who find their best friends between the covers of books, Dave also sought out adventure series that featured the same heroes. For two or three years, nothing gave Dave more pleasure than the dozens and dozens of dime novels written between 1896 and 1930 by Gilbert Patten under the pen name of Burt L. Standish, each featuring the trials and triumphs of Yale's star athlete and scholar Frank Merriwell. Frank was a superhero thirty years before Superman, although he lacked a flyer's cape, the strength of steel, and X-ray vision. Instead, Merriwell relied on his arsenal of virtues, and on every page he exemplified the qualities that he used to defeat nasty and rapacious scoundrels—honesty, loyalty, charity, fairness, courage, perseverance, trustworthiness, and so on. While Dave admired these attributes, and exemplified some of them in his daily life, he never preached their value to his children. He was no moralist. In the struggle of life, Merriwell's virtues and White Fang's instincts, a musketeer's swordplay and a sheriff's sharpshooting were all equally useful. A boy had to do what was necessary.

Like London's bold and savvy White Fang, a quarter-wolf mongrel, Dave Rabinowitz had also emerged from a brood of five pups, scarcely knew his father, and depended on his mother completely until he could start taking care of himself. Did Dave actually measure himself against Jack London's heroes? Did it matter to him that Merriwell was always yammering on about sportsmanship, while to Jack London's Buck, "fair play was a forgotten code"? Did he notice the contrast? I doubt it.

Given his reluctance to identify with anything outside the household, it seems more likely that he just read to escape to other worlds, to olden times, to foreign lands, to exotic adventures. It was the pleasure of the plot, the entertainment of the chase, that he valued. Heroism was not for people who shopped at the Hester Street pushcarts. Dave's impulse was to race to a book's conclusion, thrilled that his hero had finally prevailed.

More Like a Man

In the summer of 1926, after twelve-year-old David Rabinowitz had graduated from elementary school and was admitted to the "RA" or Rapid Advance program, which would allow him to complete three years of junior high school in two, his mother announced that the family was "moving to the country," that is, to Brownsville, Brooklyn. Indeed, the lower scale, wider avenues, and empty building lots in Brownsville and its next-door offshoot, East New York, made it seem more spacious than Lower Manhattan, but these areas of Brooklyn were already more populous and just as poor as the Lower East Side, then beginning its long, steady depopulation.

Dave quickly assumed a new persona in East New York, feeling "more like a man." He was as disdainful of the nearby Hebrew Educational Society (HES) as he had been of the Manhattan settlement houses. He found his first real sidekick, a boy named Al Berlin who was equally devoted to reading, and the two of them ransacked the Stone Avenue branch of the Brooklyn Public Library in search of exciting books. Dave recalled their sitting side by side on a ledge one summer day, reading Frank Merriwell books, chewing and spitting out "polly" (sunflower) seeds, and swapping the books as they each arrived at the last page. Al, whose family was even more dysfunctional than Dave's, was a perfect alter ego, expressing a tough, impulsive, and even violent side that Dave repressed. As kids, the two of them pulled off many pranks, with one creating a disturbance in the back of a store while the other swiped merchandise from its front counters. Berlin had a fierce temper. In a fury, he once pulled out the four-foot-long post that anchored a pushcart and used it to bash the cartman. (Decades later, he told me that at sixteen, "I just loved to hit.") Since Al's parents were useless in such a crisis, it became a challenge for Eva Rabinowitz, with scant English, to rescue Berlin from the Raymond Street Jail, a "greystone bastille" near downtown Brooklyn, and vouch for his future conduct. Berlin later became a wildcatter on Alaska building projects, joined the Civilian Conservation Corps, and hoboed his way across the United States.

By whatever magic, Al's craziness and bold exploits over time allowed Dave to become the more cautious one. From the moment of his arrival in Brooklyn, Dave started looking for jobs. Like others born in his time and place, he missed out on adolescence. During junior high, he worked afternoons and evenings unpacking and shelving shipments at Clara and Max Fortunoff's hardware emporium on Livonia Avenue, under the newly constructed IRT New Lots Avenue elevated train. He was earning a dollar a day, and taking on more responsibility every month. He spent one summer as a "missionary salesman," promoting a line of sweeteners that, added to milk and left in the refrigerator overnight, would produce a tasty, cheap alternative to ice cream. "I got to know every grocery in Brooklyn, Manhattan, and the Bronx, just from that job." Self-consciously proud of his skills as a salesman, Dave's success impressed his old man just this once in his lifetime. During high school, in 1928–1930, he took two trolleys every afternoon to get to work at the National Packing Box Company, which handled shipments for many department stores. School itself was of little interest, except for the debating team, but he couldn't afford to give up his after-school work for what he called "frivolities." He completed his courses to graduate from Franklin K. Lane High School, but he never bothered to pick up his diploma. In any case, he had probably skipped too many days at school to qualify. And when the shock of the Wall Street crash began to ripple down to local businesses, Dave had to scramble to find any work at all. He prayed for the days when snowstorms snarled traffic. Then he could join the snow-shoveling teams, clearing streets for a dollar and a quarter an hour.

His luck turned again in 1933 when a neighbor, a man named Shiner, lined up a supply chain of men's caps, produced by nonunion shops and meant to be sold cheap. Boxes and boxes of caps filled Shiner's apartment. For most of a year, Dave took a bundle and hawked them at factory gates, lunch places, construction sites, on trolley cars and subways. He soon had a thousand dollars in the bank.

After work and on weekends, Dave hung out at his cellar club on East 95th Street in the East Flatbush section of Brooklyn. One of the other members was a musician named Hal Gorman who had a six-man "orchestra" that played at wedding receptions. Dave knew that even in the depths of the Depression, you could count on having a fine meal at a wedding banquet, and he cleverly convinced Gorman he could help transport and set up the band's instruments at the banquet hall. His career as a finely dressed "techie" hit the jackpot at Ida Schlachtman's wedding on June 9, 1933. When the band took a break, Dave mounted the stage, read a few telegrams sent by relatives from as far away as the Bronx or Philadelphia, repeated a few jokes he had heard at vaudeville shows, and scouted the room for good-looking girls. When the band took the stand again, Dave was ready to ask Sarah Schwartz to dance with him. Few of the guests were as skilled in the fox trot and the waltz as he, and so he and Sarah had the dance floor mostly to themselves for a lot of the evening. He was a great dancer, and she followed gracefully.

Well after midnight that evening he walked her home, about ten or eleven blocks, from the hall on Williams Avenue, near Atlantic. He asked if he could see her again, and she gave him the phone number of Lerner's candy store. Forty-four years later both Sarah and Dave recalled that their first date was at Radio City Music Hall. But the movie they remembered, *Morning Glory*, with Katharine Hepburn and Douglas Fairbanks Jr., did not open at Radio City until August 18, 1933, about ten weeks after they met. So it could not have really been their *first* date, but it's no wonder that this outing stood out. After an hour-long subway trip from Brooklyn, Dave and Sarah descended from the Sixth Avenue El train and entered Radio City's lavish landscape, a lot like the sets of the movies shown on the huge screen. But these were in fact real, constructed with the finest materials and craftsmanship. The magnificent theater, claiming to be the largest on earth with six thousand seats, was less than a year old. This must have been a hot ticket for Dave to get. (Legendarily, 100,000 people sought tickets for the opening during the previous December.) Radio City's use of exotic woods, delicately carved sculptures, and plush carpets—all in the most advanced Art Deco style—was unlike anything the young couple (or anyone else!) had ever seen. The carpeting was so plush that thousands of attendees could scarcely be heard as they together ascended to the auditorium. Elegantly attired ushers led them to their reserved seats, as if they were honored guests. They were agog at the spectacular egg-shaped proscenium, at the gigantic murals, and at the superb details in the re-freshment areas and lounges. And the show! In addition to the movie, the young Brooklynites heard arias by the great lyric tenor Jan Peerce, who was just making his big debut and would later become a star at the Metropolitan Opera, and they watched as the Roxyettes (the house's dance troupe, soon to become the "World Famous Rock-ettes") performed their perfectly synchronized chorus-line numbers on the enormous stage. What a date that must have been!

And what must Sarah and Dave have thought about the film it-self? It poses some real puzzles for me. Released a year before the Hays Code curbed hints of sexual license in the Hollywood cinema, *Morning Glory* features Hepburn, who won an Oscar for the role, as an ambitious Vermont aspirant for Broadway stardom. Crashing a producer's cocktail party, she drinks too much and recites at full volume the soliloquies from *Hamlet* and *Romeo and Juliet*. Maybe

Dave had encountered these speeches in a school text, but probably not either play as a whole. To Sarah it must have been altogether new, as ornate as anything in the theater itself. (Like so much else in America, she had missed out on schooling and all the tools it provided for understanding the culture, but she was determined to enjoy herself.) Viewers next see Hepburn on the following morning, having spent the night—without much notice or any consequence!—in the bed of the producer, played by Adolph Menjou. What did Sarah and Dave, still presumably sexually inexperienced, make of all this? Watching the film left me with more questions than I started with.

Sarah and Dave's relationship intensified through the autumn, until Dave's crisis of self-confidence over the bottle of Evening in Paris perfume. They spent that New Year's Eve apart. But in the following weeks Dave's spirits sank lower and lower. His club pals asked him often about Sarah and chided him for his foolishness in letting her go. His resolve in breaking off the relationship "wasn't working out," and he started seeing her again. Neither Sarah nor Dave had previously had a serious romantic attachment, and they each used these months, as many courting couples do, to define their own ideals of femininity and masculinity. Sarah acquired the image of herself that she wanted from several sources. She shared her mother's instinct for modesty and decorum. She was certainly never a "dance hall dolly," leaving the house after supper to try her luck with young men. She almost never tasted a drop of alcohol, and the culture of Jewish New York, even after the end of Prohibition, forbade young women from going to bars or restaurants on their own. She inherited her mother's prudery about women's appearance and behavior.

Yet, as much as she despised frippery and ostentation, she found no room in her self-culture for too much plainness and simplicity. The finest women, she thought, were always "nicely dressed." What precisely did that mean, and where did it come from? When she looked at herself in the full-length mirror inside the family's armoire, her daughter Beverly recalls, Sarah saw herself, first, as a small woman. She had a nice figure, about right for size 4 dresses—if they were available. But she found few of them on the racks at Fisher Brothers and other fine stores on Pitkin Avenue, the neighborhood's premier shopping street. Everything she loved required alterations. In itself that pushed Sarah's taste toward refinement. Buying a suit, a rare occasion, meant marshaling a company of family experts—her mother to check the tastefulness of what was on offer and her father to test the quality of its fabric, plus an aunt or two to "ooh and aah." Even on the tightest of budgets, Sarah became accustomed to clothing that was almost made to measure.

She was usually a sweet person, but she had one unfortunate prejudice. She disdained people who were overweight. Though she was never impolite, she regarded *zaftig,* or heavy, women as bearing a curse. Escaping that fate helped her define her own self-presentation. And, as we have seen, she devoted an extraordinary amount of energy to maintaining that self-image by keeping busy, by doing everything in just the right way. Cleanliness came first. Sarah, fortuitously, arrived in New York just as the plague of "body odor" had been exposed in newspaper and magazine advertising. All manner of social disasters would befall a person who did not use Lifebuoy soap, introduced by Lever Brothers in 1926, or its chief competitor, Camay, produced by Procter and Gamble. The cosmetics craze was on. Sarah learned to use Pond's Cold Cream each morning and evening to maintain her "girlish complexion." She never left the house without putting on a bit of lipstick (after the mid-1930s) and some rouge, with her hair neatly arranged (seldom covered with a kerchief), dressed in a skirt, blouse, and jacket. On fancier occasions, she was more carefully made up. Her thick black hair was marcelled in the 1930s and later set in a pompadour, bulwarked by padded "rats." She wore one of her two or three elegant outfits, but with little jewelry.

Sarah never read the women's magazines. *Good Housekeeping* and *Woman's Home Companion* were too impractical, assuming there were dollars when she had only dimes. Fashion magazines, she felt, made too much fuss over being fashionable. But the movies—ah, that was a different story. Extremely attentive to costume, to manner, and to personal carriage, Sarah mimicked the movie stars. She did not focus on how they dealt with crises in melodramas, nor to the sultriness of seductive roles, and not to the foolishness of the screwball comedies. She did not care about the actors' love lives and never picked up a fan magazine. Sarah was most impressed by the way the women moved and presented themselves on screen. Claudette Colbert, the star of 1930s films who had coloring and hair most similar to hers, became a favorite model.

Into this world of self-control and discipline came Dave as a lover. For him, innocently, the gift of a bottle of perfume perfectly exemplified the role to which he aspired—as the generous patron of Sarah's elegance. For the rest of his life, nothing was so pleasing to Dave as indulging Sarah, prudently but to the best of his means, with beautiful adornments—a ring, a jeweled brooch, a Persian lamb coat. His love, however, did not ever extend to asking her what she really wanted. Evening in Paris, it turns out, was not her favorite scent, and she eventually hid the blue bottle behind others on her dressing table. Dave was in fact never a great help when she shopped for clothing. He was glad to pay. (In fact, he distrusted her ability to handle a checkbook, and after his death she needed Beverly's help to learn how to do her banking.)

Dave loved dressing up himself, and he was pleased when Sarah's appearance complemented his. He slicked his hair back with Vitalis or Wildroot hair tonic and started a decades-long attachment to Old Spice aftershave in 1938 or 1939. In fact, I think that Dave and Sarah discovered the ideal of their couplehood on the dance floor. Both of them were tasteful and modest in their elegance. As in their dress, their dancing avoided garishness of any kind, but it guided them into observing and holding onto each other, without a lot of showmanship. Dave's own model from the movies was the stylish George Raft. Like Raft, Dave was a Manhattan-born Jew who danced gracefully. But Raft also had a sleek and seductive manner, which could turn into a cold lethality entirely missing from my father. Perhaps Dave's anger found some imaginative release, in the safety of a dark movie house, in George Raft's gangster characters.

Sarah could not and would not repay Dave's generosity with material gifts. Instead, she offered Dave a psychic resting place he had never known before. Sometime during that winter of 1934, she played the tactically brilliant card of inviting him to come to dinner at the Schwartzes' table. There was a sweetness about Sarah's father, Dovid Schwartz, a sharp intelligence about Shenka, her mother, and an ease about the brothers that Dave had never seen in his own family. He was beguiled by the respect that Dovid and Shenka had for each other, even when Dovid's job prospects were dim, and he was deeply gratified that the Schwartzes treated him with such respect. He gradually grew into the role that they accorded him as a decent, hardworking young man. The virtues of fair play, forged on the playing fields of Yale College and celebrated in the Frank Merriwell novels, meant little in the talk around the Schwartz table. Instead, they revered two different values above all others, respect and consideration.

Respect, derived in some sense from the Biblical commandment to honor one's parents, conferred an aura of inviolability on its object. Respect created distance, a heightened regard. A respected person was taken at face value, not to be questioned. Respect accorded autonomy to the person you were addressing, acknowledging that he or she was the best judge of what to do and how to do it. And in the family setting, paying respect to the parents strengthened the bond of the group. Dave's respect gratified and reassured Sarah.

Consideration was rather different. It signaled your awareness of a person's needs, weaknesses, motives, and interests. While respect was paid in the very moment of engaging someone, consideration required forethought. It demonstrated that you could anticipate how this particular person would, for his or her own reasons, respond to an invitation, or to words of reproof or praise. It assumed that you were competent to register the anxieties of the people around you. Daydreaming at a dinner table was strongly discouraged. Instead, everyone was expected to pay attention to everyone else's feelings. A sarcastic remark was, therefore, all the more offensive, as it could not have been careless. Or rather, thoughtlessness was just as insulting as the words of assault themselves.

This must have been all new to Dave Rabinowitz. He had grown up in a raucous family of five brothers, with a mother eternally nurturing her grievances and a hot-tempered, often absent, father. No one stuck around long enough to do more than eat, cadge a half-dollar, and escape. Dave had learned to be nimble in that madhouse, and he had been swimming in the shallow end of the pools of life until this moment. This was a turning point. In the middle of 1934, he and Sarah decided to get married, and they set a date in summer 1935. This was no casual engagement. They committed themselves, aged twenty and eighteen, to open a joint banking account so that they could really be ready for housekeeping. Dave would put in $25 per week, Sarah only $5. Still, given the finances of the Schwartz household, she often couldn't meet that target.

Though they were still so young, both had had their childhoods and youths stolen from them. They knew adult responsibility firsthand. Eva Rabinowitz was not happy to lose Dave's contribution to her pocketbook, but he had no reason to remain at home. As for Sarah, I think she'd had enough of sleeping on a folding cot in a half-bedroom screened off from her brothers' beds. In 1935 Brooklyn, there were few places for a couple to "canoodle," in the vernacular of the day, without being observed and disturbed by onlookers. (Wintertime was especially discouraging, when parks and beaches were off limits.) So, though only 8 percent of Jewish couples married before age 25, Sarah and Dave, now 19 and 21, got a license at Brooklyn Borough Hall and planned their wedding for August 31, 1935.

And what a plan it was! Bubbe Schwartz volunteered to cook for the invitees, but the young couple would have none of that. They found a hall at Alabama and Sutter avenues willing to feed everyone with a chicken dinner, and soda rather than beer, for $2 per couple. Close to a hundred guests were invited, but only Eva and one of her brothers from the Rabinowitz side of the family were included. Dovid Schwartz would bring along some moonshine with which to offer toasts. They spent $7.50 on the flowers for the bride's bouquet, the groom's and ushers' boutonnières, and the table decorations. Hal Gorman's six-piece orchestra was paid $15. Goldsmith Studios on Stone Avenue charged $12 for the posed photographs. (They kept the solo image of Sarah in their shop window for five years. "She was the prettiest," Dave explained.) Sarah lent her mother a dress, and bought her own for five dollars. Dave rented a full white-tie outfit, and all the ushers were similarly decked out in formal finery.

I'm impressed, and a little alarmed, by my father's exact memory of these details. Even four decades after the wedding, he could still recall and recite the price of everything. He could remember everything, too, that they bought to furnish their first apartment, on the third floor of a building on Riverdale and Hinsdale Avenues—a bedroom set (including that vanity), a kitchen table and chairs, an icebox, an electric iron and ironing board, curtains and curtain rods, and a bridge table and chairs (which I still use regularly). The Fortunoffs presented the newlyweds with a washboard. (It was then on sale at their store, which gave everyone a laugh.) Friends from the cellar club dropped by with presents—almost all of them housewares like waffle irons.

His perfect memory was a clue to how deeply considered this commitment was. He had married a woman who had been taught a great deal about womanhood and how to run a household. Since Sarah and Dave were the first couple married in their "set," their apartment soon became a hangout for the old pals, and Sarah had to figure out how to feed these hungry card-playing "galoots." For one Sunday afternoon, she went out and bought two pounds of herring, two or three loaves of Stuhmer's pumpernickel, and four dozen ears of corn. The friends passed their hat to help defray the costs to Dave and Sarah, and they always took responsibility for bringing the beer and sodas. Perhaps Sarah had to borrow the Edlund bottle opener from her mother's drawer in the third-floor apartment kitchen. When they told stories of those old days, both Sarah and Dave would start to laugh, Mom almost uncontrollably.

Sarah and Dave each had developed a complex identity out of their childhood experiences, out of the wounds of displacement and poverty, and out of the strategies each family used to heal those injuries. Dave assigned himself the role of steady provider, the solid foundation on which Sarah, as the homemaker, could create a well-managed household. At the same time, he fantasized that he could also be the adored spouse who could indulge his beloved, even spoil her, when circumstances would permit. He would not seek or accept help from anyone in his manly responsibilities. He loved being his "own boss." Now enmeshed in a family shaped by the Jewish labor movement, he still called himself a "capitalist." Sarah, by contrast, was a woman balancing many obligations and many loyalties, to her husband and future children, to her parents and especially her mother, and to other New York Jews with whom she felt solidarity. He could shift quickly and temperamentally from celebratory exuberance, then to explosive anger, and then again to warm possessiveness. She had to ride out these storms. Staying busy, keeping her head down, learning when to brace herself for the first rumblings of thunder, became a way of being.

These identities, clarified by their late teens, would now be put to the test of circumstances and events. For Dave Rabinowitz, marrying Sarah was the best decision he ever made. But he was ill-equipped for the life that followed. The peddler either makes or misses a sale, but nothing in marriage is hit or miss. For Sarah, Dave was the love of her life, supportive of her devotion to Shenka, respectful of his father-in-law, but frequently a frustrating partner. She dreamed of a quiet and safe household, all interruptions forestalled. She wanted to lock the door against danger. But Dave brought anxiety and tension into the house. Sarah wanted to save her mother from having to deal with any tumult, but she could never quite quiet the rage within her walls.

That was just the beginning of a seventy-two-year-long marriage. Those youthful identities got bounced around, broken and repaired, reshaped by family crises and social changes. Over the decades, though, they were each other's most important mentor, and by the end of their long lives they had nearly come to adopt each other's personalities.

A Family Picture Album

Dovid Schwartz, circa 1923, taken in a New York photo studio and sent to Poland to reassure his family of his progress in the new land.

Shenka and her three children, circa 1924, probably taken at a studio in
Wysokie Mazowieckie, and sent to Dovid in New York, reminding him of
each child's distinctiveness—Sarah with a flower, Sam a book, Isaac a ball.

Baruch (Barney) Rabinowitz, hanging out in front of a NYC shop, circa 1935, on a day off from work at the fish store.

Dave and Sarah Rabinowitz, wedding photo, Brooklyn, August 1935.
Taken at a studio on Stone Avenue in Brownsville, Brooklyn.

Dave and Sarah Rabinowitz, on their honeymoon at Rockland Lake,
New York, September 1935.

Dave and Sarah Rabinowitz, Beverly at age 5, and Dovid and Shenka
Schwartz, taken at a Brooklyn studio and sent to Sam and Isaac Schwartz,
then in the army, circa 1942.

Dave, Sarah, Beverly, and Richard in front of Dave's 1941 Packard,
ready for the return from a summer in the Catskills, circa 1951.

Dave, Sarah, Beverly, and Richard, taken at a bar mitzvah celebration of the son of friends, circa 1953. Richard wears a suit that once belonged to the bar mitzvah boy.

Dave and Sarah, dressed up for a fancy dinner at Brown's Hotel in the Catskills, circa 1962.

Sarah and her two brothers, circa 1976. This picture of the affectionate siblings provoked an explosion of jealous anger from Sam's wife.

Sarah and Dave at home in Deerfield Beach, Florida, circa 2007. Each comfortably enjoyed a distinct domain in their retirement apartment— keeping track of the news, planning next week's meals.

During World War II, the mailman customarily blew a whistle if he had a letter from the War Department. The sound pierced the hearts of sixty or seventy residents every time.

6

Sarah Awaits the Mailman's Whistle

The Catholic Church of St. John the Baptist in Wysokie Mazowieckie had a bell that tolled the hours during the day and called pa-
rishioners to mass several times on Sundays. Sarah liked the sound
of the bell, but she mostly stayed inside on those Sunday mornings,
warily watching her Polish Catholic neighbors pass to and from the
church. So far as I know, there was no other town clock or time-
piece. Not much in the shtetl ran on a schedule. The Jewish men
assembled for prayer largely by a collective and informal awareness
of dawn and dusk. Perhaps the schoolteacher called children to class
with a handheld bell.

In New York, of course, everything was different. Subways and
buses ran on schedule, mostly. Workers and students arrived at and
left work and school at specified times. Clocks were everywhere—
on the street in front of jewelry stores, on classroom and office walls,
and increasingly, on the wrists of people rushing to and fro in the
great city. Stores opened and shut, mornings and afternoons, at predictable times from Monday to Saturday. The radio synchronized the
attention of many thousands of people to its scheduled programs at
the same exact time. The newspaper printed a "movie clock" indi-
cating when the feature films would start. (But from my experience

no one paid any attention to that. We arrived in the middle of a film and remained in our seats through the cartoons, the newsreels, the second feature, and the beginning of the first feature until it became familiar—and then we left.)

For Sarah and Dave, and for most of their neighbors, World War II intensified all that. Sixteen million Americans served in uniform, most of them obeying instructions about where and when they were supposed to be occupied. More people, including Dave, now worked regular hours in war industry and civil administration jobs. Every public facility now had more scrupulously maintained hours of operation. But while there was more regularity in the everyday lives of Americans, there were also more frightening interruptions in that regularity. Dave's alarm clock rang at 5 AM. Sarah took Beverly to school precisely at 8 AM, with the children expected to line up in "size place" (by height), girls and boys separately. The calm of the school day was often shattered by schoolwide alarms, signaling fire drills and shelter drills, concluding with an all-clear signal. Offices and workshops also conducted such drills. In a neighborhood with many small factories, sirens blaring from fire trucks and ambulances became more common. With residential phone service so spotty, fire alarm call boxes were placed on street corners, three or four blocks apart. At night, civil defense workers conducted blackout alarms, when the streetlights and traffic signals went out and blackout curtains blocked the lights from inside homes and shops.

All this provided an edge to daily life, compounded by fears of German subversion, underground cells of Nazi sympathizers, and a ceaseless barrage of rumor and propaganda. Again and again, everyone was reminded to button their lips. But the most terrible fear and the most frightful alarm of all came from the postman's whistle. I don't know how widespread this practice was, but at 502 Alabama Avenue, Beverly remembers, the mailman customarily blew a whistle if he had a letter from the War Department. The sound pierced the hearts of sixty or seventy people every time. Nothing was dreaded more than bad news about a son at war, five or fifteen thousand miles away.

Sarah and Dave Rabinowitz had carefully prepared their first household on Riverdale Avenue, but they had no clue about how they would keep a roof over their heads or food on the table. "We didn't have a serious view of the future. We didn't think about having children. We just went along, day to day." Without a clear alternative, Dave determined to give up on peddling. Every unsold piece of merchandise had become a personal humiliation. Marriage brought him into familiarity with Sarah's extended family. Almost all of her American-born cousins graduated from high school, and two or three were at Brooklyn College studying accounting and management. Dave was welcomed into the family by these strivers, but he was embarrassed and defensive about his limited education. He felt no dignity if "his office was in his socks," so to speak.

For Sarah, a newlywed at 19, it felt as though the weight of the world was on her shoulders. The people who loved her, they were her problem. Her young husband was loving and generous. Dave was not given to vices like drinking or gambling. He was not careless with money. Quite the opposite, he had inherited his mother's talent for hard work and prudent saving. He never stopped trying to be a good, consistent provider. But in those middle years of the 1930s, he had a terrible time making a living. A sweet-talking salesman, he knew that the chief ingredient in sales success was the acquisitiveness of the buyer. And in the mid-1930s, nobody was buying. Night after night, he returned home frustrated and angry—not at Sarah but at himself.

Dave could not get a head start or amass a nest egg on his own, and he had no one to tide him over the rough spots. Though he made friends easily, and these might tip him off to a possible deal, not much came of this. Was there something else at work in his persistent failure? Dave's father's anger had also been episodic, unpredictable. And, like many such children, Dave could never afford to be entirely trusting. Sometimes he could mask this with a New Yorker's cynical snarl, a what-do-you-expect attitude. But his distrust disqualified him, literally disconnecting him from anyone in better shape than he—a person with more money, more education, or a more secure job. He dropped out of school, quit jobs, and consistently failed to parlay a short-term gig into an ongoing position. In the era of Tammany Hall's dominance over New York City politics, before Mayor La Guardia's housecleaning, smart kids like Dave attached themselves to patronage-dispensing local pols and rode the corruption escalator to long-term jobs. But not Dave. He never competed for a civil service post or signed up with the federal or state efforts to combat joblessness. This reluctance to get involved fed both his determination and his self-doubt, and at times made this charming fellow into an angry, bitter, competitive victim. He could not accept the basic indifference of the people he met, so he invented and presumed hostility even where there was none.

Beverly was born just before Sarah and Dave's second wedding anniversary, in August 1937, and they moved to a second-floor, three-room apartment at 502 Alabama Avenue, between Livonia and Riverdale. Everyone assumed that it was best for Shenka and Sarah to stay close to each other. Sarah, age 21, still depended on her mother's guidance in food shopping and planning meals, in furnishing the house, in tending the baby, and perhaps in anchoring her prudence and frugality. But both mother and daughter also knew that Shenka would lean more and more on her very capable oldest child. In the following year, when their lease on Williams Avenue expired, Dovid, Shenka, and the two boys moved into a more spacious third-floor apartment in the same building as the Rabinowitz family.

About the time Beverly was born, Sarah and Dave hit rock bottom. They scrimped and saved, and they located bargains before purchasing anything. Mayor La Guardia's government set up free dental clinics, eye exams, and vaccinations against childhood diseases. Still, at one of the deepest points of the decade-long economic crisis, Dave could find only sporadic work. Sarah took a job sewing in an underwear factory, with her mother-in-law as a babysitter. Shenka was furious with Sarah, first for getting pregnant so imprudently and then for leaving the child to go to work. Shenka would not blame Dave for his earning difficulties, but he was embarrassed all the same. "The worst part was I lost a lot of confidence in myself," he confessed. On a good week, Dave was proud that they were living at 502 Alabama, one of the better buildings in the neighborhood. The next week he was afraid that all their belongings would be pitched out onto the street by the sheriff's men. They did not consider moving to a cheaper apartment in Brownsville or, as an even more desperate measure, doubling up with Sarah's parents.

His own parents could not help him. They were not regular members of a *landsmanshaft*. Dave himself never joined a mutual benefit society. The five senior Schwartzes, Dovid's brothers, never pooled their resources, and their children did not form a cousins club until the 1950s. Instead, Sarah and Dave survived by borrowing money, more than once, from the Provident Loan Society. In the late 1930s, they applied for cash relief from the city. I have not found official evidence of their application, and my mother only mentioned it to Beverly once, explaining that they were rejected because the inspector discovered a bowl of beautiful apples on the dining table when she visited their apartment. Even if that story is not true, it reveals the family's proud concern for appearances.

These two or three years scarred Dave for life. He had wanted so much to be a hero to his wife and daughter, and he was a failure. He was a member of a very unlucky cohort, born in 1914 and coming of age in the depth of the Great Depression. Many newsboys a generation older than Dave, it was reported, became real estate speculators and apartment-house developers in the expanding Jewish neighborhoods of the Bronx and Brooklyn in the 1920s. That building boom crashed with the stock market, but the mythology of self-reliance, the "bootstraps myth," remained vivid in Dave's mind. He always considered believers in collectivity or solidarity as suckers. There was no fulfilling his dream of success, no denouement or dramatic turnaround to his personal adventure story. Sarah understood this. It was surely one of the reasons she quit her job and never again worked for someone outside their home. She respected those women who continued to work in factories even after they were married, helping the family income. But the trade-off in her household was too great, given her husband's investment in his self-image as a successful provider.

Dave desperately needed some sort of trade. He hired on as a housepainter for a contractor but could not abide working for somebody else. He considered buying a news and candy stand on Flatbush Avenue but could not get Sarah's Tante Minnie to lend him the $500 he needed. In desperation, he decided to try the needle trades. He made a deal with an elderly manufacturer of infant bathrobes, in a factory where his friend Al Berlin was already working. Dave would be a shipping clerk for a month or two and then be trained and employed as a cutter, gradually assuming an elite position in the shop. His first task was as a "stretcher." He and Al would each hold the end of a bolt of fabric and walk backward, pulling hard all the way. Voilà, in twenty minutes, fifty yards from the mill would become sixty-five yards of cloth on the shop floor. Already a net profit of 30 percent! But after a few months of this, Dave was still stuck at the loading dock. He went to Siegelman, the owner, who told him that "he saw no advantage in changing the way things were." Dad told me years later that he had never been angrier in his life, until he perceived that the old man feared for his life. At that point Dave walked away. Thus concluded his association with New York's leading industrial sector. I heard and overheard my father's anger plenty of times, but this must have been quite a doozy.

What did he do with his time, when he couldn't find work? The neighborhood offered two sanctuaries. One was the Supreme Theatre on Livonia Avenue, just under the IRT elevated tracks. (There were times when the suspenseful discovery of "whodunit?" was interrupted by the rattle of the express train above.) Dave may well have seen every 1930s grade B movie, the specialty of the Supreme. When I was growing up, and the movie libraries of the 1930s became the stock in trade of 1950s television stations, Dad became my walking motion picture database. He knew Madame Curie's story (from the MGM biopic) better than the committee that awards the Nobel Prize. He always claimed to have read all the great nineteenth-century classics like *Wuthering Heights* and *A Tale of Two Cities,* but I think he mostly remembered the movie versions.

Beverly fondly recalls that her mother would often pack her up and take her to an afternoon movie, bringing along a jar of fruit or some cookies and milk to consume during the hours when kitchen work could be ignored. They often took the long way around the block so that none of the other children would catch them, and whine until they were taken along. I have to wonder that Dave and Sarah never ran into each other in the movie house. For both, the silver screen was acknowledged as a necessary nostrum to hard times. On weekends, the three of them would all go together to see the first-run movies at the Loew's Premier or the local movie palace, the Loew's Pitkin. Once or twice a year, the whole family put on their finest and headed off to Radio City Music Hall for an afternoon show, followed by dinner on Mott Street in Chinatown. Beverly can still recall what each of them wore to the showing of *National Velvet* in 1944, as well as almost every line in the movie.

Dave's other refuge was the local pool hall, atop Fox's dairy at the corner of Alabama and Livonia, popularly and sarcastically known as "the Yeshiva." Dave played skillfully, but he steered clear of the tough guys, the sharks and hustlers. Partisans of the local welterweight hero, Al "Boomy" Davis, hung out there, as well as card-carrying associates of Murder, Inc., our local gangsters at the peak of their notoriety. If Dave studied anything at this yeshiva, it was to sharpen his street smarts even further. In Eastern Europe, of course, the yeshiva or study hall was the daylong sanctum of the most studious Jewish men, who could spend endless hours out of sight, deflecting Talmudic texts off one another. So I find it especially delicious that Mom would occasionally tell Beverly, "Go get your father from the Yeshiva."

On days when, like an old cash register, he had to hit the button that popped up "No Sale," he would trudge home, climb the twenty-three grimy steps to the apartment, each of his steps heavy with frustration, and enter quietly. Sarah and Beverly held back, allowing Dad to exhale, to vent, to waste a few moments looking at—but scarcely reading a word of—the newspaper on the kitchen table.

Still, the Schwartzes kept up their confidence in Dave. He was not a *nishtgutnik,* a lazy good-for-nothing, or a spendthrift, and he behaved respectfully. Many men would have been undone by living under the microscopic scrutiny of his in-laws, but the Schwartzes were easy-going, tolerant, and kind. Mom found her own kitchen table too often occupied by my father's old buddies from the cellar club, many of them still unmarried and threatening to "eat her out of house and home." But she recognized that Dave needed these companions, and she learned to roll her eyes and avoid a confrontation. She weathered his storms, as when he exploded at Zayde for wasting a dime on soap bubbles for Beverly, and she passed over his foolishness, as when he bought a dumb Christmas present for Beverly, a toy machine gun that shot out sparks. Everyone waited for better times, when it was expected that Dave Rabinowitz would finally become a *mensch,* a generous and thoughtful adult. The novel of his life got thicker and thicker, but the climactic chapter, the one with a turn in his fortunes, kept getting deferred.

As Dave customarily said, the family "didn't go too deep" in thinking about the future. It seemed that every time that Sarah and Dave celebrated a milestone, their financial prospects worsened. When they were engaged, when they were married, when they had their first child: all these *simchas* (joys) were followed by months of sheer desperation. Everybody agreed that Sarah and Dave's baby, Beverly, came too early. And from that moment, everybody had an opinion about how she should be cared for. Dave's mother, Eva Rabinowitz, a talented woman hardened by years of abuse, was full of superstitions. She still resided among demons and spirits who crossed over into the same material universe as living mortals. Shenka had no patience for this nonsense, and Sarah had learned to ignore it, most of the time. A "protective" red thread on the baby's left wrist was one thing, but Sarah walked in once to discover a knife under the baby's pillow—a piece of Old World folklore that should have been left behind in Odesa.

In the argot of Alabama Avenue, everybody was a meddlesome "Mrs. Buttinsky." The baby was too fat, too skinny, too placid, too colicky, and certainly too much for the young mother to handle. The architecture of 502 Alabama Ave. did not help. The thresholds between the common hallway and private family space were entirely theoretical. Parenting, after all, was pandemic, and expertise was everywhere. Worst of all, Sarah was a sucker for punishment. She was too generous, too welcoming, too willing to listen. Her innermost cravings for a quiet family life, "everyone all together," were impossible to achieve in this world. Her mother, who loved her dearly, could not protect her from prying neighbors and relatives, and Shenka's own yearning for isolation sometimes led her to hasten Sarah and her baby out of her own apartment.

The little girl also took good advantage of being the only grandchild and the only niece. Beverly was treated to pastry and candy treats by her zayde. She shadowed her often-idle uncles, Sam and Isaac, around the neighborhood, and she probably knew more about the social geography, pool hall gossip, and cinematic offerings of East New York than any other toddler in history. And she has remembered almost every detail to this day.

Just a few weeks after Dave's debacle with Siegelman and the bathrobe factory, the drumbeats of war changed everything in the Schwartz and Rabinowitz households. Everyone's pulse quickened in 1939, when the Nazis and the Soviets both invaded Poland, and it raced even faster through the spring blitzkrieg, the fall of France, and the Battle of Britain in 1940. By the time of the Japanese attack on Pearl Harbor, the family expected that war would come soon, so shocking was this demonstration of the vulnerability of our national territory. The men of the family, hollowed out by the economy for so long, felt themselves filled by the rush of public events. Dovid Schwartz's work became steadier. Sam and Isaac were drafted in 1942, went through basic training at army bases in the southern states, and then were shipped across the Atlantic.

In January 1942, Dave's brother Al gave him a lead on a job at the Federal Shipbuilding and Drydock Company yard in Port Newark, New Jersey, where the company had announced that it was expanding its facilities and hiring an additional 10,000 workers. Faced with a shortage of skilled workers, the Roosevelt Administration issued a series of executive orders allowing federal and private contractor shipyards to appoint temporary workers, without Civil Service protections, to work as apprentices and helpers. These "unclassified" positions often came with age and experience qualifications, expectations of "high standards of ability, intelligence, conduct, loyalty, diligence and good manners," probation periods, and provisions for evaluation. But labor shortages amid the national emergency following Pearl Harbor, lax enforcement, and bureaucratic confusions led to frequent breakdowns in these standards.

Dave signed up as an apprentice test electrician at the shipyard. Week after week, a destroyer escort slid down the ways at Port Newark, and the officers on the bridge communicated with the engineers and the men through a DC (direct current) wiring system that a master mechanic and twenty apprentices like Dave Rabinowitz would test, over and over again. The shipyard job was a godsend, his first full-time, long-term employment, finally, at age 28. For this consistent and reliable work, Dave drew a paycheck—fifty cents an hour, sixty cents an hour, even a dollar an hour—with "time and a half for overtime." And his war work allowed him to claim a 2-B classification and exemption from the draft as an essential defense worker, though he always quipped that he was classified "4-F, a married man with furniture."

He may also have made money on the side. Once he told me, "I had a board." Seeing my puzzlement, he explained that he ran a craps game, in which players tossed their dice against Dave Rabinowitz's board. (How this fits his aversion to gambling I do not know, but clearly he preferred to be the banker rather than the bettor.) As each vessel neared completion, he spent more of his time aboard ship, far from the eyes of supervisors.

His shipyard hours were long. The bedside Westclox alarm clock woke him at five o'clock. He was waiting outside fifteen or twenty minutes later, ready to join three or four fellows in a neighbor's car. "Fifty cents," he recalled, "for the trip to Joisey," as they all called it. The commute was accompanied by a lot of joking and backseat driving. It's on these trips that Dave mastered telling the Damon Runyon–like stories of a companion of his youth named C. C. Delancey. "Where did his name come from?" you would ask. "Clinton, corner Delancey. That's where I was born," he would say. A decade later, at my bedtime, I became his best audience for these tales.

Although there were dozens of cafeterias within the yards and many lunch stands around the gates, Dave chose to bring his own meals in a black metal lunchbox, with a thermos for coffee. Sarah had prepared some sandwiches the night before—tuna, egg salad, or a leftover hamburger. She had supper on the table when he returned, at 5:30 or 6 PM when he was still working one shift, much later when he took on overtime. Dave took on as much work as possible, and then he got a chance to do a double shift in New Jersey. This was too much. A doctor certified that he was too exhausted to work as many as eighty hours a week, plus traveling an hour each way to Port Newark. At that point, Dave successfully petitioned for a shift to the Brooklyn Navy Yard. In Brooklyn, as an electrician installing a ship's communication wires, he worked for the Broadway Maintenance Company, which built the USS Missouri and other battleships. Dave fell into a regimen of daily and weekly work schedules, happily foregoing for these months the thrill of making the sale, closing the deal, that dramatized the life of a salesman. But he still could not "catch fire." Other men might have parlayed the camaraderie of the shipyard into a friendship or, God knows, a business partnership profitable to both parties. After his last day on the job, he never said a word to anyone he had met over those three years.

I should have asked more questions about this period of Dad's work life. It was probably the first time that he met and worked alongside African American men (and, perhaps, took a chunk of their money at his craps board). FDR's Executive Order 8802 outlawed "discrimination in the employment of workers in defense industries or government because of race, creed, color, or national origin," and established the Fair Employment Practice Committee to oversee its implementation. Many Blacks migrated to New York City from southern states to work in the shipyards and factories, as the city's role as the nation's most important industrial center expanded. Quite possibly he could have traveled to the Yard from East New York on the Myrtle Avenue El, in which case he would have encountered many Black workers moving into rental housing in the Brooklyn neighborhoods of Fort Greene and Bedford-Stuyvesant.

This work regimen made Dave unavailable to Sarah during the week. On many Saturdays and Sundays, he took Beverly for outings—semipro baseball games, including Negro League games at Dexter Park just over the Queens line, Dodgers games at Ebbets Field, and summer days of swimming and boardwalk "rides" at Coney Island and Brighton Beach. Sarah often took the opportunity to stay home and rest, especially when it was a ballgame day. Picnics at the park usually involved more formality than one would ever see today. Dad wore decent slacks and a sport jacket, Mom wore a dress. They customarily carried a blanket and a suitcase full of food. "It smelled of hardboiled eggs," Beverly remembers. They sought out a comfortable spot near the Abraham Lincoln statue on the eastern side of the park, not far from the carousel that Beverly loved. Dave, of course, made a point—nearly universal among his social circle—of never helping with the housework, the cooking, or the food shopping. But he was obsessive about packing up a few sandwiches made at home—salami on rye with caraway seeds was a favorite—and filling a jug of iced lemonade. It was a cardinal principle of the family to avoid buying food and drink on such excursions. I can't remember my parents ever springing for a Coca-Cola.

Dave's weekday work schedule helped structure Sarah's day. She hated having to rush though her cleaning, shopping, and cooking. She welcomed the chance to enroll Beverly in a Yiddish preschool run by a local cell of the Communist Party, and in another program for tots sponsored by the federal Works Progress Administration at a park on Snedicker Avenue. (The Gentile teachers there introduced the children to Halloween, but Mom said she "had no time for making costumes or other such nonsense," much to the little girl's disappointment.) Sarah discovered that the scarcity of children born in 1937 left plenty of room in kindergarten classes at P.S. 190 and succeeded in getting Beverly admitted at age four. My mother wore an apron in the house, of course, and Beverly was very much tied to her apron strings. When she entered kindergarten, she wanted Mom to stand outside and wait for her. Sarah laughed, but then she signed up to stand watch at the locked entry doors to the school for a few hours each morning during the early days of the war.

Beverly looked forward to her father's coming home from work, especially when he brought home bracelets a fellow worker had made by winding colored wires together in wonderful patterns. But just as often she remembers that he could be angry when he came in the door, full of complaints about this boss and that coworker, about traffic, snafus in production, and foolish regulations issued from on high. Beverly was very frightened of his temper, and on one occasion when he was home alone with her, he pushed her into the bedroom dresser and broke two of her teeth. When Sarah returned home and found Beverly bleeding and sobbing, she screamed at her husband. For a long time it remained a painful memory for all three of them.

The war was inescapable. It imposed its regimen on everybody. With sixteen million men and women (of a total national population of 130 million) in uniform, the country marched to a more unified beat—reading and listening to the same news, sharing the same entertainments and humor, obeying (or trying to evade) the same rules for rationing, recycling, and civil defense.

Public life expanded into the corners of every habitat. Shenka mounted two blue stars in her window facing the street. Everyone in the neighborhood knew that her "boys" were abroad, in danger and out of touch except for rare letters. On the street, there was a fear that U-boats would invade New York Harbor, or that Nazi sympathizers and "the Japs" would sabotage the country. Children were constantly drilled to exit classrooms silently and to stand in straight lines along school hallways. Each child was issued a plastic dogtag on a nylon cord. Wearing it was mandatory. "Remember Pearl Harbor" posters hung on the walls of classrooms and libraries. Boisterous drives for savings bonds and stamps, for recycling of oils and fats and metals, for home gardens and window boxes, were constant reminders of the common urgency. The movie houses, the subway platforms, and the newspaper pages were filled with propaganda, calls for volunteers, and campaigns to raise civilian morale. New cars and appliances disappeared from the market. Movie melodramas modeled the proper emotional responses to anticipation, worry, and tragedy. "Claudette Colbert," Beverly says, "was a good crier" in many of these films. The Rabinowitzes read the news in the *Brooklyn Eagle* and *PM,* scorning the *Daily News* and Hearst's *New York Mirror* as "right-wing rags." Dave's angry rants each evening were diverted by listening to the news reported by H. V. Kaltenborn on CBS (and later NBC) radio, with a calmness and thoughtfulness that is largely absent in today's television journalism. But, as is often the case today, the news reinforced pre-existing ideas and loyalties.

Everyone in the neighborhood, even the most ignorant, followed the progress of the fighting through the radio news, the front pages of the tabloids, and the newsreels at the Supreme. But the newsreels in particular, with their stirring musical soundtracks, also served the ends of patriotic propaganda, interpreting small victories as auguries of ultimate triumph and explaining even large defeats as minor setbacks. More frightening truths were suspected but defensively set aside. The possibility of defeat went unspoken.

No one on Alabama Avenue needed a war to be convinced of Hitler's villainy. His fierce invective, announcing his intention to rid Europe totally of its Jews, had instilled terror in Brooklyn's Jews almost daily since 1933. With perfect hindsight, it would have been possible to piece together the evolution of the Shoah, step by step: first, the exclusion of German Jews from public life and the suppression of their basic liberties, and once the war began in Europe, the arrest of Jews from every corner of the continent, from tiny Greek mountain villages to the streets of Amsterdam and Paris, the confinement of Jews in ghettoes, the sweep through Poland of the Nazi *Einsatzgruppen* brigades, the murder of hundreds of thousands of Jews in Poland by mass shootings and mobile vans using poisonous gas, the transport of millions to "the East," and, finally, the construction and operation of enormous death camps in Poland and Germany. Despite the suppression of this information by the Nazis and even by British and American intelligence agencies, bits and pieces of this story came to light in the accounts of escaping prisoners, partisan fighters, neutral observers, and officials of humanitarian organizations. In June and July 1942, the *New York Times* reported that a million Jews had been murdered. Though the article was buried on inside pages, its horror reached the tenements, synagogue pews, and park benches of East New York. But in general rumors of Nazi atrocities were not easily verifiable, and many reports were distrusted as Allied propaganda. Jewish leaders in America, as in Europe and Palestine, often grasped at straws, allowing hope to obscure fragmentary evidence. For many in the Gentile world it was hard to see the difference between the centuries-old persecution of the Jews through pogroms, almost a fact of nature, and the Nazi effort to destroy the entire Jewish people. Not in my family, of course. Still scarred from twenty-year-old memories of the 1920 pogroms, they heard the slightest rumor of Nazi violence as a sure sign of the worst outcome for European Jewry. "Mass murder? I wouldn't put it past them, the bastards!" But the scale of the Shoah, the priority the Nazis gave to the "final solution," and the extraordinary industriousness with which they executed, monitored, and recorded their crimes were simply unfathomable. Sarah recalled, "We didn't know, we couldn't imagine." The entire story remained elusive until the camps were liberated in 1945.

The Schwartzes had been mostly cut off from their Polish roots as anti-Semitism expanded throughout Eastern Europe in the 1930s. Few tidbits of news had been exchanged for over a decade. Shenka expected the worst, assuming that her friends and family in Wysokie, Dovid's in Sokoly, and even her half-brothers in Warsaw were all dead. And yet, when the war ended, and survivors of the camps began to be listed by refugee agencies like the Hebrew Immigrant Aid Society, Shenka and Sarah pored over the names. Shenka and Sarah could never confirm the loss of family members. The subject, too painful for public discussion, was summed up by the presumption that "Hitler must have taken care of them." Until the late 1950s the Shoah remained a horrible secret. Displaced persons, like the family that owned the grocery on our corner, often wanted to avoid the subject and get on with their lives. Sarah did not want to know anything more. She didn't want to read about the Holocaust, as it became known in America, or to watch documentaries. About forty years after the war, I discovered an account of the fate of the Jews of Wysokie Mazowieckie during the Shoah. I sent it to my parents, but my father intercepted the package, lest it upset Mom. In the end, she was actually glad to know the details, especially to learn that some of her old schoolmates had performed heroically in leading a community doomed to extermination. But Sarah never entirely shed that armor of deliberate ignorance, of aversion from the horror.

Recognizing once and for all that the United States had saved her family from the Shoah, Sarah's attachment to the nation intensified and never relented, though she remained a fierce critic of many injustices within our borders. World War II was no time to rethink what it meant to be American, Jewish, the parent of a young child, or the child of an elderly parent. And there was no need. Amid the anxieties of daily life, New York City was now definitively the family's home. There was no other. It was comforting to experience the continuity of leadership in both New York City and the nation. Franklin Roosevelt had served as president for twelve years, and Fiorello La Guardia as mayor for eleven of them—almost all of Sarah's and Dave's adult lives. They were in their thirties before they cast a vote for anyone else.

During the war, the old hollowness was externalized. It migrated from inside the men, from feelings of individual inadequacy, to the entire household, where feelings of absence and anticipated loss crept into every corner. Beverly was old enough to follow the news and sassy enough to express the fears that none of the adults could speak aloud. Personal feelings went into hiding as the business of life became more complicated. Brooklyn filled up with migrants, the buses and subways were crowded with workers on early and late shifts, and transactions at the shops took longer because of ration cards and coupons. Every residential neighborhood was converted into "the Home Front," constantly described as necessary to victory.

Sarah spent lots of hours waiting in line at the Office of Price Administration on Blake Avenue to get the family's ration cards. Tuesdays and Thursdays were meatless days. Used cooking oil was collected, as were food cans. Beverly had a book of stamps, bought for her by her zayde, which would ultimately be turned into US Savings Bonds. Blackout curtains covered Shenka's windows facing Alabama Avenue—they weren't needed at Dave and Sarah's apartment, which faced the back and sides of the building. Sarah found it hard to avoid arguing with her neighbors about politics. The street was full of people too busy and too cynical to vote, even in wartime, but Sarah was insistent. From toddlerhood, Beverly got to pull the lever when Sarah (and her father, too) voted for the American Labor Party, which provided a vehicle for socialists to support FDR and other major-party candidates rather than those of the more militant Socialist Party. Sarah was always too shy to speak in public or to take a leadership role. But she had a strong sense of herself as a responsible citizen. She chaperoned every school trip that Beverly's class took and never missed an Open School Night.

Dave was different. Even in summer, he preferred to spend his leisure hours lying in bed and reading. He had "no use" for the neighbors, or, for that matter, for most anybody else except Sarah and his in-laws. Though he could be sociable, even winning, in company, he almost never made an effort to make new friends or to nourish older ones. He continued to see the friends he had made before his marriage—but now only when Sarah arranged it. She, on the other hand, cultivated a strong group of women friends from the wives of these men. They got together to play cards or to go to the movies. More than a shared immigrant background, or inclinations toward politics or religion, Sarah's criterion for the friends she chose was self-respect, evidenced in being "dressed nicely." As we have seen, personal appearance and self-care were essential for her. She always did her hair at home, not in a beauty parlor. She wore mascara and bright red lipstick, but no nail polish. She always wore cocktail hats and gloves to social occasions, with an extra pair of white gloves to wear once she arrived at the site of the wedding or party.

But Sarah's mind was also occupied by less predictable anxieties. Her mother's digestive problems began to worsen during the war years, and Sarah took responsibility for a round of doctor's appointments and hospital stays that would occupy most of the decade. Her father Dovid was healthy but persistently underemployed—periodically laid off for "slack seasons" in the coat-making industry, even in wartime—and worried about finances. Periodically he borrowed money from Household Finance, a street-corner lender. Zayde's fears became morbid, and they grew to surround every contingency in the family's life: Would Dave be injured? Would Shenka feel better enough to resume her cooking? Would Sarah be able to carry her groceries home herself? Would Beverly hurt herself by playing in the street? Roller skates? Oh, no, impossible. A two-wheeler? Absolutely not. (Consequently, I only became a real cyclist at age 55.) Dovid cosseted his granddaughter, fussed over her sniffles, and made everyone crazy with his worrying.

And then there were "the boys," Sarah's brothers, drafted in early 1942 and shipped off to the European theater right after their basic training—Sam in the infantry, Isaac in the engineers. Isaac was an eager recruit. He had been spoiling for a chance to fight fascists since he tried, against his mother's iron will, to enlist at age 15 in the Abraham Lincoln Brigade in the Spanish Civil War against Generalissimo Franco. Sam was another story. He hated the idea of joining the fight. Caught between his mother's insistence and his father's constant worrying, the war for Sam was neither a cause nor an adventure. I never heard him talk about it afterward.

The boys wrote home via Victory mail, or V-mail, in which their letters were first censored by the military, then microfilmed and shipped as thumbnail-sized negatives. Arriving in the United States, they were enlarged by the Post Office to 60 percent of their original size, printed out, and sent on. On most mornings, the Alabama Avenue mailman mechanically and unobtrusively keyed open the mailbox in the building's entryway, sorting the letters and postcards into the sixteen or seventeen slots. But he also made a practice of blowing a whistle loudly whenever he had a letter from the War Department. The whole building seemed to stiffen with fear at that sound. Anticipating a blast, Sarah stood as a sentinel every morning, ensuring that her mother would not be the first to hear bad tidings. Her vigilance was rewarded after Isaac was wounded in the stomach during the Italian campaign. Upon news of his being awarded a Purple Heart medal, the family felt even greater fear, no matter how much reassurance accompanied the notice. Sam, meanwhile, contracted malaria during his time in Sicily and was sent to recover in England. Thus he missed the D-Day invasion of Normandy, much to the family's relief.

Every emotion in the two households ran through Sarah. Though still in her twenties, somehow she had learned to perform all these roles—as wife and mother, as daughter and sister, as nurse and psychologist, as citizen and neighbor, as an articulate and stylish young woman. She did not read the women's magazines, which were full of advice on handling household problems. She listened intently but skeptically to the difficulties described by her group of woman friends, but she kept her own counsel. She made it a rule never to boast and never to groan. She could not complain to her mother, fearing to upset her. Though she respected authority figures like First Lady Eleanor Roosevelt and Frances Perkins, FDR's secretary of labor and the first woman in a president's cabinet, Sarah knew that her life was far different from theirs. She felt the lack of American mentors for young foreign-born housewives like her. Her aunts repaid her sweet affection and concern with unwelcome advice, and sometimes nasty commentary. "Everyone could live your life better than you could," she recalled. But she soldiered on. *Nisht geferlach:* it wasn't so bad. Beverly recalls that her mother had no patience for complaints. She could have mounted a sign above her sink that said, "*kvetching* is forbidden." God forbid, if a child announced that she was bored, or had "nothing to do," a string of sarcastic comments shot forth: "Go knock your head against the wall!" This would be followed by even more caustic, wickedly off-color expressions of dismissal. At the first inkling of a whine, she was quick to banish the offender from the premises.

While she tried to stabilize the life of the household, Mom could not overcome the endemic stubbornness of all her loved ones. She could not stop the incessant shouting matches between Beverly and Dad. Her parents did not always follow her advice, and she never had any luck in dissuading her brothers, after the war, from attaching themselves to very difficult spouses. Her love was fraught with frustration.

But the situation at home was vastly better at war's end. Dave was earning more than a hundred dollars a week. As horrible and frightening as it was, war could also be bracing. Dave and Sarah Rabinowitz had begun to put money away. They felt confident enough again, as in the reckless first days of marriage, to want another child, and I was born in the very last weeks of the Pacific war. Dad got the news of my birth while working on the early shift at the shipyard. He remembered his first thought. His new son should never have to live through such terrible times. My life would flourish in an era of peace.

He got it wrong.

*When she noticed the pair of bandage scissors, Beverly gasped in
horror. "Oh, God, where did you get that?" she asked. But, of
course, she knew. These were the scissors that Mom had used
seventy years ago to cut gauze to wrap Bubbe's bleeding ulcers.*

7

Beverly Is Startled by the Scissors

The house at 742 Bradford Street was the largest and most valuable object Sarah and Dave Rabinowitz ever owned. Purchased in September 1948, it signaled Dave's self-proclaimed success as a breadwinner—independent, self-employed, beholden to no one. He could now stand on his porch in a suit and tie, full of pride, a cigar lit, his body bulkier than it had been in shipyard days just three years before, looking out on a quiet street lined with sycamore trees. Sarah, on the other hand, loved being inside, in command of its domestic order. In short, the house fulfilled what each of them had dreamed of, individually, when they married thirteen years before.

Impressive as the Bradford Street house loomed in the minds of its new owners, it was actually quite modest, less than 1,000 square feet. It was situated in the middle of a line of a dozen semi-detached, two-story brick rowhouses, exactly duplicated by another twelve facing it across Bradford Street. Like other New York City row- or townhouses, they were all built on speculation by a single builder. The date, 1929, the year of the Wall Street Crash, was inscribed in the keystone above the entry, a date that helps to explain the builders' difficulties in finding buyers. Eventually, we learned, the properties were doled out to their still-unpaid tradesmen—the plumbers, the electricians, the floor guys, the roofers, and so on.

Seven forty-two Bradford Street mimicked the city's grander townhouses on a smaller scale. Its exterior and interior architecture derived, I believe, from the nineteenth-century effort to separate home and work, to insert as much space as possible between the street life (characterized as male, commercial, impolite, and noisy) and the domestic sphere (female, cultural, religious, polite, and quiet). Along the city's new residential streets, male breadwinners increasingly worked outside the home—in factories and offices, at transport facilities, and in retail establishments. Their spouses assumed responsibility for creating and preserving the home as a refuge from the rough-and-tumble world of competitive capitalism. Even in such a humble abode, the family's most private spaces, its small bedrooms and the bathroom, were placed at the furthest reach from the street and the front steps.

Entering the house itself, one had first to pass through a small vestibule with a tiled floor, appropriate for leaving umbrellas and boots. Then followed the living room, dark and formally furnished, and seldom used except with "company." Through an arch, its doors removed, one then came upon the sitting room, eventually called the "TV room," the heart of family activity. Beyond this room was a small area with a choice of three paths—down the stairs to the side door, ahead and left to the dining area and its dinette table, or ahead and right into the kitchen. Once through the kitchen, one finally arrived at the two bedrooms and the bathroom. Altogether one might traverse the whole house in the time it takes to read these few sentences. Because our house was on the west side of the street, the back was much the sunnier side. Walking through the whole house, one progressed from dark to light. Sunlight flooded the bedrooms. From their windows were suspended the clotheslines on which Sarah's laundry, all except the sheets given to a pickup and delivery service, was hanging. It was the first place one looked at to find out what sort of day lay ahead.

Like much fancier residences, the Bradford Street house even had a side entrance, up a flight of stairs from the adjacent alleyway, so that deliveries of groceries and laundry could be brought directly into the kitchen without using the front door or soiling the wall-to-wall carpeting in the living and sitting rooms. Also along the alley was a door into the cellar, where fuel oil and later merchandise for Dave's business were delivered.

On the second floor of the house the Rabinowitzes now owned a rental apartment, even more spacious than their own, which contributed roughly enough in monthly rent to cover their mortgage payments. The backyard garage was also rented to a businessman on a neighboring block. In a single moment, Sarah and Dave had become landlords, fellow stewards of their block, protectors of its safety from the intrusion of the outside world. They could now dedicate space and expense to interior furnishings and décor, presenting their self-image to the world. After decades of tenement life, they had become bourgeois, if only in a "petty" (petit) sense.

There were limits to our social ascent, of course. There were only two bedrooms, and Beverly at age twelve was more deserving of the second one than I. So I didn't have a room of my own, or a playroom. I was put to sleep in my parents' bed, nestled into my fantasy tent or Conestoga wagon, reading (like young Abraham Lincoln) by imaginary candlelight. In the morning, I awoke on a "high-rise" trundle bed in the sitting room. I have no memories of having been transported from one to the other in the entire five or six years of this arrangement. During the day, I roamed the house, finding nooks and crannies, tabletops and carpeted areas, on which to play. There was no preschool for me or my neighborhood friends in those days. During quiet weekday hours, when I was home alone with Mom, I re-enacted the Hopalong Cassidy movies I watched on television. The chenille spread on my parents' bed provided a really good imitation of a sagebrush desert. The flowered wallpaper in the darkened living room turned the room into a haunting landscape. My toy Indian heroes hid out behind the red club chair, waiting to ambush (a favorite word!) their cowboy rivals. After each climactic scene, I could venture into the kitchen to find Mom grinding liver, mixing chocolate cake, or cutting up celery and carrots for snacks.

My earliest memories go back to our family's very first days at Bradford Street in 1948, when I was just three. The years before that are lost in the mists of my infancy, but I now know that they were convulsive for my parents, alternately thrilling and awful, painful and comforting. The immediate aftermath of World War II had brought the most distressingly mixed emotions of Sarah's life. Her brothers returned home to Alabama Avenue in the autumn of 1945, safe if not entirely sound. Now in their mid-twenties, they sat around their parents' apartment for months. Demobilization made them eligible for the "52–20 Club," that is, a government check for twenty dollars per week for a year. Most of the money, Sarah remembered, seemed to go for cigarettes, cheap beer, and Cokes. The ashtrays filled up as the sofa cushions wore down. Martin Block's "Make-Believe Ballroom" on WNEW Radio played the Ink Spots and Frank Sinatra, and the Victrola wore out several 78 rpm discs of "To Each His Own" and that annoying novelty song, "Open the Door, Richard." The number one song of 1946 was Perry Como's "A Prisoner of Love." Plaintively, the vocalist complains that he cannot break the invisible chains imposed by his unfaithful spouse or lover (who has presumably been swept off her feet by some coward who evaded military service). What an irony! To be demobilized, unshackled from military discipline (and sometimes actually liberated from POW camps), and then to feel yourself held captive by your feeble affections. How much pain clouded the joy of homecomings! Hardly recovered from injury and illness, emotionally deadened by the toll of war, haunted by memories of violence, and then urged on all sides to pick themselves up and start rebuilding their country and their lives, veterans like Sam and Isaac were a mess.

The decade-old, green-handled bottle opener now seldom found its way back to the kitchen. For a whole year, nothing interested the boys. "They wouldn't move themselves," Sarah complained. "Mama didn't know what to do with them." Not quite stymied by post-traumatic stress, they lived in a nether world of penny-ante poker games, trips to the pool hall and the racetrack, and long, long naps. Isaac's war stories, full of cynical complaints about the stupidity of the officer corps ("college boys"), soon became too tedious to repeat for the civilian audience. Sam's silence about his war experiences was even more disturbing. Their eventual recovery, painful and limited as it was, is as much a testament to the American fighting man as their courage on the battlefield.

Dave's fate was different. He was quickly dismissed from the Navy Yard in August 1945. He had not expected to remain in the shipbuilding trades, and even those who counted on it, like those Black co-workers also hired as "unclassified" employees, were thrown out of work when defense expenditures were slashed in 1946 and 1947. Employment at the Brooklyn Navy Yard declined from over

65,000 in 1943 to 19,000 three years later, and half that the following year. Dave had instead toyed with the idea of joining the Local 3 of the International Brotherhood of Electrical Workers, which had apparently promised to absorb wartime electricians like him. A power center of New York City's working-class elite, the union's leadership soon reneged. Privileged workingmen were not going to welcome the competition of so many newcomers. Everyone feared that the end of the war would mean the resumption of the Depression. For many Local 3 members, their own sons were coming home and needed good jobs. There were no farewell parties or gift watches for the men and women who had built up the US Navy during the war.

Once again, good news—in the form of my birth in July 1945—paradoxically brought financial panic to Sarah and Dave. Their regular government paycheck was gone. Twenty years after he first swelled with pride about "being a man," fifteen years after his initial enthusiasm about hitting the streets and finding customers for his merchandise, Dave hated the idea of picking up his peddler's pack again. Besides, selling caps one by one, as in the desperate days of the Depression, was not going to pay the bills in the mid-1940s. With a path to the electrician's trade closed off, street trading was pretty much all that Dave knew how to do. But he needed to find a way to make it pay.

The peddling economy thrived in the shadows of the normal distribution channels from manufacturer to wholesaler to jobber to retailer. War had disrupted the availability of ordinary consumer goods, curtailing production of many items and giving priority to military orders. Many New Yorkers learned the intricacies of payoffs, kickbacks, and other methodological refinements of the black market, trading in illegally acquired merchandise or its grayer varieties—"buying direct" and bypassing the retail outlets. At your workplace, in the candy store, or even at your sister-in-law's table, the word might be passed that Joe down the block had a few dozen nice cans of olive oil to get rid of. Where they came from or how they escaped the retail market was never revealed.

In 1945, demand was high, and shortages were everywhere. Dave searched for anything on which he could turn a profit. And along came his brother Carl to tell Dave about a guy who had boxes and boxes of watch movements, the actual inner workings of a wrist-watch, which he was ready to unload for a song. Suddenly Dave was "in business." He scraped together the funds, bought the goods, rented a corner of a 47th Street office, and began to make the rounds of local watchmakers. They were desperate for these tickers. No watch movements had been imported from Switzerland since 1939. Dave sealed the deals, and even better, he built a network of pals in the jewelry trade. Then a few cases of leather watchstraps fell into his lap. And then watch cases. And display boxes. And some gold rings. Soon he was carrying a satchel, peddling his goods to jewelry stores along Flatbush Avenue in Brooklyn and Jamaica Avenue in Queens.

Within a year he had become a jeweler. Watches and jewelry were a good business in the immediate postwar years, as reunited and newly acquainted couples rushed to marry after years of wartime separations and delays. By this time diamond engagement rings and gold wedding bands had become requisite for every self-respecting bride. Sometimes a father-in-law might be resourceful in providing a job, but a gold watch was the most common survival of the dowry or bride-price in 1940s New York. By 1948, Dave had finagled himself into his own jewelry store at 35 Maiden Lane, in Manhattan's longstanding downtown Diamond District. For a small child like me, the glory of his shop was its huge York Lock Company safe, with a secret combination and double doors, where the jewels were stashed every night for safekeeping. At the shop's front entrance was a glass display case, which seemed to get more use, actually, as a counter for the elbows of kibitzers and hangers-on. At the back of the store sat Harold Kwait, a real watchmaker, with about a thousand different tiny tools and boxes of parts. I loved to watch him work. When I told my first-grade teacher that my father was a watchmaker, my mother felt impelled to march into the school the next day and correct me: "He's really a jeweler, with his own shop." I thus imbibed a lesson about the relative social classes of merchant and craftsman.

One of the earliest elevator-equipped business buildings in Lower Manhattan, 35 Maiden Lane had a faded grandeur about it. The Romanesque Revival street entrance issued into a beautifully tiled central hallway, which led to a majestic wide staircase and a grand mezzanine. Dad's shop, the Raven Watch Company, was tucked into a corner on the ground floor, just to the left of the stairwell. The ten floors of 35 Maiden Lane were filled with a fascinating collection of offices, six or eight on a floor. Some arranged the shipping of goods in and out of the port of New York, or the distribution of imported products around the United States. Someone in that line must have helped ornament the Raven shop with a giant lithograph of a Moore-McCormack freighter, which made Dave feel as though he had a role in global commerce. My favorite office was the headquarters of the Ray-Max Stamp Company, where two gentlemen catered to the collecting impulses of eight-year-olds like me by sending them "approvals" (e.g., eight commemorative stamps from the Union of South Africa for $1.25, returnable for a full refund). On Saturdays, when I accompanied my father to work, I would spend a few hours up in Ray-Max's top-floor aerie sorting piles and piles of used postage stamps from everywhere in the world. And at least an hour each week was devoted to the tutelage of Gus, the elevator man, who dispensed meteorological and political commentary as he expertly landed the car at exactly the right level for each floor. I ignored his commentary but loved showing off my skills to the building's patrons.

Among the thousands of men and women who worked the desks of Lower Manhattan's banks, insurance companies, and investment houses in the postwar years, many hungered for a few extra bucks. During lunchtime, the Diamond District was only a short walk from Wall Street, and you could come to Dave Rabinowitz and take away three or four watches on consignment and sell them to your co-workers. Or you could tell your office mates that you knew a great place to get an engagement ring. Then a bright-eyed young couple could come to 35 Maiden Lane, scattering the hangers-on at Dave's counter. Far from the chic precincts of Tiffany and its neighboring Fifth Avenue emporia, and equally remote from Main Street mass-market jewelers like Zales, the downtown jewelry stores offered a custom, fly-by-the-seat-of-the-pants business.

Dave Rabinowitz might show you and your sweetheart five or six stones. He told you the "four-c" variables: cut, clarity, color, and carat weight, always stressing the value of the first three over size. For a thousand dollars, you might get a carat-and-a-half stone, smaller if it was free of all imperfections and had the nicest color. Once you had your heart (and your fiancé's wallet) set on the right diamond, Dave would show you alternative settings. You could get a Tiffany or solitaire setting, in which the prongs pushed the stone up like a crown above the ring. Or a fishtail setting, where the stone sat low and was surrounded by tiny diamonds known as "baguettes." Then Dave sent you to a "setter" to make up the ring. Dozens of dealers and craftsmen worked in close collaboration with one another in this building and in others on the neighboring streets, trusting one another informally with many thousands of dollars' worth of diamonds and other gems on the basis of a quickly scrawled memo. On any given day, while Brink's armored cars cruised between retail outlets and bank vaults, men and women in shirtsleeves carried precious jewels from dealer to dealer in their handbags and back pockets. Thirteen-year-old Beverly once carried a bag of diamonds, wrapped in blue paper and hidden in the inside pocket of her overcoat, on the subway back and forth to Green and Sons on Canal Street, at the edge of the downtown jewelry district. "Who's going to bother you?" Dad told her, not quite reassuringly. Jewelry downtown was indeed a "word of mouth" business, with the mouth invariably tightly clenched around an expensive cigar.

Dave Rabinowitz had finally hit his stride. Once an Italian American club wanted to honor Joe DiMaggio at a dinner and needed to find a beautiful Longines gold watch, neatly inscribed with the details of the honor. So they asked Dave Rabinowitz to pick out a few beauties, drive up to Joe D's hotel, and have him select his favorite. (Too bad I was not a Yankees fan, though I trekked along!) Arlene and Darlene and Marlene from the Five Towns area of Long Island passed the word that Dave Rabinowitz could be trusted. The business built up Dave's bank account and, equally important, his ego, in a way that twenty years of work had never done before. He bought a sharkskin suit from Richfield Clothiers on Pitkin Avenue, and a third pair of snappy shoes from Florsheim's. Sarah got a beautiful Persian lamb coat and a diamond brooch. Dave supplied engagement rings at a significant discount to all of Sarah's cousins, and this enhanced the family's admiration of the couple's style at family weddings and bar mitzvahs.

The most obvious marker of Dave's newfound prosperity was a home of his own. A "private house," as it was called, was a mark of great status in this generation. At this particular moment the returning veterans and the beginning of the baby boom had created a housing crisis in New York City. The apartment buildings in Brownsville and East New York had become dilapidated over the course of the war. Little new housing had been built in the city since the late 1920s. The fancier apartment buildings on Eastern Parkway and in Flatbush were not to Sarah's taste. She had had enough of hallways, stairwells, and nosy neighbors. Snootier ones would be even worse. The arrival of more Blacks and Puerto Ricans during World War II seemed to threaten the comfortable insularity of the Brownsville "ghetto," which in 1920–1940 was the largest Jewish neighborhood in the world. Sarah's cousins and many others were moving out from the old and tired city to tidy new suburban boxes in Nassau County, usually leaving their parents behind. To Sarah that was unconscionable. For years she had talked about buying and sharing a house with her parents. Her mother was ill, and her father still traveled by subway to work in the garment district. Sarah had never gotten a driver's license and would have had difficulty shepherding her mother and her children around the suburbs. The family were still pleased with the New York City school system. Why leave Brooklyn?

The dramatic history of Dovid Schwartz's family was coming to an end. Both Sam and Isaac were married in 1947 and left Alabama Avenue for homes of their own.

During the summer of 1948, Dave sprang into action. He rented a bungalow at Rose Tree Acres in the Catskills for Sarah and the family, including Shenka. He arranged for Sarah to leave everyone in the mountains for a day so that she could catch a bus from Monticello, New York, to Brooklyn, to check out a two-family house on Bradford Street, between Linden Boulevard and Hegeman Avenue. It was a half-mile east of Alabama Avenue, in a quieter, lower-scale part of East New York. Most of their prospective neighbors were also refugees from the Brownsville neighborhood. Sarah could still do all of her food shopping at kosher butcher shops, fish stores, and greengrocers located only a few blocks from home. Sam's "Service and Self-Service" grocery store stood on the nearest corner, just three hundred feet from her new front door.

To reach the price of $13,600, Dave borrowed small sums from his father-in-law and secured a bank mortgage. In those tight credit times, obtaining $5,000 from Brooklyn's Hamburg Savings Bank required that he place three crisp $100 bills, delicately but decisively, into the open drawer of the bank president during their interview.

Dave was part of the second generation of homeowners along Bradford Street—men in their late thirties, often veterans or ex-war workers, all but one of them Eastern European Jews. Almost every family had two or three children, at most, as well as an aged mother-in-law, wearing black and speaking only Yiddish. (Sometimes she was the actual owner.) A few of the men were civil servants, department store salesmen, and garment industry craftsmen, but most, like Dave, ran small businesses. (The Italian exception, the Murgolos, were in the fuel oil business.) None of the women, at that moment, worked outside the home.

Sarah was happy to be free of the constant snooping and meddling at 502 Alabama Avenue. For the first time since she had arrived in America two decades earlier, she had a threshold to her dwelling, a house without *nextdoorikehs,* the Yinglish term for intrusive neighbors. "You could close the door and be alone with your thoughts. Oh, how I loved that!" The early months at Bradford Street were, however, anything but happy. The family had hardly begun to move in, when Bubbe's stomach ulcers grew cancerous and life-threatening. Sarah had little time to get to know her new neighbors. They installed their bedroom furniture in the sitting room, leaving one of the two back bedrooms for Shenka. Beverly and I shared the other one. Mom was distrustful of the nurse she had hired and spent almost all day and night taking a hand in the nursing. Her face became paler, more drawn, and weepier. She paid almost no attention to Beverly, and Beverly reciprocated by hiding away from her mother. Bubbe's wounds were suppurating, oozing blood and pus, and Mom was constantly cutting gauze rolls to form bandages and cutting adhesive tape to keep the bandages in place. The acrid smell of tape reminds me of that time.

Shenka died in January 1949. She was 58, Sarah just 32. Beverly still shudders to recall the visit from the undertakers, who took the body out of the house. I can only recall standing on the front porch, waiting for the long black cars of the funeral parlor and hearing the phrase, "She died in her sleep," which convinced me that I must never willingly nod off again. Mom was a wreck—bone-weary, angry, somehow convinced that she should have done this or that to save her mother from all the pain and the early death. Except for a week or two around the birth of her brothers in Poland, and three or four nights in the United States, Sarah had never been separated from her mother. They had never written to each other or phoned. No, this was a love of hand in hand, of lips on cheeks. Sarah wept, she mourned, and she continued to grieve, long past the times prescribed by the rabbis for the stages of bereavement, past the time when everyone who loved her began to worry. She obsessed about her loss and seemed to lose touch with her father, her husband, and her children.

Then, on a June night that year, she told Dave that she was going to a movie, leaving him with the children. She put an apple in her jacket pocket and walked toward the Biltmore Theatre on New Lots Avenue. But she turned right on New Lots and walked a few blocks to the old church at the corner of Schenk Avenue. She had never entered the church or even noticed the graveyard before. Now, among the stones of Dutch farmers dead and left unmourned generations ago, she found a smooth spot and sat down. Through the long night, almost until dawn, she recalled the incidents of her mother's life: Shenka's cruel childhood and its loneliness, her sweet but unfulfilling marriage to Dovid, and that powerful and impatient independence which sometimes pushed even her beloved Sarah away from her.

This devoted daughter remembered, and she wept, and she forgave, and above all she confronted her loneliness—her aloneness, evermore. Sarah thought of how much she had disregarded her husband's business concerns in the past twelve months. She knew that she had ignored Beverly's problems in her new school. She knew that just as her long days as her mother's nurse had ended, now her endless nights as her mother's mourner would also have to end. For years Sarah had put her mother's health and comfort first, and everyone else in the family accepted that. Dave had been absolutely supportive, never critical, always caring and respectful in visiting the ailing Shenka every day. Now that her mother was gone, Sarah's life had seemingly lost its purpose, and she was a muddle. At the center of her heart, where her love for her mother had held sway for years, there was only emotional emptiness. At the same time, in practical terms, she was now suddenly liberated from the endless worry and labor of caring for her mother, day and night, at home.

What would fill those hours? Who would she now be? What would she become? She had come face to face with the tragic truth that love, too, has its limits. All the selfless caretaking in the world could not save Shenka from the relentless ravages of cancer. Another waking hour at her mother's bedside, one more soothing balm, or even a flood of loving words and prayers could not stem that menace. As the eldest of the immigrant children, Sarah had taken the lead in acclimating everyone to New York life. She had shrewdly used her mother's fastidiousness as a way of separating herself from intrusive, unrefined neighbors on Alabama Avenue. Sarah now felt that she was starting all over again, but this time without any guidance. Her friends were not in the habit of sharing emotional *tsuris,* or distress, with one another. The magazines offering women's advice were useless. The rabbis she knew were of the Old World, and all of them men—ignorant of situations like hers. Professional psychological counseling was the province of a different, uptown class of people. Where could she turn?

She listened hard and seemed to hear her mother's voice, encouraging her to think about the future. She felt her mother's spiritual strength descend into her. Sitting there in the darkness, she re-imagined herself. She had heard her little boy object to her black dresses and necklace of black beads. It scared him. And so now she resolved to put away the mourning garb, have her hair done up again, and carry herself tastefully. She would pay more attention to Beverly and tell Dave how grateful she was for his support. As before, she would manage the household carefully, with her twin by-words of frugality and beauty.

She picked herself up and went home in the summer dawn. She climbed into bed for an hour or two. Dave awoke as usual and read a few pages of one of his thrillers. She never told him what she had done, or what she'd thought about. She had never heard of a "dark night of the soul." No one ever spoke of a spiritual crisis or a spiritual journey in her hearing. She would never have acknowledged that such a thing was possible. In fact, she was thereafter thoroughly skeptical of the value of such introspection.

Something snapped inside Sarah that night. She never again was so selfless as she had been with her mother, never again so trusting with her love. From then on, for the remaining sixty-six years of her life, she became more cautious, more protective of herself, less vulnerable to life's abuses. On the other hand, she was finally able to assume some responsibility in the outside world. She had always been a modest but diligent citizen, voting and contributing in small ways to the war effort. Now, as a homeowner and a parent of two school-age children, she took on a more proprietary attitude toward the public realm. She would never be as politically engaged as her brother Isaac, but she began to express her opinions more vividly. Among the American-born and -educated women surrounding her on Bradford Street, she slowly came out of her shell, even if she was still easier with the old *bubbes* on the block, who loved her warm Yiddishkeit.

In her night at the graveyard of the Dutch church, she located the regimen of common-sense wisdom, what in Yiddish is called *seykhel,* that ruled her life from that day forward. That Yiddish word is rich with connotations, but in my family its core meaning is a wisdom that is neither inborn nor acquired, and certainly not obtained through study. It is discovered deep within your head and heart at some point in your maturity, and it often seems associated with the end of a self-indulgent youth and the assumption of adult responsibilities. For Sarah, it signaled the end of her limitless love and, correspondingly, the beginning of her more nuanced and balanced stance toward the world around her.

Like the moralistic term *consideration, seykhel* was often marked by its absence: "What do you expect? He has no *seykhel!*" From the moment of her arrival in the United States, Sarah had learned an enormous amount about character, morality, and dignity. She attributed a lot to meeting and judging her American aunts, uncles, and cousins for the first time. The probing conversations between Sarah and Shenka about the two dozen members of their extended family "were better," Sarah used to say, "than a college course in psychology." As she visited each of her father's four brothers and their families, Sarah found plenty of love. But she also saw enough to create her own Dantean list of cardinal sins: selfishness, stinginess, vanity, insensitivity, and sloppiness.

Her uncle in Borough Park, Brooklyn, for one, had foolishly favored his American-born children over those who had emigrated with him from Europe. Her Tante Chaya in the Bronx strutted around pretentiously, acting out her two-bit superiority. Chaya gave her husband, Uncle Erschel, ten cents a day for carfare and a single teabag—and warned him not to waste any of it. Shenka and Sarah laughed. Then Chaya discouraged every suitor for the hand of her daughter, also named Sarah, even the nicest men. Shenka and Sarah sighed. And finally, the girl was married off to a peddler, who promptly brought the whole family under criminal investigation. Shenka and Sarah wept. "You shouldn't know from it."

Invited once to join Tante Minnie's daughters Frieda and Rose for an afternoon of games, Sarah arrived to find the girls gone, perhaps embarrassed to be seen in the company of their greenhorn cousin. Sarah stayed to keep Minnie company for an hour, but she never forgot the slight. Shenka and Sarah together constructed a vocabulary and a mental image of what was proper and what was not, binding themselves together.

Finally, Shenka taught Sarah to have compassion, *rachmones,* on the impoverished, the unfortunate, the desperate people around her. Well into her nineties Mom would return from a supermarket shopping trip, complaining about the prices—but not for herself. She never stopped worrying about "the burden on young people today, . . . I don't know how they can afford to live." One of my favorite stories concerns an obviously troubled neighborhood character in the early 1940s who scared many children by standing near the entrance to the local movie house and exposing himself. Once, when my sister ran home in deathly fear of this man, Mom calmed her down and explained that though he was *meshuge,* or crazy, he was basically harmless. But for the pervert's mother, whom my mother knew, oy the pain of that woman! "Just imagine having to deal with a son like that! What could be more horrible?"

Seykhel meant shrewdness as well as judgment, but in Sarah's case it was seldom combined with a plan for action. Her wisdom was reductive, defensive. She had simply gone through too much pain already, and she was not interested in exploring life's new possibilities. Sarah was a woman of wonder but not of profound curiosity or investigative energy. Dave was always a handful. Keeping him in tow was enough of a challenge. So Sarah's common sense had an air of finality about it—it was a way of ending a conversation. She was not dogmatic, but neither was she genuinely inquisitive. She might try cooking a new dish. I recall her tackling a variety of stews. But she seldom adopted an adventurous new recipe. She knew the basics of each cooking method—roasting, sautéing, deep-frying, baking, poaching, and so on. And she knew how to handle every one of her pots and pans as if they were childhood companions she'd grown up with. Most of all, she knew how every piece of meat, every vegetable, every dash of herb and spices, and every other ingredient could be expected to be transformed in cooking. In her world her knowledge was encyclopedic. But she was not a world traveler in the kitchen. Those beautiful Time-Life cookbooks with their elaborate dishes prepared in exotic settings were wasted on her.

In a similar way, she loved her children and grandchildren, and she could call to mind every aspect of each one's distinct speech patterns, playfulness, temperament, taste for food and clothing, and social character—but she had no interest in learning about childhood in general. Her politics was all about sympathy for the underdog. She criticized politicians and labor leaders, whom she generally viewed as self-serving. But she did not dig deeply into the manifold causes of social distress, or remedies beyond simply providing better income for the distressed. The symptoms—unemployment, malnutrition, homelessness, domestic abuse—needed to be taken care of. Case closed. She had no interest in learning why someone could deny men jobs, limit women's health care, or restrict children's education.

Her common sense always came across as hard-won wisdom. Though she spoke English with her friends, *seykhal* was often embodied in Yiddish phrases. In this world of survivors and strivers, almost every conversation concerned people trying to get ahead. Nothing created a warmer feeling of commonality than puncturing pretentiousness, and Yiddish expressions supplied a shopping cart full of stickpins. *"Ayn klaynigkeit"* (Yeah, oh sure!) was the first line of attack, followed by an exclamation like "she thinks her s—doesn't stink!" On the other hand, a conversation after being informed of an *umglik,* a calamity, followed a different rhythm in Sarah's house. After a few dozen "tsk, tsks," the women would detail the situation in an English sing-song tone—"first she tried this, then she tried that," all to no avail—and then conclude, *"Azoy gait es"* (That's how it goes)!

More and more she assumed the role of the wiser and cooler head. She always shied away from accepting the presidency of the local women's club. Even after twenty-one years in America, and in all the years to come, she still deferred to American-born women to write the petitions and proposals for funding and to gavel the meetings to order. But she was the trusted counselor of those women, the most sensible one. She baked and brought the best cake to the meetings. And while her comrades were eating and admiring it, she was advising them on the direction forward. She gradually assumed her mother's role in the shtetl, the most senior and the most trusted guide. Around her were gathered the younger mothers who had never had Shenka's tutelage. Sarah became their Shenka.

Women a little or a lot younger than Sarah came to her, as they had come to her mother, and she listened well. She always counseled caution, being satisfied with one's lot in life, acceptance. In this way she maintained the pulse of the family, of her friendships, of the community around her. One after another, people would drift into Sarah's kitchen, celebrating, kvetching, demanding, beseeching, and she kept a steady beat. The meals would continue to come to the table, today's problems would be succeeded by others, each person was admonished to expect little and enjoy the unexpected excess.

Shenka's death closed Sarah's youth. Always wary of change, now she had come into her mature self. There were no more options to become this, or that. She was not interested in weighing alternatives or debating choices. She remained a sounding-board for Dave's schemes, but she was quicker to close off his rants. "Oh, please," she would say, *"hak mir nisht keyn tshaynik,"* literally, "don't bang on my teakettle," and figuratively, "don't give me a headache with your nonsense." He would slink away, having lost his jury. In the process she slowly became the emotional center of the family, determining what was worth worrying about and what was unimportant. Dave was dislodged, her father and her children fearful of going against her wishes.

There was, of course, a dark side to this moralizing. Over time, almost every question became a moral issue to Sarah. Her morality was inextricably bound up with the protection of her mother. It was as if the two of them, mother and daughter, had remained in the shtetl cottage, clutching each other tightly to protect against any assaults from the *goyim*. As she grew older and her mother grew ill, Sarah registered every fault she witnessed, whether immoral or just stupid, as an injury to her mother. And every injury to Shenka was a pain for Sarah to share. Although they were generous and compassionate women, and although they almost always "bit their tongue," they were never really very tolerant. In private, they were often judgmental. To the end of her mother's life and even after, Sarah's emotions were tied up with her mother's well-being. "I could never do enough for Mama," she confessed. "I couldn't stand that my mother suffered so much." In her view, Shenka's doctors and nurses were callous, inattentive, even foolish. *Fun vigele biz grub,* from cradle to grave, "Mama didn't have a good life." Sarah was never really reconciled to my bubbe's death. She was still in mourning, to the point of tears, on the day that she herself died, over six decades later. Anger and bereavement were Sarah's only sisters. *Azoy gait es.*

The Scissors Cut Two Ways

A beer stein emblazoned with my college's insignia now sits on my desk, and in it is the object with which I've had the longest continuing relationship. It is a pair of bandage scissors. When my sister,

Beverly, noticed it during a visit not long ago, she gasped in horror. "Oh, God, where did you get that?" she asked. But, of course, she knew. These were the scissors that Mom used to cut gauze to cover and wrap the oozing from Bubbe's ulcerous stomach. For months, Mom was on constant alert, waking again and again through the night, to check on her mother's condition in the back bedroom of the Bradford Street house. For months, Mom had barely had time to make breakfast for Beverly, to brush her hair, to see that her skirts and socks matched, or to perform any of the other maternal tasks that she loved to do. She focused all her energy on Bubbe.

That pair of scissors, seven and a quarter inches long, chrome-plated, has a blunt tip on the bottom blade, which helps in cutting bandages without gouging the skin. They are named after Joseph Lister, the pioneer in antiseptic surgical practice. I've seen them protruding from the pockets of physicians for decades. This particular pair remained behind when all the other furnishings and equipment of Bubbe's final illness—the hospital bed, the bedpans, medicine bottles, enema tubes, salves, ointments, and hot water bottles—were removed. Deposited in one of Dad's cigar boxes along with my broken crayons and a six-inch ruler, the pair of scissors outlived the cleansing of the little bedroom. With a new bed and dresser, it became Beverly's room. Instead of a bedroom, I had a big cardboard box for my toys and other stuff, hidden away in a closet.

I am not sure when blunt-edge children's scissors became available, but the bandage scissors remained in the tool kit of my youth for years. I cut out the backs of macaroni boxes so that I could mount "television stories" through the cellophane panels on the front. I cut out and taped together fences for mock corrals for my plastic toy horses. I cut and labeled rectangles with the abbreviated names of baseball teams—STL, CHI, PHL, BOS—so I could recreate the

Ebbets Field scoreboard on the wall-to-wall carpeting in our television room.

To put it mildly, Beverly had different and more painful memories of this object than I did. For me, this single pair of bandage scissors is a symbolic bridge between two moments in my mother's history—from devoted daughter to indulgent mother. The most important transition of Sarah's life.

Now we piled the aluminum and plastic beach chairs into the car's trunk, along with lemonade and bags of fruit and sandwiches—on our way to Long Island for a day of picnicking, boating, or ocean bathing.

8

Dave Takes Out the Beach Chairs

Nostalgia often sits on lawn chairs. Different designs and materials for outdoor furniture inspire intense devotees. Outdoor furniture itself belongs to the body language of leisure. An orange crate or a displaced kitchen chair may have you ready to spring into action, but it's harder to get up out of a lawn chair, especially as you get older. Each type recalls a different sort of relaxation and reverie. The wooden Adirondack chair, patented in 1904, evokes summer evenings on northern lakes, accompanied by the plangent calls of mating loons. The metal shell-back lawn chairs with sculpted seats and tubular steel arms, which emerged in World War II, were peddled by Sears Roebuck. From a million backyard patios in the postwar suburbs, these chairs provided the weary parents of the baby boom a comfortable view of their children and selected friends at play. Thousands of them are probably still rusting away in suburban garages and at tag sales. On Bradford Street, my parents did not have a long, wide porch with a lake view or any sort of lawn or patio. For them, the lightweight folding chair with a frame of aluminum tubing and a seat of webbed plastic strips (in many colors) was ideal. Both of these materials were first deployed in wartime. Designed by Frederic Arnold, a combat pilot, in 1947, 14,000 of these chairs emerged every day from his factory on the waterfront in Greenpoint, Brooklyn, less than nine miles from Bradford Street.

Two of these chairs, and another in reserve for a guest, were carried out every summer evening to the top of the stoop at Bradford Street. Sometimes a TV tray with legs came out with them, on which perched a pitcher of lemonade and a plate of Mom's homemade after-dinner cookies. The occupants of these chairs, looking out over the street, felt a bit like royalty, as if they were the masters, even the owners, of the street below. A casual pedestrian had to ascend to the throne. Local protocol dictated that one needn't rise to welcome the newcomer, as one might for a visitor to the home itself. Nor was there a dress code for the resident homeowner. Men's Bermuda shorts, another innovation of World War II, left the rather unsightly knees of these royal personages exposed. Women still mostly wore dresses. Walking up and down the block on a hot evening did not offer a pretty sight.

A low wall divided our porch from its duplicate atop the stoop of the adjoining castle, where Goldie and Moishe Winter lived. They loved Mom's cookies. On both sides of the street, other neighbors could be seen sitting on exactly the same sort of chairs. As they emerged, after a long week of work and housekeeping, people waved greetings to one another. If someone's relative was, God forbid, in the hospital, or if a child had, thank God, succeeded in school or business, it was customary to approach and offer support or congratulations in person.

The aluminum "beach chair," as we called it, also altered leisure-time activity beyond the neighborhood. No longer did Mom and Dad pack their lunch in an old satchel, carry a rolled-up blanket, and head off to Prospect Park by subway. Now they piled the folding chairs into the car's trunk, along with a picnic jug of lemonade and several shopping bags of food in Tupperware containers. And forget Prospect Park. Now we were headed along the Southern State Parkway to Jones Beach, Belmont Lake, or another of Robert Moses's state parks on Long Island for a day of picnicking, boating, or ocean bathing. I am not sure that we were aware that these outings also separated us from most Black and Puerto Rican families, with whom we had picnicked and swum in the city's parks and playgrounds for decades. Buses would not fit under Moses's elegant overpasses on the state parkways. In effect, a private automobile was required for admission. The increasingly racialized public landscape of the 1950s came to us wrapped in a package of convenience and comfort.

The folding chair allowed Mom and Dad to sit a few feet above the sand or grass, and in a metaphoric sense above people as poor as they had been twenty years earlier. These outings, planned in advance and long remembered afterward, became our common way of visualizing our family unit. Now we had a bucolic green and blue scenic backdrop, rather than the steel grey and red brick my parents knew from their early years in New York City. At home, we were often each going our own way. At the state park, we practiced what the 1950s treasured as "togetherness." If picnic pictures became the family's image of itself, they also showed how we had isolated ourselves from our fellow citizens. "Togetherness," one of the great virtues celebrated during the 1950s, also implied aloneness.

People Like Us

Dave's jewelry business prospered, until one day it did not. Quite suddenly, in 1952–1953, his sales fell prey to shifts in the jewelry trade and the city around him. Price-cutting discount department stores like E. J. Korvette and Alexander's took away much of the retailing of wristwatches. And as Midtown grew in the postwar years to become the focal point of New York's economic life, the Diamond District at 47th Street and 6th Avenue outpaced its downtown rivals. Dave should have moved his business to Midtown in 1953, but he didn't.

But what really did in the Raven Watch Company was Dave's failure, probably common among his ilk at the time, to collect and forward the federal (excise) and state sales taxes levied on the retail sales of luxury items like jewelry. He had posed as a wholesaler, but his many retail customers seeking engagement rings attracted attention from the local jewelry merchants. One of them squealed to the tax authorities. Slapped with a hefty tax bill and then threatened with an even heftier fine, Dave sought help from a lawyer who had earned his stripes with the FBI. For all his bluster, Dave was actually a rather timid person, and he contained his rage within the walls of the Bradford Street house. Sarah kept most of this out of the hearing of the children, but the rage contributed nothing to the resolution of the crisis. The lawyer helped him escape with a manageable payout but a crippled business.

What would he do now? Was there a place in the jewelry world less dependent upon retail sales? Curious about those possibilities, he devoted several weeks to working in a company that made gift cases for watches and rings. The Rite-View Display Company had a good track record under its founder and owner, who wanted to sell out and retire. He promised to teach Dave the business—the production technology, the networks of suppliers, the lists of regular customers, everything. But the old man died a week later, and with that the deal collapsed. All that remained around our house were three or four empty samples of the company's line.

For the next three or four years, until about 1957, Dave wandered haplessly. His wide-lapeled suits were not replaced when they became unfashionable, the silver tie clasps in his dresser drawer tarnished with disuse, a film of dust covered his shiny wingtip brogues, and a dozen crisp white dress shirts yellowed in the closet. The cigars, much to the family's relief, became rarer and less costly (and never smoked inside the house), and his stock of jokes was seldom replenished. The Borscht Belt routines were retired.

Dad scared me by traveling to Buffalo to check out a discount store. I hated the idea of moving to a city that did not have a major league baseball team. Mom and Beverly were equally opposed, but probably for much better reasons. Luckily the deal was unappealing to Dad. Every Sunday, while I pored over the sports section in the *Times,* he rifled through the pages of "Business Opportunities" in Section 5. No luck. He went to work refilling racks of ballpoint pens for a local competitor of Paper-Mate. He sold fluorescent light bulbs for industrial buildings for a company that had hired Beverly as a temporary secretary—a humiliation. Everything frustrated him. His bosses were "disrespectful," ignorant, wasteful. His customers were too stupid to see the value of what he was offering.

Even at age 43, Dave had no useful business connections beyond his immediate family. He acted out the role of a man on the make, sliding into the driver's seat of his car early enough in the morning to avoid being conspicuously underemployed. He uncharacteristically kept silent about jobs in front of Sarah's cousins. All this made him angry. And then, late in 1956, his brother Al introduced him to another local business, the Union Supply Company. Its owner had built a jobbing route, supplying everything that a grocery store, bodega, or candy store sold other than food—toiletries, school supplies, small toys. The route was well established in Queens and Nassau County. The principle was simple: he offered his customers two weeks' credit to pay for deliveries. Each Monday Dave went to the distributors on Ludlow Street on Manhattan's Lower East Side to stock up on goods. From Tuesday to Friday, he drove his ten-ton truck to about a dozen customers each day. He quickly figured out that his margins were much better if he skipped the Ludlow crowd and bought "direct" from manufacturers—Johnson & Johnson (Band-Aid), Bristol Myers (headache and antacid remedies), Colgate Palmolive (toothpastes and shampoos), Pen-Tab notebooks and paper goods, Dixie Peach and Royal Crown hair pomades, and twenty other giant firms. Sometimes he took advantage of special offers and loaded up on merchandise that he could hold and sell for a year to come. At that point our basement became a supply depot, and Sarah became the receiving agent for deliveries. She quickly learned that a couple of dollars in tips and a piece of almond cake would compensate for the lack of a loading dock on our residential street.

Dave probably never asked Sarah how she felt about being a part of the business. Receiving these shipments brought her into regular contact with non-Jews, the truck drivers, for the first time since she'd arrived in New York thirty years before. These men, burly and brusque, reminded her of the threatening Poles she had left behind in Wysokie Mazowieckie. Dave never put Sarah on the payroll, which would have allowed her, much later, to collect Social Security on her own account. He stubbornly acted as if he was uniquely responsible for the family's financial well-being. He unloaded his frustrations on his family almost every day. No one could ever do anything to help. Always impatient, never used to working alongside anyone else, Dave's frustration had become as routine and self-perpetuating as his biweekly travels. Mom kept her own fears and frustrations under wraps.

But, happily, this business gambit paid off. At its core this was a solid business. Dave worked all day, every day, paying off the note to the previous owner within a year, way ahead of schedule. The work was hard: he climbed in and out of the truck twenty or thirty times a day; wheeled heavy cartons on a hand truck; sliced open the boxes and unpacked their contents; loaded and resupplied the truck's shelves with packaged merchandise; filled empty cartons with items the customers had ordered; asked to get paid; warned customers that they would suffer if his bills were unpaid . . . the whole process was physically and emotionally exhausting. But he made a go of it. There was just enough margin between his discounted costs, though he often had to battle manufacturers who did not like servicing his relatively small orders, and the advantage he could take of storekeepers who wanted small quantities of these highly profitable items. He could sell a half-dozen tubes of Crest toothpaste, retailing for 39 cents each, for $1.25. He prized loyal customers and got rid of those who bought from other jobbers.

There was not much pleasure for Dave in the business. Over and over again, all through my own working life, he papered over all the tensions that I was experiencing—also as a self-employed person without a safety net—with the catch-all phrase, "as long as you're doing what you like." He would have laughed at the idea that work like his was "fulfilling." I'm sure he missed the camaraderie of Maiden Lane, of wearing classy suits and elegant ties every weekday, and of associating with men of a similar background and enthusiastic opportunism. The proprietor of a small business has no comrades, no allies, no one who shares your interest. He made no friends among his suppliers or his customers. If more of them had shared his age and background, he might have swapped better jokes in the first few minutes of taking an order or making a delivery. The one Jewish storekeeper he serviced for fifteen years, a candy-store owner on Cross Bay Boulevard named Lipschitz, was himself an angry, tough old bird. He and Dad barely tolerated each other. When I worked on the truck with him, Dad seemed to be fond only of his biweekly visits to Eddie Parietti's grocery in Queens. Eddie would make us hero sandwiches of the most thinly sliced prosciutto, soppressata, Genoa salami, provolone, peppers, onions, and ripe roma tomatoes, laid carefully on his own home-baked rolls and drizzled gently with very fine olive oil. We never told Mom.

Still, as hard as Dave worked, his prosperity depended equally on wider social and economic conditions. During the 1950s, many Manhattan industries were moving to the ring of suburbs in Queens and Nassau County. As middle-class New Yorkers like Sarah's cousins bought single-family houses with two-car garages on Long Island, the rental market in older neighborhoods was filled by many working-class white, Black, and Puerto Rican families. Only a little over two in ten city residents owned rather than rented their dwellings, far below the national average. This expanding population still found it convenient to shop at small neighborhood stores. The shopping center, the shopping mall, and big box retail came late to this region.

Dave's business had another advantage. He did not have to push his merchandise. Radio and television advertising celebrated the virtues of brand-name toiletries like Crest, the first fluoridated toothpaste, or deodorants, or headache remedies like Anacin, Bufferin, and Bayer Aspirin. Schools set the expectations for their students, who had to bring their own supplies, like three-ring binders, ballpoint pens, and loose-leaf paper. Dave did not have to know or argue the qualities of anything he sold. He sold many cases of canned

Sterno brand cooking fuel, always suspecting that some folks were "squeezing" its denatured alcohol to make an intoxicant. "That's not my department," he always said.

For fifteen-plus years, Union Supply gave him a steady living. Equally important, the route created a routine. Summer and winter, he made money every single day. For the peddler turned shopkeeper turned self-employed businessman, this began to fill an always shallow pool of self-confidence. The trade in diamonds had always carried a risk, their value proved only in the actual sale. The merchandise that Dave sold now was mass-produced and slated to sell at a list price printed right on the packaging. A 39-cent bottle of White Rain Shampoo cost the same at the groceries who bought from Dave as it did at the pharmacy next door or the supermarket five miles away. With the industrial economies of Europe and East Asia still recovering from wartime ruin, no place could compete with American manufacturers and distributors. Dave Rabinowitz's prosperity swelled along this cresting moment of the American industrial economy.

The house on Bradford Street, too, throbbed to a regular rhythm. Beverly and I came home from school and checked in with Mom. I treated myself to tall glasses of milk, slices of chocolate cake or apple pie, or three or four freshly baked cookies, and then I escaped to read, do homework, invent new games, sort my stamp collection, or, in better weather, to spend a couple of hours in street games with my pals and our ubiquitous "Spaldeen" pink rubber balls. For Beverly, always mindful of her plump toddlerhood, indulgence was a more complex calculation, and then she disappeared as well. Dad returned from work at 4 or 4:30 and worked at his desk for an hour or so on bills. Sometime during the next hour, sounds from his corner desk would make us aware that a temperamental cold front was forming. The idiocies of a customer or a supplier earlier that day were like squall lines, and then expletives would crash through the house like thunderstorms. A half-hour later, the winds would shift, and calm would return. Dad would forget what offense had set off his ill temper. Slowly, over the years, Dave's thunderbolts got milder, and this vexation evolved from a full-blown monsoon season into something like sporadic afternoon tropical showers. Mom, Bev, and I would look at one another, thankful that the hurricane had not reached Category Five, and we gathered for supper at about six o'clock. We always ate together, the conversations flavored lovingly by Mom's cooking.

After the meal, Mom cleaned up. Dad did not help out. He retreated to a quick perusal of the *New York Post,* which was then a voice for liberal Democratic politics, and a full evening of television. He cared little for the news shows, then only fifteen or thirty minutes long, and was not a rapt audience for the network sitcoms and dramas, either. Often he enjoyed a big bowl of ice cream or fruit in front of the television. The family retired for the night at around eleven. Dave started his day at four or five in the morning, reading for an hour, napping for an additional hour, and then quickly shaving, showering, bolting down breakfast, and getting to work—all before eight o'clock.

I wish I could recall what he read. Four or five glossily wrapped library books sat on his night table, right up to the day he died in 2008. Following his boyhood habits, he never read nonfiction, never opened a magazine of any sort, but in the 1950s seems also to have abandoned the genre fiction of his youth—whodunits, westerns, crime novels, sci-fi, and the like. Beverly recalls that he read lots of the books on the bestseller lists of the 1940s and 1950s, especially those made into films—*The Grapes of Wrath, A Tree Grows in Brooklyn, Captain from Castile, Gentleman's Agreement, The Caine Mu-*

tiny, Giant, and *Exodus*—but he skipped almost all of what we would call "literary fiction."

I remember his enthusiasm for films like *The High and the Mighty,* based on a novel by Ernest K. Gann (1953, film 1954), and *Run Silent, Run Deep,* based on the book by Edward L. Beach (1955, film 1957). He had read both of these books and took me along to both of these pictures. In the immediate aftermath of World War II, such stories featured male heroes, scarred by personal and wartime tragedies, who were called upon to perform heroically, if always reluctantly, in a moment of crisis. Existentially isolated, despising fame and glory, full of self-doubts, these heroes succeed where shinier but shallower men fail. They brilliantly rescue the (abjectly dependent) women and children around them from injury and death. In the process, they often commit some terrible but ultimately excusable act—like killing enemy combatants in violation of the Geneva Conventions, often in revenge for the hurts and losses they have themselves suffered. They return home to Kansas or Maine, fated to feel pangs of conscience evermore. But the reader or the moviegoer comes away satisfied by the ending.

Dave Rabinowitz spent a lifetime fantasizing himself the hero of an adventure story, although only in the pajama-clad immersion of his early morning reading. In middle age, heroism was not what it had been in the pages of Jack London and the Frank Merriwell pulp fiction. Jaw-to-jaw combat among London's huskies in the Yukon was no longer his model of courage, and good old Frank's rescue of damsels from burning buildings was a lot less complicated, morally, than sinking an armed merchant ship in the Pacific in 1943. Ambiguity had entered the masculine world of heroic narrative along with bureaucracy, sex, and racism. Dave had not been in the war, but his favorite authors enlisted him in their imagined military as surely as if he had been 1-A. Wartime enemies were subhuman "Japs" or machine-like Nazis, and the technology was always less than perfect. But in these fantasies American men saved the day with improvisational ingenuity and loyalty to their comrades.

The melodramatic moment of decision, with the hero standing alone against the challenges, obviously appealed to Dave. He cared nothing for patriotism, or for any other principle. He never regretted not going to war himself. Poverty in youth had made him single-minded about economic security in adulthood. He simply refused to think hard about the moral questions raised in these war stories. He shunned effortful thinking of any kind. Intellectual pursuits were inherently suspicious. They were just dangerous diversions from the main purposes of life, which were to make a good living for one's family, take advantage of opportunities for good, clean entertainment, and keep one's head down. That's all. Dad did not have hobbies or interests beyond his family and his business. He had hardly any friends anymore, except the husbands of the women Sarah had cultivated since moving to Bradford Street.

Dad was entirely consumed by the role of provider, and all the rest of us could then only be the ones he provided for. In the household of the small businessman, everyone was spending "Dad's money." Beverly began to get clerical jobs while in high school, on weekday afternoons and during vacations. But she didn't feel quite free to spend even the money she earned herself. She contributed a portion of her earnings to the household expenses. (In the end, Mom had put all that money aside and gave it back to Beverly when she married.) Even though I was growing up during the family's more prosperous years, I too internalized this anxiety about money. I worked on Dad's truck during my weekends and summers and parlayed my reputation for good grades into tutoring gigs all around the neighborhood. But I was always nervous about whether Dad would second-guess my purchases. In high school, I recall buying myself a copy of the *New World Dictionary of the American Language,* list-priced at $7.50, and bargaining with the shopkeeper to get it for $6.00. It was obviously necessary for my schoolwork. On the way home, I erased the "6" and rewrote the price as $5.00. Why? Would I ever be free of the question, "What did it cost you?"

Although Dad and Mom were frugal, they were not ascetic. The whole household was devoted to elegance and stylishness. We still lived with the scent of the perfume bottle Dad bought for Mom in 1933, maintaining my parents' and maternal grandparents' strict standards of fine appearance. Mom and Dad dressed beautifully when they went out for the evening or when there was a family wedding or bar mitzvah. No classmates outshone Beverly and me on school days. In the seventh grade I carefully chose knit ties to match my plaid shirts (well-ironed by Mom) every day. I shined my school shoes several times a week. Beverly spent hours ironing her blouses and dresses in our kitchen. We did not save our best outfits for special occasions.

In fact, the Rabinowitz household did not have special occasions. Both Beverly and I had summer birthdays, and so we missed out on birthday parties at school or at home. In fact, our parents scarcely recognized our birthdays at all. We grew up getting gifts, but not for Hanukkah (beyond a few pieces of chocolate *gelt*), Passover, or any other holiday. Mom did not make us birthday cakes, but she baked wonderful treats all year round. Gifts came when Mom (or less often, Dad) found something terrific and brought it home. On a rainy March evening when I was about eight, Dad brought home a brand new Grady Hatton third baseman's glove, out of the blue, in its original packaging. (Why Grady Hatton, a journeyman in-fielder who played for Cincinnati? I was happy to have the glove and didn't ask.)

Beverly recalls a more sobering incident. During the summer of 1946, the family shared a kitchen at a cottage (a *kuche alein*) in the Catskills. The neighbors celebrated Beverly's ninth birthday in August, chipping in to buy her a lovely dress from a shop on the Main Street in Monticello, New York. Beverly was thrilled. Mom was very upset. "How could we reciprocate? We may never see these people again. It's a terrible thing that they've done."

Mom's strict routine in her housework kept us on an even keel. Her cardinal principle was a deep devotion to the sanctification of the everyday. In a sense, Mom's Bible left out Genesis 2:1–3, where God finished his work, called it holy, and rested on the seventh day. In Mom's practice, "Godliness" ran a distant second to "Cleanliness." She found plenty of faults in pious people, but there wasn't much she could do about that. Ah, but *schmutz,* dirt, that she knew how to roll up her sleeves and fix. Once she had finished cleaning, her house was as hushed and orderly on every weekday as it was on the Jewish Sabbath. She was not compulsive, but she enjoyed being busy all day. She loved the solitude. First thing in the morning she set out to clean the house, to make it appear that none of us had left anything out of place on tables, chairs, floors, and furniture. She scrubbed down the kitchen and the bathroom. As she worked, she was occasionally interrupted by the doorbell. Each week the laundry man brought the newly washed (and still damp) sheets and towels, which were hung on the backyard clotheslines with wooden clothespins. (These same clothespins were the ubiquitous building blocks in my toy chest.) In our early days at Bradford Street, deliverymen also brought milk every other morning, and butter and eggs from New Jersey once a week. The seltzer man brought a wooden case of ten bottles every Wednesday afternoon and took away the empties. Sarah had the help of a cleaning woman once a week. Everything else needed to keep the house in order was her responsibility.

As she had learned from her mother, the entire week of meals was in her head before it was in her refrigerator, on her chopping board, or on her stove. We never seemed to run out of the food we loved, nor did anything ever spoil in Sarah's pantry or fridge. She never learned to drive and preferred to shop two or three times each week at the small food stores on New Lots Avenue, just as she had at Livonia Avenue in the 1930s. As Dave's business prospered, our diet featured more steak and lamb chops and roasted chicken, with potatoes or rice, and some green vegetables. Twice a week, these alternated with dairy meals—broiled flounder, (canned) salmon croquettes, noodles (with ketchup). Cans with bright Del Monte and Green Giant labels gradually gave way in the course of the mid-1950s to mid-1960s to bags of fresh vegetables, as Sarah read the advice of nutritionists like Adele Davis and listened to the radio food guru Carlton Fredericks. Sarah never baked her own bread, not even challah for Shabbos, but she did abandon Silvercup white bread and adopt healthier, whole-grain varieties. (Cornell Bread, made with soy flour, was a favorite.)

Sarah kept a kosher kitchen, and in the early years used to kosher her meat and poultry at home—washing off any visible blood left after the proper slaughtering, soaking it for a half-hour, salting it and letting it drain for an hour, then washing it thoroughly again. For some reason, Sarah loved knowing the meat she was preparing so intimately. By the late 1950s, ready-to-cook rabbinically certified koshered meat was available in grocery stores, even in the frozen food section of stores, and Sarah gave away her treasured koshering pan.

She could not have told you where in the book of Leviticus it forbade the consumption of animal blood. Mom followed the rules out of respect—not so much for the commandments themselves, or for the memory of her mother, who was even more of a free thinker than Sarah. Her observances came from adherence to an imagined community of good Jews—one that she carried in her head even when she could not see them in front of her eyes. On Bradford Street, it was embodied in the good opinion of the older women, the *bubbes,* on the block. They seemed to be permanently fixed, sitting in the second-floor windows, watching the street. Sarah did not want to offend them by shopping (that is, carrying money) on Saturdays. Respectful men, in the same vein, tried to avoid parking directly in front of their houses on Saturday, preferring to walk the extra block or so. More positively, Sarah never failed to stop off during the week and ask the bubbes if she could pick up something they needed while she shopped.

As the months went by after Shenka's death and Sarah's long night in the graveyard, she reveled in the peace and quiet. Beverly and I both did well in school. My uncle Isaac showed up on many evenings to have a cup of coffee and another sandwich. My zayde, Dovid Schwartz, went back to work and had less occasion to sit at Sarah's dinette table. When he visited, he almost always brought a tale of woe, some chicanery pulled off by his second wife. Mom tried valiantly to keep her frustration to herself rather than upset her father even more. My other bubbe, Eva Rabinowitz, remarried and took up storekeeping on the opposite side of Brooklyn. Always a zealous saver, she closely followed the advertisements that promised free gifts for new savings accounts at Brooklyn banks. Sometimes she would ask Beverly, the first woman in our family with a driver's license, to carry her to Greenpoint or Bay Ridge or some other corner of the borough so that she could secure her prize. Her closets overflowed with frying pans, electric irons, and clock radios—many still in their original wrapping. And even though Beverly was just then furnishing her first kitchen, Bubbe Rabinowitz never went to the closet and presented her granddaughter with one of these treasures.

But the biggest change in our lives came, I think, from the architecture of Bradford Street. Very few cars and trucks came down the block. The twenty-four semi-detached brick houses were exactly alike, with no room for external ornamentation. The backyard stretched without fences for almost the whole block. It was originally meant to provide access to garage space, but it had become a shared play space. Each house fronted on a porch and a five-step "stoop." Beginning in May and through September, in those days before air-conditioning, many families gathered on the top step or on the porch on folding chairs every evening. Cold drinks and cookies were passed around. Often one neighbor or another would come by and pose the basic question, *nu?* This meant everything from "What's up with you?" "Still the same old nonsense?" to "After all this time, don't you have anything interesting to tell me?" or "Enough with all this, what's really important?" A whole philosophical system in two letters, an "n" and a "u"! After four or five refusals to have a seat, Mom or Dad would say, "Richard, go in and get another chair," and then an hour of kibitzing would begin in earnest. It was interrupted, regularly, by the arrival of the Good Humor and Bungalow Bar ice cream men. They jingled their way into our street at about 7 o'clock, and we passionately debated the merits of Popsicles vs. Creamsicles, butter pecan vs. black cherry ice cream cones, and so on—as if we were provisioning an around-the-world voyage rather than an after-dinner treat. Then, tiring of eavesdropping on adult chatter, the kids would go back to stoop-ball, or box baseball, or a hundred varieties of Hit the Penny.

My mother had come to America three decades earlier and discovered cousins who became—despite her self-consciousness as a "greenhorn"—her closest companions. While still emotionally attached to one another, many of them had by now dispersed to the suburbs. Then, while in school and work, and while courting my father, Sarah had made a few close friends. They, too, were visited four or five times a year. But not until Bradford Street did my mother acquire a band of peers, of "people like us." These were not the closest of friends, but their lives interpenetrated with hers in a thousand ways. The eight or ten women who lived to our left and right in the 1950s were all stay-at-home mothers. Most were American-born of immigrant Jewish parents, speaking English from childhood but well acquainted with Yiddish as well.

They did more than borrow sugar and eggs from one another. Inevitably they forged norms and framed expectations—how to dress, what to cook, where to vacation, where to celebrate, where and when to look for bargains, what movies to see. Social expectations were on constant display. On our block, the 1950s were very much an age of conformity, as opinion columnists in magazines and newspapers kept insisting. Everybody read the *Reader's Digest. Life* and *Look* were everywhere, but I never saw the *Saturday Evening Post, Collier's,* or the *New Yorker* on Bradford Street. "Keeping up with the Joneses" (in Brooklyn, more likely "the Goldbergs") meant more than seeking the newest kitchen appliances, weeklong vacations in the Catskills, or a fancy car. It also implied curbing one's opinions and stifling eccentric tastes. Still, in reality, the distinctions among Mom's peers came out as much as their similarities. One neighbor had very elevated tastes in music, evidenced by the Steinway grand in her living room. One had been a Communist in her youth, a secret they all kept to themselves. The husband of one shaved very rarely, afraid to damage his delicate visage. In fact, everyone had a husband who was a little bit crazy, and family arguments with foul language (but only from the mouths of men) traveled quickly across the driveways and along the porches, usually to be forgotten the following day.

One Saturday night each month, about six of the couples gathered for dinner. In the Rabinowitz house, it was all about the food, as Sarah expanded family recipes for the buffet "spread"—chicken chow mein one time, halibut collars at another. At Eleanor and Julius November's Saturday nights, they all gathered around the piano to sing. Abe Sussman was a superb jokester, Moishe Winter told dirty stories. The ladies seldom hosted daytime meals for one another. Coffee, yes, and some sweets to accompany the weekly mahjongg game, a mainstay of Jewish women's social life—that was always available.

Even as a child, I knew that the adult world of Bradford Street was full of worries. I eavesdropped on my parents' financial anxieties, and I sneaked peeks at television news reports about the arms race with the Soviet Union and about massive resistance to desegregation rulings. Out of the corner of my eye, I once caught a glimpse of a very scary Ku Klux Klan rally, with men in hoods and burning crosses. But, in general, the mood was optimistic. Men and women who had grown up with immigrant parents, desperate to escape the ravages of pogroms and the Depression, now enjoyed unprecedented security and comfort in their everyday lives. Revealingly, they constantly spoke of their new acquisitions as "good deals." No one on the block would admit to "buying retail." Our living room furniture was a good example. A man in Bradley Beach, New Jersey, owed Dave some money from the old jewelry business and gave him a bargain on very expensive furnishings: a deep green mohair sofa and a red mohair club chair—both of them fringed at the bottom. In addition, Mom and Dad also bargained for two gray "lady's" (or "occasional") chairs placed around a leather-topped drum table and a step table in the window area at the front. On the drum table sat a tall lamp, and that shone onto a porcelain figurine of a troubadour serenading his lady. I loved tracing his delicate fingers on the lute and hers on a bouquet of flowers.

In the summer of 1953, when the jewelry business was still aglow, Dad came home with a new two-toned Packard Clipper sedan, with "Ultra-Matic" (automatic) transmission. It outshone the green DeSoto recently bought by Moishe Winter next door. Once Beverly had a baby in 1957, Mom laid out the money for a washing machine (but not a dryer), and Beverly paid her back. Our kitchen now featured an electric Mixmaster, but dishwashers and air-conditioners remained beyond reach through the 1950s. Each summer Dad installed a 24-inch window fan in the front window. We were instructed to leave the back windows open to create a flow of air through our five rooms. On plenty of sweltering nights this was a fantasy.

The layout of the block made it easy to keep watch on everything that was going on. We did not need surveillance cameras to take note of every unfamiliar car. The clopping and squeaking of the old clothes-gatherer's horse and wagon, the clang of the knife-sharpening van, and the amble of the Fuller Brush man from door to door marked the passage of weekdays in spring and fall. Young men coming on Saturday evenings to pick up the block's daughters for dates were given the once-over, and pretty soon everyone knew their names, their intended professions, and the likelihood of their success. But where the eyes of mothers really focused was in watchful responsibility for the children. When Sarah was hospitalized for a hysterectomy, I had lunch, after-school snacks, and supper at the table of Debbie Sussman, whom I considered a second mother. And during the hot summer of 1953, when fears of a polio epidemic spread through the neighborhood, Michael Heit's mom caught us at her kitchen washtub washing (and, in theory, refreshing) a batch of old "Spaldeens" we had rescued (with bent wire clothes hangers) from the corner storm drains. Without first calling our moms, she pulled off all our clothes, frog-marched us into her bathtub, scrubbed us down with stinging Octagon soap, dressed us in Michael's shirts, socks, and shorts . . . and then took us to each of our homes.

The mothers of Bradford Street desperately fought back against all incursions of the natural environment. Weeklong vacations in a Catskill bungalow colony offered fresh air and occasionally milk direct from a cow, but Sarah overcompensated for these gifts by worrying about poison ivy. No one at Bradford Street planted a garden, though a few potted plants were admitted inside the house. No one had a pet, except perhaps for some fish. I remember that a French Canadian woman who lived two or three blocks away had the occasional temerity to walk her dog on our street, and in full daylight no less, while residents stood ready on every porch to fend off the deposit of poop or pee within our property lines. Feral cats were enemies of the people. In that heyday of DDT, the neighbors banded together to slaughter every creeping and flying creature that dared encroach upon Bradford Street. But since we lived only a single block away from the edges of the marshland bordering Jamaica Bay, summertime might bring wildlife, horrible sulfurous smells, and—with our windows wide open—the noise of airliners aiming for the runways of Idlewild (later JFK) Airport. In the late 1950s, the area south of our block was turned into land for a park, a school, and huge city housing projects. That pushed the natural world a little further off.

Most important, the ladies of Bradford Street developed—with other women in the community—a passion for civic improvement that transformed the neighborhood. They formed the women's committee of the East New York Young Men's and Young Women's Hebrew Association, and raised money through theater parties, bake sales, auctions, and a hundred other events until wealthier "uptown" Jews could kick in and help build a sparkling new community center, with an indoor swimming pool, a fancy gym, craft shops, classrooms, and an auditorium. Each year the ladies hired a bus and went to Albany to lobby the local assemblyman and state senator for items on the capital budget agenda—a beautiful new public library branch and the George Gershwin Junior High School.

Collectively, the mothers created a safe and homey neighborhood for children like me. Inside these well-understood boundaries, roughly matching the catchment area of my local elementary school, maybe twenty-five square blocks in all, kids over seven or eight were free during daylight hours to roam alone, to visit friends after school, to attend our after-school Hebrew lessons, to do "last-minute" shopping errands for Mom, and to go to the movies, the library, and the playground. Without asking special permission, we could cap off our sandlot hardball game by getting a malted, 25 cents, at Stevie Rodgeveller's grandfather's soda fountain on New Lots Avenue between Pennsylvania and New Jersey Avenues, or a Three Musketeers bar, five cents, at Charles Weiss's father's candy store between Bradford and Miller.

In the mid-1950s, Public School 213 was about 90 percent Jewish, with a few children from Italian families (and from families of Italian-Jewish intermarriage). I recall only one African American classmate in all my seven years at the school, a girl named Jane Price, to whom none of us said a single word. Our juvenile cruelty was inexplicably reinforced by the teachers' disregard for Jane. Junior high school brought us into the ambit of a much more diverse student body, with lots of Black, Puerto Rican, Irish, and Italian kids, but the classrooms in New York City schools—devoted to "tracking" students by test scores—turned out to be as segregated as they might be by legal edict. My seventh-grade homeroom was still almost entirely Jewish, and down the corridor there were other homerooms with few or no white children at all.

Our little corner of East New York was a tightly knit community, more like a jersey than a patchwork quilt. Our parents and neighbors communicated a distrust of other, alien parts of the city. From an early age, I ventured with my father on Saturdays to his jewelry shop in "the City," by which we meant Manhattan. As a family, we were comfortable in going to New York's civic, commercial, and entertainment centers—to Fulton Street in downtown Brooklyn and Herald Square for department store shopping; to Times Square for movie spectaculars like *The Ten Commandments, Ben-Hur,* and *Exodus;* to the Hang Far Low restaurant in Chinatown and Don Peppe's Italian place in South Ozone Park for celebratory dinners. And the family took advantage of connections to family and friends in order to "buy wholesale" in corners of New York's old industrial geography. When we wanted a new set of dining room furniture, for example, we went to a manufacturer near the Flatiron Building in Manhattan. Winter coats came from a family friend's contacts in the West 30s, car repairs from Mom's cousin Rose's husband Larry's garage. While Mom and Beverly could look for nice clothes at the big department stores, especially those along Fulton Street in downtown Brooklyn (Abraham & Straus, Mays, and Martin's), or bargains at S. Klein's in Manhattan's Union Square, Dad would have been humiliated shopping at one of those stores.

I wonder if he ever crossed the threshold of Macy's or Gimbel's in Herald Square. He was a devotee of Richfield Clothiers on Pitkin Avenue, the main drag of Brownsville–East New York.

The city's great cultural institutions lay outside this family ambit. We never visited the art museums or attended performances at Carnegie Hall, or even strolled through Central Park. It took the visit of out-of-town guests, the family of Dad's friend Al Berlin, to get Dad to the Statue of Liberty—his one and only visit, around his forty-second birthday. But Mom was glad to volunteer as a chaperone on school trips to the Brooklyn Botanic Garden, the Brooklyn Museum, the Museum of the City of New York, and the Museum of Natural History—and that was my introduction to the elite cultures of my home town. After one such school trip to the last-named of these, at age twelve, I got a friend to return with me to the museum's Hayden Planetarium, on our own—an hour-long subway trip away. And by age fourteen, I was traveling by train to high school in Manhattan every day, and spending my afternoons and evenings roaming around Greenwich Village, masquerading as a college student to get into the Forty-Second Street Library, and voraciously consuming every museum gallery and theater performance I could afford.

My parents had few social or business relationships with non-Jews, and almost no non-Jewish friends. They taught me to be wary of the underlying Christian bias of American public culture. Christmas was full of jolliness, but for us it carried an ominous message, surely colored by my mother's shtetl-era memories. We didn't go to see the department store windows or the tree in Rockefeller Center, and the idea of celebrating it with a "Hanukkah bush" never entered my parents' minds. One incident stands out. My third-grade teacher, Theresa Cosgrove, to us an ancient Irish lady, sent us home one day in the autumn of 1953 with advice to watch the Bishop

Fulton J. Sheen show, "Life Is Worth Living," on television that night. Sheen was a charismatic theologian and television presence, the smooth public voice of New York's Francis Cardinal Spellman. But he wasn't welcome in our house, even electronically. As soon as I disclosed Miss Cosgrove's recommendation, my parents strapped on their combat boots for a visit to Miss Stitt, the principal of PS 213. I don't know if these events are connected, but Miss Cosgrove lasted only two more months before she was replaced by Annette P. Goldman, returning from a maternity leave, who turned out to be the very best teacher I ever knew.

The New York metropolitan area had over two million Jews, and they spread themselves over the entire range of trades, occupations, and professions. Unlike small-town America, or even the New York suburbs, where most Jews had reached an economic and social standing above the community norm, New York City still had plenty of working-class and lower-middle-class Jews. Those engaged in the small-scale production and distribution of goods probably outnumbered Jewish industrial workers, professionals, and big-business types. One did meet Jewish clerks when it was necessary to fill out forms in public offices and banks in one's own neighborhood or downtown. It was likely by 1955 that your children's teachers were going to be Jewish. Homeowners could and did call Jewish carpenters and plumbers to make repairs, buy from Jewish retailers and wholesalers, and consult Jewish doctors, lawyers, and accountants. Occasionally one could meet a Jewish cop, firefighter, or sanitation man. Everyone now spoke English, but Yiddish expressions often communicated deeper truths. They also served to seal business deals and to convey congratulations on a blessed event. Beverly, who had grown up living alongside our grandparents, understood and could speak Yiddish, at least in childhood. My

Yiddish was largely composed of catchphrases, aphorisms, and elaborate curses.

Insularity could only go so far. We were safe inside the cocoon of lower-middle-class New York Jewry. But safety could also imply exclusion. New York City was a patchwork of tiny enclaves like our corner of East New York. Most were then as much dominated by a single ethnic group as ours. With a historian's hindsight, I now realize that in the aftermath of the 1924 US immigration restrictions, the only major new groups in New York City were Blacks from the American South and Puerto Ricans, who were American citizens by birth. New York's ethnic enclaves—Irish, Italian, Jewish, Polish, Greek, German, and others—had by my time calcified into sharply bounded second-generation "turfs," antagonistic and defensive toward outsiders. We knew not to go where we were not wanted. My friends and I went to Brooklyn's Prospect Park, but we mostly stayed on its east side, close to the Jewish neighborhoods of Eastern Parkway and Crown Heights.

Our parents' worries were different. McCarthyism badly scarred our community, sparking fear and ultimately undermining our confidence about being "at home in America." During the Red Scare of the early 1950s, newspapers, newscasts, and radio and television dramas avidly promoted fears about "Communist cells," secret bands of dangerous conspirators and subversives. New York's state legislature, like most others, imposed a loyalty oath on public-sector employees, and several of Beverly's high school teachers were forced to resign because they had once been members of the Communist Party or refused to sign the oath. Such repression registered more mildly on Bradford Street, however, among the households of small businessmen, where few cared about political reputations. Almost everyone, after all, had leaned left during the 1930s and during

World War II, many had joined the Communist Party for a few years, and there was little interest in stigmatizing neighbors for their politics.

My favorite person in the whole world, my Uncle Isaac, was a member of the Communist Party from the 1930s until his death in 1997. Zeke was unabashedly open about his membership. His children, my cousins Jeanne and Carl, tell me that he never served as a sector leader or in any other official party position. He never stood on street corners selling the *Daily Worker,* the party newspaper. He went to meetings, he helped organize events (like the famous 1949 Paul Robeson concert in Peekskill, New York), and he had a wide circle of friends within the party. But Zeke also retained all of his childhood buddies, including those whose politics were far to his right. He remained active in the painters' union all through the years when New York unions were purging Communist members. He was a popular patron of coffee shops and luncheonettes in his neighborhood. He was elected president of the tenants' organization in the public housing project where he and his brother Sam lived. Later in life, he even became a member of the Brooklyn Democratic Party county committee.

The children of Shenka and Dovid Schwartz—Sarah, Sam, and Isaac—remained extremely close, often to the chagrin of their spouses. But the two older siblings were much more fearful than their younger brother. Sam's wife, my Aunt Ida, spoke bitterly of Isaac's politics, fearing that Sam's application for a job at the postal service would be waylaid by his brother's well-known membership in an outlawed movement. While the FBI came around, once or twice, to interview Zeke, nothing ever came of it, and Sam's hiring was unimpeded. My mother periodically warned me not to "get into trouble" by subscribing to my uncle's political leanings. But her warnings were unnecessary and unavailing. Both Beverly and I were deeply influenced by Zeke's warm-hearted embrace of social justice, racial diversity, and economic equality. Because of him, racial slurs, ethnic stereotypes, and dialect jokes (even including the common use of Yiddish inflections in Borscht Belt humor) were all outlawed in our household. He lived out his beliefs. He had strong friendships with Black peers, unlike any other adults we knew. Zeke was a party-line loyalist, but not a doctrinaire one. He laughed when you were feeling good and comforted you when you weren't.

Of all the events connected with McCarthyism, the most palpable distress came from the conviction in 1951 of Ethel and Julius Rosenberg for spying, and especially from their execution two years later—the first American civilians to be put to death for such charges and the first to suffer that penalty during peacetime. The news sent a shock wave through our neighborhood and the city. Sixteen-year-old Beverly heard of the execution while waiting for the show at a drive-in theater to begin. "I told my friends that we had to go home immediately. I was shaking. It was terrible." Everyone around us interpreted the Rosenberg case as an anti-Semitic attack, although many of the principals on the prosecution side were also Jewish. Mom's confidence in American justice was irremediably sapped. If the United States was capable of such injustice, then you had to stay away from involvement in anything that risked the family's safety. Was it 1920 all over again?

Mom's response, typically, was to pull in her horns. The move from Alabama Avenue to Bradford Street had given her the power to control her own space, to bar the intrusion of nosy Jewish people and threatening non-Jews. She had outlasted the pogroms of the shtetl and the madhouse of the tenements. She would tighten the cocoon around her family by keeping out of "what was not really our business." As tumultuous and temperamental as her husband and children were, she had now become the stable core of our family, community, and civic (though not political) life. She had now acquired exactly the desirable mix of an accessible stoop and a locked front door, the perfect balance and alternation of a comfy housedress and an elegant wool suit.

Acquiring a new combination stereo-TV brought our family together, but it also signaled how we were coming apart. As our tastes diverged, parents and children began to live in different worlds.

9

Richard Puts a Record on the Magnavox

Just in time for the televised inauguration of John F. Kennedy as the US president in January 1961, Dad bought a Magnavox combination television and stereo phonograph from Bressner's appliance store on nearby New Lots Avenue. In a beautiful light-toned wooden console, it occupied the place of honor in our family sitting room, which had in fact been renamed the "TV room." The chairs and the sofa were arranged for each person to focus on the eighteen-inch screen rather than on one another. Except for the house and Dad's car, it was our most valuable possession.

Advertisers bragged that this new home entertainment center would "bring the family together." On increasingly rare moments, like that Kennedy inauguration, it did. It was a snowy day along the Eastern Seaboard and school had been canceled. We all gathered in front of the screen and gripped our coffee cups tightly. Even my three-year-old niece was attentive. Kennedy was our hero. I had distributed leaflets for his campaign during the previous fall and seen him speak at a gigantic rally at Brooklyn's Eastern Parkway Arena in October. I came home gushing with excitement for his endorsement of civil rights legislation and aid for housing and education. But acquiring the new Magnavox that winter also signaled the ways the family was coming apart. New technologies often have unintended consequences. As they aged, Mom and Dad relied even more on their television. Their circle of friends and relatives continued to disperse. Neighbors tended to stop in less frequently. No one wanted to interrupt a neighbor's viewing of their favorite scheduled shows. The furniture in the TV room was comfortable. The kitchen was only a few steps away. Dad's physical labors often left him too weary to get too far from his easy chair during TV's prime time. If 742 Bradford Street was Dave Rabinowitz's castle, his Magnavox was the moat.

For me, it was the stereo phonograph that enlarged my world. I was much less interested in watching television. I was bored with the pratfalls of American variety shows, dramas celebrating the shrewd intuitions of Los Angeles detectives, or sitcoms cluttered up with canned laughter. Instead, the Magnavox and my New York Public Library card conspired to expose me to the aural architecture of European music from Michael Praetorius's *Terpsichore* to Stravinsky's *Oedipus Rex*. Inside the modest dimensions of our TV room on Bradford Street, I could imagine Gothic towers, Georgian drawing rooms, and the crammed streets of foreign cities. Thenceforth, as far as my parents were concerned, mentally I was often elsewhere. So much for togetherness.

Bradford Street was an idyll for Mom and Dad. Reaching their mid-forties in 1960, they seemed to have achieved enduring security for the first time in their lives. Each had good health. Dave's income from the Union Supply Company was reliable, though his labor was physically very demanding and the business endlessly frustrating. He got down to work quickly every morning, spared himself little time to rest between stops along his route, and returned home in early evening to release the anger built up by frustrating days. He was making up for lost time, it seemed, compressing into his forties and fifties all the opportunities he had missed during the hard times of his youth. Seven or eight years after the tragedy of losing her mother, Sarah had absorbed the lessons of Shenka's life. She had prospered. She, too, had transformed obligation into opportunity and now reveled in her clean, well-ordered household. She was respected on the block and in the neighborhood. Their children were growing up healthy and successful in school and in social life. Beverly married an ambitious and energetic college graduate and soon had a child of her own. Sarah was a very young grandmother, just forty-one when Beverly's daughter Ilene was born. Sarah and Dave were able to evict their upstairs tenant and give the three-bedroom apartment to Beverly's family. A constant traffic between upstairs and downstairs reinforced the ties of mother and daughter. My zayde, Dovid Schwartz, still only in his late sixties, was a frequent presence in the life of his great-granddaughter. He would live into his mid-seventies and Dave's mother, Eva Rabinowitz, survived to almost ninety. Ever frugal, Dave was already putting money away for retirement. "On the whole," he would announce, "things are good." Mom would cautiously add, *"Halevai,"* "would that it remain so."

Hard times were now behind them. Pogroms, immigration, poverty, war: all that belonged to the past. By its nature, as I've said, my parents' East New York had initially been a refuge rather than a destination, a welcome stop on their lifelong exodus from the decades-long nightmare befalling Eastern European Jews. Many of them had journeyed from a shtetl to a larger European city, then to the Lower East Side, then to Brownsville, and finally to these few streets along Linden Boulevard in East New York. To their surprise, "our area," as Sarah called it, had become foundational, a permanent home rather than just another port in a repeatedly turbulent journey. Scarred as each of them were by their youthful trials and still wary, they hoped the stable present would persist. They declared their own migration over. A tiny local mini-culture had evolved with its own set of associations and loyalties. The residents of Bradford Street, though they had taken different routes to get there, almost all voted the same way, worshipped the same way, amused themselves in the same way, and brought up their children in the same way. They recognized one another as peers, with some surprise and relief, and they recognized that they were different from the mini-cultures of Eastern Parkway Jews, or Midwood Jews, or Valley Stream Jews, and vastly different from Upper West Side, Westchester, or "Five Towns" (Long Island) Jews, not to mention Jews from Chicago, Los Angeles, or smaller cities. The mores of Bradford Street and its surroundings were consistent. Eccentricity was allowed, and every family had its own *mishegas,* but the extravagant, the abusive, and the squalid were impermissible. Our street knew its place in the American social hierarchy. Our family's mobility, social and geographical, had reached its farthest extent in East New York. (In those days of the space race, the word "apogee" was frequently on our lips.) Sarah and Dave were not going anywhere. Like all of their friends, they fully expected to spend the rest of their lives here.

Something in the air of 1950s America fed this complacency, at least for white families of their generation. Cold War patriotism reinforced their belief that the United States was the best place on earth. It had become a little dangerous to voice contrary opinions in East New York. As for the future, they might be hard-pressed to predict what lay ahead, except for more of the same or better. They expected better gadgets (the rotisserie and the electric knife), greater comfort (recliners covered in Naugahyde), and even less tension in international affairs (as evidenced by Soviet-US "summit" meetings). Their houses would be lifelong dwellings, if possible, not (as they would become a quarter-century later) "fungible assets." No one on Bradford Street, I'm sure, ever refinanced the family home. Debt was a dirty word, and Dave and Sarah considered their desperate Depression-era loans like childhood diseases, never to be suffered again. On a personal level, they could only foresee retirement through the lens of their own parents' experience. They would try to live close enough to spend lots of time with their children and grandchildren, maybe take a few weekend trips, spend a week or two at a Catskill hotel. Their highest aspiration was to avoid being a burden to their children as they aged. That they might later spend almost four decades living thousands of miles away from Beverly and me, traveling to Hawaii, San Francisco, and New Orleans to see the sights, and making two long trips to Israel—that would have been an unimaginable dream in 1957.

Poor as synagogue mice in the 1930s, Sarah and Dave had taken on a few trappings of abundance to give themselves hope. Conversely, in flush years of the late 1950s, they often reminded each other of dangers around every corner. They were always too fearful to be immodest or smug. It wasn't the *ahora,* the evil eye, or some sort of *tsukunft,* or fate, that frightened them. They were haunted instead by the inexorable seesaw of financial ups and downs, and by an upsurge of anti-Semitism. What had gone up could, they were convinced, also go down . . . again. Heartened by victory in 1945 and terrified by Joe McCarthy in the early 1950s, Sarah in particular could never unequivocally bet on America. But they had no alternative. Keep your head down, that was the best plan. Focus on the immediacies of the household economy. Frugality, again, was a byword.

Each of them had outlasted the struggles of their youth. And they had developed a clear image of their personal strengths and weaknesses. They were sure about how to live their lives. They applied these strategies to everything, to Jewish religion and liberal Democratic politics, and equally to making financial decisions and family choices. They saw no need and had no capability to "reinvent" themselves.

Sarah was forever the consummate homemaker. Her love was limitless, but it was channeled mostly into providing comfort, warmth, and sustenance. Whether you were six or sixty, her first questions on welcoming you home were, "Are you feeling all right?" "Are you warm?" "Are you hungry?" "What can I get you?" She left the master planning to Dave, but she was tirelessly ready to solve problems. Sarah was not a person for speculating. Devoted to the concrete realities of life, she disparaged imaginings—and sometimes even simple feelings—as escapable delusions. I have never known anyone with less tolerance for fantasy or idle thoughts. She was impatient with fairy tales and never told her children silly stories. She scorned tales from Yiddish folklore, like Isaac Bashevis Singer's *The Golem,* as *narishe zakhn,* foolish things.

She had a spiritual side, a capacity for faith. Did she "believe" in God? Like most Jews, her religion was not doctrinal. In reflective moments late in life, she would ask, "Isn't there some kind of overall 'something' in the universe? When you think about sex and bearing children," she continued, "isn't all that the most amazing thing you ever heard of?" She would not have contemplated that God was dead, or even that God had gone missing during the Holocaust. That debate in Manhattan circles never reached this end of the IRT subway line.

She would have been reluctant to say so out loud, but she wanted God to be a fellow worker in keeping things orderly. Her rare reference to the divine was a simple occasional prayer, "God should be good to us." In a way, this was a recognition that He (always He) was not consistently benevolent or supportive. She never asked for God's intervention or a direct communication. That would have sounded absurd in this scientific age, and it risked ridicule from her atheistic brother Isaac. Like many Jews of her acquaintance, she instead felt that God was a companion—sometimes reliable, otherwise not—on the long journey of our people. Busy with His own concerns, easily distracted, He reminded her of people she had known.

She never quoted a Biblical verse or even a Yiddish proverb. (Elaborate curses don't count here.) She did not believe in maxims. Whenever she gave advice, she wrapped it in a long and, frankly, often irrelevant story. "Let me tell you something," she started, and then she dredged up some horrible *umglick* (misfortune) from the annals of her family. The import was this: *Life could be very painful. Stop kvetching and get back to work.* Oddly enough, telling these stories always left her feeling better about herself and the world. She sealed her narrative with one word, "Sure!" Conversation adjourned.

Hers was a religion of everyday practice. She knew, of course, that Judaism was rooted in a great tradition of Torah and Talmud, of ceaseless study and commentary on holy texts for centuries and centuries. She respected, even revered, that scholarship, but she had no personal acquaintance with it or with its practitioners. The cover of our Passover Haggadah, which laid out the prayers, rituals, and songs of the family seder, pictured a long table of white-bearded men, almost dwarfed by the volumes in front of them. Mom would often deposit eighteen cents, "for luck," into a *pushke,* or donation box, that was regularly collected by an agent of one of these academies, but she never crossed their thresholds. In fact, she had little use for rabbis or for synagogues, and we never joined one. She never overcame her childhood resistance to the authoritarian manner of the rabbis in Wysokie Mazowieckie.

The synagogue to which we might have gone but did not, as the saying has it, was a small Orthodox shul on Hendrix Street, about six blocks from home. A holdover from the immigrant generation, like the one my zayde attended on Alabama Avenue, its aging congregation assembled for prayer (*davening* every weekday morning, Shabbat, and holidays), for study (of Talmud tractates and the like), and for social connections. But, never having learned Hebrew as a girl, Sarah felt no tie to synagogue Judaism. Only on the High Holy Days was the sanctuary filled. The sale of tickets for Rosh Hashanah and Yom Kippur services kept the congregation afloat. For three or four years, when I was preparing for bar mitzvah and it would have been embarrassing to stay home, Dad bought tickets.

But at least the manner of Hendrix Street was familiar. Its sobriety distinguished itself from the charismatic, joyful intensity of the ultra-Orthodox Hasidim, who were rapidly establishing themselves as closed-off communities in Brooklyn in the postwar years. Hendrix Street was also unlike the energetic Young Israel congregations attracting enthusiastic worshippers among the Orthodox, adding social events to the calendar alongside prayer and study. And finally, Sarah could never have found a comfortable home among the Conservative and Reform Jewish congregations more often located in the suburbs and fancier Brooklyn precincts. They seemed too American, bland, ostentatiously prosperous. She did not really wish to understand everything she believed, or to believe in nothing.

Instead, she embraced the mystery, what she called the miraculous survival of the Jews and of Judaism, and she felt a responsibility for carrying it forward. If she was often uncertain about God, Sarah was totally at one with the people of Israel. Her identification with other Jews—pious and secular, European, American, and Middle Eastern—was complete. Later in life, Beverly bought Mom a lifetime membership in Hadassah, the women's Zionist organization. It was a perfect match for Sarah's pride in Jewishness and her commitment to *tzedakah*. No gift ever gave her so much pleasure. Sarah accepted the holiness of *halacha,* or Jewish law, but she always knew that she could not live within its strictures. She viewed Judaism as capacious. She was sure that a person could be a good Jew in many ways. Sentimental identification with other Jews or with our history, however, was not enough. As a practical person, faithful to a religion that emphasizes practice, Sarah's self-appointed mission was to perform Judaism at home with the people she loved, and in the process to enact in concrete and visual forms the family's identity as Jews in twentieth-century America.

She unquestioningly accepted those requirements of the law that identified the Jewish life cycle—arranging a *chuppah* (canopy) above the wedding altar, scheduling a *brit milah* (ritual circumcision) for baby boys, observing *shiva* after the death of a parent or a spouse, saying the mourner's Kaddish prayer several times a year, and lighting a *Yahrzeit* candle on the anniversary of that loss. These rituals tied Sarah and our family to uncles, aunts, and cousins, and sometimes to well-loved neighbors and friends.

On the High Holy Days, our corner of East New York was transformed. The schools remained open in those days, but the absence of Jewish teachers and students transformed them into spooky, nearly silent outposts of the Gentile establishment. Almost all the stores shut down, and automobile traffic dwindled. The streets were jammed with families parading back and forth from synagogues to residences, pushing prams, carrying tallis (prayer shawl) bags and even a few sweets and toys to keep children happy. Still, there were a few years when the World Series battles between the Yankees and the Dodgers coincided with these holidays, and the buzz of television broadcasts seeped out onto the sidewalks.

As for other holidays on the Jewish calendar, our observances fundamentally stemmed from Sarah's domestic practice rather than the formal rituals of the community. We lit the menorah on Hanukkah, but the family made no effort to create a Jewish analogue to rival the *goyish* Christmas season. Nor did any local girls doll up as Esther at Purim, commemorating the persecution and rescue of the Jews in ancient Persia. Shavuot, observing God's giving the Torah to the Jewish people, went by unnoticed. It would have felt ostentatiously pious to construct a *sukkah* (dining hut) on our porch to recall the travail of the Israelites in the desert during Sukkoth.

The center of Sarah's religiosity was her work at home. Maintaining a kosher kitchen may have originally been an obligation, but for her it was an avenue to a satisfactory home life. It ordered the weekly rhythm of meals. It insured a healthy diet for her family. It made her comfortable offering food and drink to guests. All our other experiences of holiday sanctification also emerged out of Mom's kitchen. At Passover, she worked hard to remove all traces of *hametz* (leavened bread), to clean out all the drawers and cupboards, and to substitute unfashionably ornate sets of meat and dairy dishes (stored all the rest of the year in the cellar) for our regular tableware, as well as equally ancient sets of cooking implements and flatware. During the Passover week, we loved her gefilte fish with homemade *chrain* (horseradish, strong enough to seal the esophagus shut and flood the tear ducts), her *tzimmes* (a stew of prunes and carrots), her honey cake, her matzo meal pancakes. Dad made a special intervention then, too, creating a thick and peppery *matzobrei* pancake, perfect with sour cream. And, then, of course, there were the holiday treats—*hamantaschen* at Purim, *blintzes* at Shavuot, potato *latkes* at Hanukkah. She fostered a lifelong disdain for the commercial versions of these treats. Only when I went to Venice and learned that Giovanni Bellini's paintings of the Madonna and Child were not so much representations of holiness but holy objects themselves, to be worshipped, did I understand the spiritual gifts cooked into Sarah's holiday delicacies. Most of these dishes involved the use of ingredients seldom incorporated into Mom's weekly cookery, throwbacks to her days in rural Poland.

Still, no assessment of Sarah's ideas and images about the divine, and no inventory of her religiously oriented activities, can fully document the way she (and hence her family) was infused with Jewishness. Some elements of her ordinary life in America, of course, had nothing specifically to do with being Jewish. Like other newcomers (Italian Americans, Greeks, Poles, Czechs, and so on), first- and second-generation Eastern European Jews made their extended families the center of their social lives. Other hyphenated Americans probably felt the same pain when an airliner crashed with one's country folk on board, or shared the shame when the FBI nailed a noted criminal with one's ethnic background. But in other ways, Sarah's habits of mind were characteristic of Ashkenazi Jews of her generation. Socialist leanings were instinctual, at least until the 1960s. Zionism merged Jewish identity with all the good and bad qualities of nationalism, except where (as in Isaac's case) it conflicted with the commitment to international communism or cultural radicalism. Then there were the behavioral and rhetorical traits common to Sarah's culture. Like many in her generation, she thrilled to intense arguments. Interruptions were expressions of affection. Listening too intently was often taken as a negative judgment: "You don't understand what I'm saying?" And listening patiently could be diagnosed as the first sign of some dread emotional frailty or disease: "I'm talking and you're not saying a word, what's the matter with you?"

The local East New York Young Men's and Young Women's Hebrew Association offered Mom the best platform for extending her housekeeping skills to the wider community and to seeing other *menschen* (decent, warm-hearted souls) in operation. The YM & YWHA, also known as the "Y," perfectly expressed Sarah's laundry list of the legacies she hoped to leave behind: a sense of community built on face-to-face encounters, a respect for both secular and sacred learning, the special culture of lower-middle-class Brooklyn Jewry that found expression in the performance of Jewish comedians and musicians, concern for the elderly and the less fortunate—in sum, her manifold Jewishness. She joined the Women's Committee while the fundraising was under way, and she remained active until she had to leave Bradford Street. She did not generate new program ideas, but she kept them going, praising and rewarding those who contributed wisdom and labor. In return, she was well loved, and finally, in 1968, she was honored by the "Y" [as "Mrs. David Rabinowitz"] at its annual breakfast. It was a long-overdue recognition of her contribution.

By contrast, focused exclusively on making a living, Dave Rabinowitz abstained from all these devotions, at least until he had retired to Florida in his sixties. Laudable and perhaps necessary, Dave's single-mindedness created a vacuum. It left Sarah at the helm of the family's emotional, spiritual, and social life. Dave was, indeed, a forceful character. He could express strong judgments, positive and negative, but these usually came after the fact, after you had already paid too much, arrived too late, or signed the contract (in ink). That was painful. All the positive, substantive messages about how to conduct oneself in the world came from Sarah.

I think that each of my parents had spent so much energy overcoming the strains of their childhood that they were unready for parenting—or at least the emotional part of parenting. Beverly and I were pretty good kids. We almost always internalized and fulfilled our parents' expectations. We did not perplex our parents with some of the more severe dilemmas of our generation—drug addiction, cult membership, draft resistance and self-deportation to Canada. We both turned out to be competent and self-reliant in everyday life. But there was still a gigantic gulf between Mom's and Dad's childhood experience and what the world expected of parents and demanded of second-generation children in the 1950s.

On the surface, it was easier to bring up a daughter than a son. My sister, born in 1937 and coming of age in a lower-middle-class family during the mid-1950s, was supposed to follow the prescribed path of dating, early marriage, childbearing, and household management—at least "until her children were grown up." At every stage of her education, however, Beverly was singled out by teachers for her intelligence. While her parents appreciated her good report cards, they saw no educational alternatives. For over a century, and especially since the hiring of many Jews as teachers and administrators in the 1920s, the New York City public school system was the jewel in the crown for the city's Jews. In sixth grade, Beverly was encouraged to apply to the special junior high school at Hunter College, but Mom could not imagine allowing her twelve-year-old to commute an hour each way into Manhattan.

The family had prospered through the 1940s by aiming for "enough." It would be *enough* for Beverly to get a job after high school—and to work at it until she "settled down." The model was my mother's cousin Chayele, who had, even while her children were young, landed a great job as an executive secretary for a metals-importing cartel in lower Manhattan. So, when Beverly entered Thomas Jefferson High School, she chose to pursue a commercial rather than an academic diploma—mastering typing, stenography, and bookkeeping. During afternoons in her junior and senior years, and during every summer, she took on office work, splitting her earnings with the family. In her spare time, she alternated between racing through classic novels and leafing through fashion magazines. One part of her brain was intuiting what made a novel compelling while the other developed a keen eye for good design. A few of her friends decided to start college, but she concurred with her parents' belief that this was unnecessary. Her English teacher at Jefferson was appalled. He wrote to my parents that she was as well qualified for college as anyone he had taught. "But why do you need a college degree," my father asked, in one of those rhetorical flourishes that resounded throughout this lower middle-class neighborhood, "in order to change diapers?"

And so, a few months before her nineteenth birthday, after a year of working at the same office as Cousin Chayele, Beverly was married. Would history repeat itself? Sarah, like Shenka Schwartz, enjoyed being a grandmother. But Beverly couldn't match her mother's sense of accomplishment, or Mom's pleasure in a well-ordered home life. Motherhood and housekeeping never gave her that satisfaction, and Beverly began to seek a pathway out of her boredom. At out-of-the-way antique shops in dicey neighborhoods in Brooklyn and lower Manhattan, she found wonderful stuff to refurbish—oil lamps to electrify, coverlets to hang on her living room walls. Her apartment displayed a creativity uncommon on Bradford Street. Dad thought she was crazy to bring such trash into the house. More troubling was Beverly's realization, after two or three years of marriage, that she had made a huge mistake. She knew her husband would never outgrow his playground self-indulgence. So she came to Mom, asking for help in tending her toddler so that she could go to college and find a different career path. She hinted at divorce.

Notwithstanding her devotion to her grandchild, Mom was ad-
amant. She actually recited the hackneyed motto of the unforgiving,
"You made your bed, now sleep in it." There was no hesitation in
her voice, no apology, and no further explanation. Just anger.
Beverly had pushed and pushed, and evidently reached the edge of
Sarah's loving patience. All the hurt of being the overprotective
daughter and the long-besieged wife oozed out in Mom's response
to Beverly's crisis. Sarah Rabinowitz had never been able to escape
the responsibilities of tending older and younger generations at one
time, so why should Beverly? Sarah had never had a way of shut-
ting off her husband's roars, so why should Beverly complain about
her husband's neglect of their child in favor of his ongoing obses-
sion with basketball, tennis, or golf?

Mom was embracing weakness for the first time. She had always
been the strong one, the one on whom everyone relied, and now
she wanted out. Freedom required professing her unwillingness to
help. A thick shell of reluctance began to form around her. Still a
loving person, she had seized a private island of reserve that could
not be breached by the never-ending neediness of her family. She
now began many conversations by saying, "*Ich hab nisht di shtarkeyt,*"
"I haven't the strength."

As the younger child, and a male at a time which prized boys, I
grew up in a very different world from Beverly's. My parents were
protective, nurturing. Both of them were physically very affectionate. Ours was a house of hugs. The tabloids spoke of juvenile
delinquency and gang warfare, but East New York was still a calm
and prosperous place. Even when we misbehaved, the authorities
were indulgent. My pals and I once tried to liberate some baseballs
from the outfield of the local Bat-a-Way on Pennsylvania Avenue.

Real baseballs were much too expensive for us to buy. But we were nabbed by the cops and provided with free transport to our homes, where the police explained our misdemeanors to our parents and mildly warned us against further offenses against the public order. I was not frightened by the experience. It seemed obvious that the owner of the batting range would try to prevent our pillaging. But somehow I do not think that Black children would have been treated so gently by the New York Police Department. In the 1950s, white New Yorkers like Sarah and Dave inhaled and exhaled the air of pleasant social peace.

Mom was consistent in her affection with me. I don't recall being scolded very often. I remember how I had laid out the different piles of stamps from different countries and British "possessions" on the carpet or the dining room table before arranging them in my stamp album. Did I, at age nine or ten, clean up all the traces afterward, or did Mom do it? Probably the latter. In general, Mom did not assign us household chores. I was occasionally asked to carry out the garbage. She felt it was easier to do it all herself. She didn't bother to teach Beverly her cooking tricks until much later in life. At bedtime, Mom would tuck me in and stretch out my legs "so that I would grow up tall" (it didn't work!), and then give me a big hug and kiss—as if I was the most precious thing she knew.

Dad was equally affectionate. During bedtime chats in my early childhood, I would ask him to tell me a story of when he was a little boy, and he would regale me with improbable tales of his pal, C. C. Delancey, and his adventures on the Lower East Side in the 1920s—getting his shoes stuck to his feet when stealing into a glue factory, having his neighbor's entire pitcher of milk devoured by a cat he had befriended, and so on. Some of the stories, I'm glad to say, bore the stamp of truth—like his newspaper-selling, and I have recorded them here. But Dad's love of entertaining "shtick" contrasted with Mom's ferocious disdain for fantasy of any kind, and I much preferred his companionship at bedtime. On many evenings, I went to sleep giggling.

On the other hand, Mom was a better playmate. She taught me card games and turned my three- or four-day-long confinements for mumps, measles, and the chicken pox into delightful vacations from school. She put a little U-Bet chocolate syrup into the prescribed Phillips' Milk of Magnesia to make it more palatable. I loved going shopping with her and especially having lunch at the Automat on 14th Street near S. Klein's discount department store. At the Automat, I could plug five nickels into the slots to get a tuna fish sandwich or a slice of apple pie. I have loved nickels ever since.

For Dad, sharing time with his son seemed always to have another, more obscure agenda. Four or five times a season, we would go to see the Dodgers play at Ebbets Field. We would get up really early and, right after breakfast, start making sandwiches, lots of them—salami on rye with mustard and pickles was a favorite. Then Dad filled a gallon picnic jug with lemonade, loading a tray of ice cubes into the frozen lemonade mix. (As I've said, he was constitutionally opposed to the purchase of soft drinks.) We carried our provisions, as if we were Lewis and Clark setting out for an expedition, to our car. We would never take the subway, even though Ebbets Field was only ten or eleven stops away from us. This posed a problem. Ebbets Field, constructed in 1913, had no designated ballfield parking. Dad was not about to pay some shyster, living a block or two from the park, two or three bucks to leave our Packard in his driveway. So at 11 AM, two and a half hours before game time, we would begin our circumnavigation of the streets of Crown Heights, looking for an empty spot. Once successful, I would walk excitedly to the ballpark. Dad refused to buy the regular 25 cent program, which contained a scorecard and lots of pictures and statistics about the Dodgers' season. Nope, he preferred to buy the *Brooklyn Eagle* newspaper for five cents, which included a crummy, stiff, one-page scorecard in its Saturday edition. We bought grandstand seats, $1.25 each, and spent about two hours watching batting practice—and eating all our sandwiches (and the cookies that Mom had snuck into our bag). During the game I kept track of every pitch and every play, just as Dad had taught me, and I was in heaven. Even when the "Bums" (as the Dodgers were called in the headlines of the *Daily News*) were losing, or when the game was one-sided, Ebbets Field was exciting. Our seatmates were often memorable Brooklyn types—priests and longshoremen, Black gentlemen in coats and ties accompanying kindly ladies with nice hats, skinny people who ordered a hot dog every inning and scary guys in knitted caps. As a diligent scorekeeper, I was the archivist for our row. Someone would turn around to ask, "Hey, kid, how many homers has Hodges hit this year?" After my answer, he would poke his sidekick in the ribs, "See, I tole ya the kid would know."

The downside came near the end of the game, especially if it was a close contest. To Dad, a traffic jam was a calamity, to be avoided at all costs. Only "idjits" would get stuck in traffic, and Dave Rabinowitz was no idiot. So, in the top of the eighth, with the visiting team threatening, Dad would say, "OK, let's go!" My protests were loud but unavailing. My recourse was to take his car keys and race the three or four blocks to our parking spot, unlock the car doors, turn on the radio, and complete my scorekeeping to the broadcasts by Red Barber and Vince Scully. In retrospect, Dad seemed more enthusiastic about outsmarting the system than about rooting hard for the home team. Where was he? Was he distracted by business concerns? Dad accommodated, even encouraged, my enthusiasms, but he didn't share them. He was just not a playful fellow. He brought home bags of stamps from the dealers in his building, but he never got down on the floor to help me sort them. After the Dodgers banned the entry of our picnic jugs in 1956—reportedly someone had thrown one and almost killed an umpire after a bad call at first base—Dad was less avid about attending games in person.

Something seemed to get in the way of Dad's full enjoyment of many things. In the early days of television, much of the prime-time schedule came almost directly from radio and from the vaudeville stage and the Borscht Belt. Many, if not most, of the performers were Jewish New Yorkers—Eddie Cantor, Burns and Allen, the Marx Brothers, Milton Berle, Sid Caesar, Sam Levenson, Myron Cohen, Buddy Hackett, and so on. There were dozens. For years on end, Mom and Dad had heard their jokes on the radio and seen their routines at the Palace Theatre. Dad had his preferences. He found Milton Berle's slapstick ridiculous. He couldn't quite get Groucho's cruel wit. Jerry Lewis's zaniness was exhausting. Dad liked most what he had once tried to do himself, at events like Ida Schlachtman's wedding, where he met Mom. He liked a succession of jokes, mostly about the foibles of Men's Lives in the Big City— jokes with well-timed punchlines, not cruel, never off-color, not too ethnic, not too political or "relevant," and not misogynistic. With so many grounds for disapproval, he was a very tough audience to please. Perhaps he was overly proud of having been there when these guys were just starting out, or jealous of their celebrity, or angered by his own obscurity in the world. When his standards were met, on the other hand, he loved retelling the jokes to someone who hadn't had the privilege to be there with him. "Oh, you missed something!"

Each of my parents posed an impenetrable mystery to me. There were some things I just couldn't figure out. But even as a child, I intuitively steered around my parents' anxieties. The world was full of problems. But unlike World War II days, no one (that our family knew) was being killed. I had fears about nuclear warfare, but I kept them secret. Though we had to duck under our desks for "shelter drills," we never were encouraged to talk about our fears at school. I recall being scared out of my wits by an animated short film about the atomic bomb, *A Short Vision,* that appeared on the Ed Sullivan Show on a night in 1956 when my parents were away. I never mentioned it to anyone, but it gave me nightmares for months. They were exacerbated on hot summer nights when our open bedroom windows brought in the rumble of aircraft overhead. Was this plane, or the next one, bringing the Bomb to New York City?

In the world beyond our front steps, I grew up in the luckiest of historical moments. Boys with promise were the choice crop of the local Jewish communal enterprise. If there had been a county fair in Brooklyn, we would have been exhibited and awarded blue ribbons. Even from early childhood we were propelled forward by family and community hopes. For a fifth-grade homework assignment, I remember writing an autobiography that focused almost entirely on the dreams my deceased bubbe had for me. The better I did at school, the higher the goals my teachers and my neighbors set me, and though my parents never needed to spur my ambition, they had obviously implanted expectancy in every breath I took. Many of my schoolteachers had forgone their own aspirations for public success because of their families' circumstances during the Depression and the war. They were deeply devoted to elementary education. A generation later, perhaps, such women and men could have become neurosurgeons and archaeologists. In the meantime, I was blessed by the transfer of their ambitions to me and my peers. If they were the sculptors, my classmates and I were the clay. For three full years, my favorite teacher, Annette Goldman, devoted a half-hour every morning before school discussing history and current events with me—even when I was not actually a member of her class.

I was a good student, and my teachers, as their report card comments say, were often puzzled about how to challenge me sufficiently in the classroom. To avoid the tedium of classroom recitations, they would come up with assignments for me—in fourth grade, to manage all classroom access to audio-visual resources, in fifth, to classroom supplies, and in sixth grade to textbooks. In class, I was often assigned to tutor "slower" classmates or children in lower grades. But since my learning seemed to be self-motivated, Mom and Dad were unworried by any of this and deeply opposed to finding a more challenging program for me. They refused to entertain scholarship offers for me to attend private or Jewish day schools. Dad constantly repeated, "I don't want you to get separated from your friends on the street." Our local public school perfectly represented and expressed their ambitions for both my intellectual and social development. They trusted my teachers to foster my leadership skills and responsibilities for my fellow students. The teachers, in turn, encouraged me to lead, to model self-confidence for everyone. In fifth grade, I organized a sandlot baseball team for my classmates. I found myself taking our catcher, Ivan Greenberg, who owned the only mask and catcher's mitt we had, to and from his orthodontist so that he would not miss our games. Well into our adult lives, one of our clumsiest teammates would, upon meeting me in the street, thank me for ensuring that he would also get a call to "grab a bat and get up there."

But what would we become? We East New York boys had no clear road map for our futures. Our fathers, without exception, had barely scraped through World War II and the postwar years. Each one had crossed into the world outside the immigrant ghetto to start or buy a small business, or to get a job in the post office, the school system, or some other part of city government. Unlike their immigrant parents, the language of their everyday work was exclusively English. As their sons, we were supposed to venture more deeply into the world of business, of politics, of culture. None of our fathers had "careers." Their small business livelihoods were too small to bequeath to us. They did not have the capital to give us a boost. In the mid-1950s, our parents never thought that their sons should look forward to making a living at the work that they did, or living as adults where they did. "Not with your advantages in life." "You shouldn't have to struggle the way I did." "No way do we want you to end up in our situation. . . . It was OK for us, but you have to do better."

They also felt obligated to ensure that we identified as Jews. Our sisters could fulfill their entire obligation to Judaism by marrying a Jewish man. In this era, they did not need to have *bat mitzvahs.* Boys were absolutely required to become a *bar mitzvah,* which meant learning to read, chant, and interpret portions of the Torah and the Prophets (the *haftorah*) specific to the Shabbat nearest our thirteenth birthday. How would this be accomplished? None of the fathers on our block was a synagogue regular. The most convenient way to get us trained was to enroll us in a local Orthodox Talmud Torah. Two hours every afternoon from Monday to Thursday, and another two hours on Sunday morning. Convenient for Dad, murder for me. In our eyes, our teachers were ancient, bearded men, smelling of onions and yesterday's milk, more gifted at cruelty than Biblical interpretation. They saw every error we made—and they were profuse and continuous—as threatening the demise of the Jewish people altogether. Our stupidities made the Nazis look like saints. Any hint of heresy—a question about God's justice, for example, in favoring Abel over his brother Cain—and, smack, the rabbi's ruler came down across our knuckles. We tried to mollify our teachers' anger. One rabbi could be bribed with boxes of cough drops. (Smith Brothers, Ludens, but never Pine Brothers, which was made with glycerin, derived from pigs. That would have been like introducing a squealing porker right into the classroom.) In the end, our retribution for their cruelty was vastly more enjoyable. We spent the hours from 8:30 to 3 o'clock in public school as model law-abiding citizens. From 3:30 to 5:30, in Hebrew school, we were transformed into miscreants. We stole all the chalk from the blackboard before class and chalked dirty words on the rabbi's black coat. We made sophisticated paper airplanes, scrawled with vilification—"Rabbi Gold is a Moron"—and calculated that if we threw them out the back window of the classroom at just the correct angle, they would be swept by the wind currents in the adjoining alley—THIS IS ABSOLUTE TRUTH!—to float back into the room through the front window, landing at the rabbi's feet. After two or three years of this, with my progress imperceptible both to the rabbis and to me, and my bar mitzvah looming as a family embarrassment, I was paroled from the Talmud Torah. Henceforth I could just cross Bradford Street and learn my *haftorah* from Murray Garber, a neighbor and friend who was employed as a cantor at a nearby Conservative synagogue. He soon discovered that I could not carry a tune and had no stake in the battle between Jephthah and the Ammonites (the subject of Judges 11, from which my portion was taken). I memorized as much of the words and the melody as I could and stood in front of Cantor Garber's congregation on a morning in late June 1958.

The rabbi earnestly made me promise to return for a worship service that autumn, but I never did. Instead, I rushed out into the larger cultural world of New York City. My parents, without a pause, supported my decision to take the entrance exam and go to Stuyvesant, a high school for academically gifted boys in Manhattan.

Once I had crossed under the East River in my hourlong commutes each morning, I was loathe to return to Brooklyn without drinking deeply of the great treasures of "the City." As a teenager I was constantly on the run—busy at school and spending many nights and weekends with friends. I had fewer hours at home. With every breath I was hungrily swallowing in the crazy richness of New York life, its subways and streets, its theaters and ballparks, its bookstores and hot dog stands. I spent many afternoons at the 42nd Street Library and many evenings at Broadway and off-Broadway theaters with complimentary or cheap ($1!) tickets provided by my schoolteachers. Until I was fifteen I had never been to a Broadway play and never entered one of Manhattan's ballet, opera, or classical music venues. These were not home turf for my parents and our neighbors. Now I could not get enough. Impelled by a vague yearning to anchor myself amid the most sophisticated New Yorkers, I took Beverly to a Japanese Kabuki theater piece and then Irene Papas and the Greek National Theatre at the City Center. I often spent Saturday nights at Caricature, my favorite Greenwich Village coffeehouse, across the street from the San Remo Café. Following my new friends up the rickety backstairs of downtown buildings, I could listen to beat poets like Gregory Corso and Frank O'Hara and attend experimental programs of absurdist theater and avant-garde music. My most exotic evening was a date with a beautiful but very quiet girl who lived up in Riverdale in the Bronx, at the absolutely farthest point on the IRT subway from my station in Brooklyn. In those days, a boy had to pick up and escort his date from and to her home. I left Bradford Street at 5 o'clock in the afternoon. After our trip from Riverdale to Greenwich Village, we went to see a production—at the Provincetown Playhouse on MacDougal Street, I think—of Eugene Ionesco's *La Cantatrice Chauve* (The Bald Soprano). In French! After an after-show snack of hot chocolate and cinnamon toast at an 8th Street diner, we set out for Riverdale. The subways, of course, run more infrequently in the middle of the night, and the bus to and from my date's house to the subway only once an hour, and so I did not arrive home until about 6 A.M. Mom was waiting for me, more than a little worried. "Where have you been?" she asked. "Oh," I replied. "What a relief! The first words of English I've heard all night!" My explanation left her shaking her head. She finished her bowl of oatmeal and went back to bed. I kept the tales of my adventures to myself.

The Magnavox

It was about that time that Dad purchased the Magnavox. It arrived just as 742 Bradford Street began to house two contrasting modes of life. As a refuge for my parents, it was a place of steadiness and routine. As a launching-pad for me, it stockpiled my ambition to get up and get out.

Mom and Dad loved being home, comfortably allowing their limbs to relax from days of hard work. When I breezed in at eight o'clock on a school night, I often found my father sitting in his favorite chair, a newspaper on his lap, barely attentive to the programs he was watching. He always had a bowl of apples at his side, a special bowl never used for breakfast cereal or soup. With each bite, he would savor the fruit and then deposit the peel—as if it were the ugly remains of his past and the frustrations of his workday—in a nearby ashtray. As the night wore on, the unsightly pile grew. But his anger had been spent, disposed of, and eventually he dozed off. After twenty minutes or so, Mom would call out, "Dave!" and he would awaken with a start, gather up his apple leavings, and make his way to bed.

All this widened the distance between me and my parents. I grew increasingly intolerant of Dad's endless ranting about his business and his customers and, in general, about money. I desperately dreamed of dinnertime conversations where money was never mentioned. I became secretive, defensive, even mendacious about how and where I was spending the money I earned. Stuyvesant High School was then close to the East Village and the dozens of used bookstores on Fourth Avenue below 14th Street. In those years before the full flowering of the paperback revolution, I fantasized about living surrounded by shelves and shelves of Modern Library classics. One by one, I began to purchase rather than borrow the books I was assigned to read by English and history teachers. Dad always questioned the necessity and, as I've said, the cost, of these purchases.

In a different way, Mom began to take aspects of my growing up as tiny acts of aggression. Piece by piece, she had built a thicket of truisms, a repertoire of trite responses, for everything that puzzled me. This made me an enemy of her *seykhel,* "common sense," which felt like an oppressive blanket over my curiosity. What I wanted was knowledge, uncommon sense. Knowledge that I had discovered for myself, whose origin lay in facts that I had weighed for myself. My parents told me nothing of sexual matters, so I got myself a copy of Alan Guttmacher's *Complete Book of Birth Control.* Mom insisted that I "should not bother myself with such things." And as I began to read darker and deeper books—Melville rather than Dickens, Dostoevsky rather than Mark Twain, James Joyce rather than John Steinbeck—my personal life diverged from my family's. As I've said, I didn't so much rebel as secede. My English teachers were pressing me to think of these books as part of a "literature," a "culture." In social studies classes, I was encouraged to see elections as parts of a "political system," arrangements of "power" and "authority." Business transactions, like the ones my father did all day long, now were evidences of an "economy." When I sat up late with high school classmates discussing Camus's *The Stranger* or Plato's *Apology,* we were trying to find a "philosophy" we could embrace. All these terms were alien to my family, and especially to my mother. She insisted on particularity. What benefit was it to use such high-flown language to describe what real people did every day with their money, their leisure time, their hopes and fears? To Mom and Dad these fancy words were nothing but ways of avoiding judgments as to what was right and proper. Did I really want to become a *luftmensch,* an intellectual with his head in the clouds, living remotely from the realities of the people around me? I had found a sanctuary in scholarship and what I thought was high culture, and I intuited that this was my ticket to success in life.

The new Magnavox home entertainment center concretely represented this doubleness. I could not spare a moment to sit down and watch television with my parents. My busier schedule—with much to occupy my after-school hours in Manhattan, not to mention homework and a teenager's capacity for long calls (on the house's only telephone) with friends—drew me away from the "boob tube." In addition, the lowbrow entertainments of television's "vast wasteland," as Newton Minow, then chair of the Federal Communications Commission, dubbed it precisely at this moment, conflicted with my higher-minded, increasingly snobbish self. I found that I could not "relax yourself," as my father ceaselessly urged, while watching *Ozzie and Harriet* and *Gunsmoke.*

But it was the other half of the two-way Magnavox that proved more divisive for our family. We had not had a Victrola to play LP records before. We were not a musical family beyond Lawrence Welk's mawkish hours on television. Now we wanted to show off our high-fidelity phonograph. For the first year or two, I now recall, I tried to acquire music that could appeal to the whole family. My first purchases of LP records were André Previn's *Like Young* and the Command All-Stars album, *Provocative Percussion,* both jazzy arrangements of familiar American pop standards like "You're the Top" and "Mood Indigo." (But not at all the "cool jazz" of this era.) Then we got some albums of Jewish musical theater favorites, like Mollie Picon and the Barry Sisters. My Uncle Zeke widened our taste with an album of Afro-Cuban jazz—not to widespread acclaim. He also brought over new recordings of The Weavers, the leftist folk group who were then escaping from their forced obscurity during the McCarthyite purges.

By the winter of 1961–1962, when I was a senior in high school, I had abandoned these compromising gestures. My musical tastes were evolving rapidly—first toward classical warhorses (the *1812 Overture, Bolero*), then toward the titans (Bach, Mozart, Beethoven), and finally toward the modernist avant-garde (Stravinsky, Berg, Webern). Twice a week, I brought home a stack of bright-yellow-jacketed Deutsche Grammophon LPs from the Donnell Library on 53rd Street and led myself through a ravenous immersion in European classical music. This was the aural equivalent of my growing separation from my parents' experience and tastes. Soon the television room, at least during hours when no one wanted to watch anything, was emptied of everyone but one mad teenager waving his arms in imitation of Leonard Bernstein.

Mom and Dad had lovingly nurtured a contradiction in their own house. They wanted my success, but they were puzzled by my growing detachment from their day-to-day lives. Was it necessary? They were living on Bradford Street, in a very concrete place. More of me was living, day by day, somewhere else—at school, in the Fourth Avenue book district, on 42nd Street, in the world of ideas. Mom was insulted when I stayed out late to work at the library or to go to the theater. Nothing was more important to her than having the family together. I was nuts, she said, to have dinner alone at Bickford's cafeteria on 5th Avenue or at "Tad's Steaks $1.19" instead of Mom's table. "Wouldn't you rather eat supper at home with us?" After I had graduated and gone off to Harvard, she asked, "Did you need to go away to college? What would have been so bad if you'd stayed at Brooklyn College for a couple of years?"

In my teens and twenties, I could not be the loyal and resourceful child my parents had been to my grandparents. Such unfailing support was their only standard of virtue. I was somehow failing at respect while I was, at the same time, trying to be considerate—to achieve what they wanted for me. On the one hand, I was fulfilling their dreams, especially my father's, of success in America—working hard, gaining a Harvard education, preparing for a professional career. On the other hand, I repeatedly failed my day-to-day obligation as a child. People like my parents still lived in a pre-psychological age, when identity was completely clothed in prescribed family and social roles. The man was the breadwinner, the woman the homemaker. A father took his children to outdoor sports and play. A mother could care for them, indoors, while ill. This was what a father or a mother was supposed to be, no matter how much it fit one's personal and interior experience. What, however, was an adult child supposed to be?

When it came to their innermost feelings, as men or women, as fathers or mothers, however, they lacked some of the tools to anticipate, weather, and overcome the dilemmas of their children's maturing and their own aging. But social and family roles are only secure and stable if everything around you is equally sure. They did not talk about what they wanted, expected, or feared would happen in their most intimate settings. And that silence disabled their emotional resilience to the changes that would soon come.

They could not teach Beverly or me to swim in the mainstream of Establishment America, of universities, corporations, the media, and cultural institutions. They had found a safe buoy inside their own lower middle-class community in Jewish Brooklyn. But they also, surprisingly enough, equipped Beverly and me with the tools to help us plunge into a much wider world. We both inherited Dad's entrepreneurial drive, and we each created successful businesses in competitive creative fields. The sharp wit of our family dinners prepared us for lively conversations with other impatient people. Mom's superstitious refusal to boast about her children (and her frequent invocation of *kinehora* to ward off the evil eye), paradoxically, immunized us against flattery or empty praise. We both learned to speak without self-pity about our failures, which proved more valuable to our conversational partners than talk of our successes.

Bentching Licht

Deep personal religious life survived in only one special observance of Mom's. After the Friday night supper dishes were washed and put away, and the family had retreated to watch *The Adventures of Rin Tin Tin* and other shows, Mom would return alone to the dinner table, put on a kerchief, light the Shabbos candles, cover her eyes, and mumble the simple prayer, *l'hadlik ner shel Shabbos.* Sometimes I would perch in the doorway and watch. Mom would tear up almost every time, likely in memory of her departed mother. The customary obligation was to light the candles at sunset, of course, but the household was always too busy at that hour. Now, in the darkened dining area, Mom could be alone with her memories and her love. She was not lonely, but she drank deeply of her aloneness. None of us, family members, neighbors, or neighborhood friends, could compensate for her loss. I have no memory of my bubbe's lighting Shabbos candles, but I still think of her, too, every time I see them lit in my house.

The luminosity of those candles is unforgettable. In youth and early adulthood, I sought instead clean, well-lighted places to do my work, to illuminate intricate problems and enlighten myself. As I aged, I grew aware of the shadows they cast, of the corners in my rooms (and the corners of my mind) that remained dark. But those twin points of light on my mother's dinner table shine ever more brightly in my memory.

Instead of a homecooked meal, served at her own table, Sarah had to prepare a lunch for reheating on an electric hot plate, as if she and Dave were squatters or vagabonds. She sighed with regret each time she spooned Maxim freeze-dried coffee into water boiled on the hot plate.

10

Sarah Warms Up Her Coffee on a Hot Plate

A hot plate can break your heart. "Oy, what an insult it was," Sarah complained about having to fill up a pot at the washroom sink and then heat up her soup or her coffee on a hot plate. Forced by block-busting to sell their Bradford Street house in 1968, the Rabinowitzes leased a storefront in Queens to warehouse the Union Supply Company's merchandise. Sarah was stationed there, for long hours on most days, alert to receive deliveries from manufacturers and distributors. Sarah's hot plate anchored her presence and permitted her to bring the warmth of her home life into the exile of these wearisome cold days at the storefront.

To be sure, sometimes a hot plate can seem romantic. A young couple, alone in their first apartment before the gas company has come to connect the range, heats up their takeout food on a hot plate and dines by candlelight. But in other scenarios, a hot plate can be an emblem of desperation, discarded whenever the sheriff's men break up a household of squatters on a forlorn urban alley. In any case, hot plates are an improvisation—not the thing that a *bala-batishe* (conscientious) housewife had in mind. For Sarah, it was a necessary concession to the uprooting of their domestic peace, quiet, and productivity in East New York, and also a sad reminder of their tenuous hold on bourgeois comfort.

The hot plate, like its big brother the electric range, was an innovation of the 1930s, and it has never completely shed its association with the Depression and with vagabonds. It lives in a family of objects with other tokens of a makeshift, jerry-built world—a sink too shallow to wash out pans, a rusty Brillo pad that stains the toilet porcelain, a stool and a card table, perhaps a bare light bulb with one or two extension cords plugged into it. "You shouldn't know from it," Sarah often said.

About Bradford Street my parents were clear. "I could have lived there for the rest of my life," my mother said. To a degree that now seems remarkable, that little corner of East New York, Brooklyn, seemed to stand still. When the dozen two-family houses on each side of Bradford Street had been completed in 1929, the four large corner lots were left vacant—and they remained so for almost forty years! Fashions came and went. Automobiles proliferated and grew so wide in the 1950s that they could barely squeeze down the alleyways to the garages. The sycamores arced over the street imperiously and bombarded the pavements each fall with seed pods that we called "itchy balls." But the houses looked exactly the same decade after decade, with red painted stoops and white trim on the porch railings. The parents stayed put. The roster of residents was astonishingly stable. I can still rattle off the family names of thirty-odd neighbors from my memory, each of whom lived alongside my parents for at least fifteen or twenty years. A few others came and went, but the core obviously had found their social niche and prepared to share the pleasures and pains of growing old together. They were not going anywhere. Appliances were replaced when they died, but no family "redid" their kitchen. Well into their fifties, the people of the street were still Depression kids, making ends meet, pinning their dreams of progress onto their children rather than onto themselves.

As their children completed high school, Dave's and Sarah's civic involvement diminished. They were not so dependent on public services as they had been. Dave no longer took the subway to work, and Sarah had fewer occasions to travel by bus to visit aunts and uncles around Brooklyn. They no longer availed themselves of many public health services, instead using doctors linked by Dave's membership in a fraternal lodge. Sarah and Dave no longer picnicked in Prospect Park or other city parks. They voted regularly, but intraparty competition among left-liberals diminished in the wake of the McCarthy era, and 1950s elections were more often uncontested. Politicians went on forever. John Cashmore served as Brooklyn Borough president from 1940 until his death in 1961. Eugene Keogh was our local congressman from 1937 to 1966. The Democratic machine was loyal to its adherents. Our local ward heeler, a lawyer named Joe Herbstman, could be counted on to get rid of my father's parking tickets or summonses to jury duty. Every Election Day, he dropped off a few hundred ballot cards and paid me, aged eight or nine, five dollars to slip them under every doorway in the neighboring streets. The ties of citizenship forged by shared sacrifice during World War II paled before the economic prosperity of the postwar boom years. Now it was through their work and spending that Dave and Sarah were most connected with the larger stories of American society—as producers and consumers, rather than as citizens.

The early 1960s were an unexpectedly calm moment in their long contest with uncertainty and anxiety. Dave could keep his head down and make a good living. "Capital H" History, the major events of their time, could only visit the household through the Magnavox television, and not through the front door, as the pogroms, the Depression, and World War II had. When Sarah spoke with friends about their lives, it was invariably about biological milestones (births, marriages, and deaths; illnesses and recoveries; children's achievements) rather than public events. If you asked her to describe their lives at this moment, she would reply with incidents of family life: "Richard got into Stuyvesant. Our granddaughter Ilene is enjoying school. Beverly is having the living room painted." National problems were not worth mentioning, and the issues closer to home— their son's inattentiveness, their son-in-law's irresponsibility, their daughter's frustrations with her marriage—were not to be shared. They lived in what one could call "peacetime," which we in the frenzied 2020s can barely remember.

But stable as Bradford Street was for Dave and Sarah, it was not detached from the forces transforming the lives of other Americans beyond their neighborhood. History catches up to us when we are least suspecting it. Sometimes it comes as a shock, like the fall of France in 1940. But more often it happens when a dozen apparently independent currents—some of them economic, others demographic, social, and cultural, all of them touching in some way on commerce, law, and government—converge into a wide stream. And then, one or two triggering events, like a sudden storm or the collapse of a dam, overwhelm the banks and flood the nearby communities. Changes that each appear tangential to millions of people can, when they converge, crush individual families like the Rabinowitzes. The security they had constructed, the defenses against change they had erected, can disintegrate in a moment.

When I was sixteen, I spent the summer at an international boys' camp in Rhinebeck, New York, and many of my evenings were devoted to high-flown philosophical debates about who or what was responsible for major historical transformations—and the important personal choices we might have to make as we grew older. During that summer, the East German Communist government built a wall to divide Berlin. Everyone was afraid of what was coming. As we gathered around campfires, all this cohort of bright adolescents could do was talk, as pretentiously and assertively as possible, about parallel incidents and current alternatives. We tossed out names and events haphazardly and imprecisely—Napoleon and Hitler, the Black Plague and the Battle of Britain, the Supreme Court decision in *Brown v. Board of Education* and the Kaiser's U-boat offensive in 1917—bits of secondary-school learning and teenage melodramatics.

At the end of that summer, we each went back to our separate homes and our personal concerns. But, to be sure, the Berlin Wall standoff did leave its mark in several ways. Globally, it reinforced the immediacy and danger of the Cold War rivalry between the United States and the Soviet Union. More personally, it aroused and renewed the patriotism I felt listening to John Kennedy's inaugural address six months earlier. It strengthened my desire to "live in capital-H History" and to follow closely the big stories—Sputnik, NASA, Kennedy and Nixon, the Bay of Pigs, and so on—as if they were the "real meaning" of my life. But meanwhile I was missing the big story happening closer to my family, one of much greater significance but harder to discern amid the headline news. My childhood home, my parents' secure refuge, was being uprooted. And my attention was elsewhere.

New York, my hometown, was on the edge of an upheaval. Where does that story start? The mechanization of agriculture in the southern United States after World War II—cotton, rice, and sugar in Mississippi and Louisiana, fruits and vegetables in Florida and Georgia—displaced many Black farmworkers and revived a decades-long Great Migration that filled the working-class housing of northern cities. Jim Crow laws, legitimating discrimination and outbreaks of violence, shattered family ties to the land and their community. Similar push-and-pull factors triggered a massive migration of Puerto Rican citizens to the New York metropolitan area. They moved first to the Upper West Side of Manhattan, from which they were displaced by gentrification to ghettoes in Brooklyn and the Bronx. With a further influx of Black and Brown factory and dockside workers during the war itself, central Brooklyn, including Bedford-Stuyvesant and Brownsville, grew to outpace Harlem as the largest nonwhite neighborhood in New York City.

New York City surrendered its title as the great industrial metropolis of North America. Manufacturing jobs began a decades-long out-migration, often assisted by an unresponsive municipal government. The city instead encouraged and welcomed dozens of headquarters of Fortune 500 companies. Two hundred major new buildings, many of them along the avenues on Manhattan's East Side, added 67 million square feet of office space, twice as large as the next nine American cities combined. The shift from manufacturing to office and service jobs undermined the prospects of many local nonwhite workers, whose education and job skills could not meet their requirements. The Brooklyn Navy Yard, for example, which had employed 71,000 people during the war, closed entirely in 1966.

Almost no private housing had been built in the city since the onset of the Great Depression. World War II veterans returned home to find available only an old, tired, and fast-deteriorating supply of apartments in central Brooklyn and the Bronx. These neighborhoods also housed thousands of new, mostly nonwhite migrants to the city. The stock of housing was further depleted by the expansion of commercial and institutional buildings, as well as highways, which fractured and displaced poorer communities throughout the city. What could be done?

In response, the federal and city governments adopted policies and practices that effectively sorted and segregated New York's working-class, lower middle-class, and middle-class populations by race. Federal programs like the GI Bill, Federal Housing Administration loans, and funding for expressway construction encouraged the exodus of veterans and their families to whites-only suburban housing developments along the edges of Brooklyn and Queens, and throughout Long Island. Sarah's cousins took advantage of these programs to resettle in Elmont and Valley Stream, nearby suburbs on Long Island.

Sarah's two brothers, Sam and Isaac, newly married, lacked the funds and the ambition to escape to the suburbs. They remained in run-down Brownsville tenements through the early 1950s. By that time, the city's "urban renewal" and "slum clearance" programs were in full swing. The New York City Housing Authority embarked on a huge public housing program, most of it fitting the modernist design of "towers in the park." Thousands of Brownsville apartments were demolished and replaced by new "housing projects" for low-income residents, almost entirely Black and Puerto Rican, as well as better-constructed and -maintained projects for middle-income families, mostly white. NYCHA built more low-income housing projects in Brownsville than anywhere else in the city. For Sam and Isaac, and their young families, NYCHA provided an excellent alternative. In 1956, they both had moved to Bay View, an especially fine middle-income project in Canarsie, surrounded largely by white families.

As the reconstruction of Brownsville proceeded, many of those displaced moved farther east, into East New York. By the early 1960s, Black families had occupied almost all the apartments in buildings like 502 Alabama Avenue in East New York, where the Schwartzes and Rabinowitzes had lived for a decade until 1948. Poorer white families, aging in place after the more prosperous had departed for the suburbs, felt threatened by the arrival of younger Black and Puerto Rican families. The average age of East New York residents in the mid-1960s fell to 18, about ten years lower than in neighboring, still predominantly white areas. Forgetting that their own children, decades earlier, had also used the streets and alleys as playing fields, many Jews, Poles, and Italians complained to politicians and the press about "noisy and disrespectful" teenagers. The term "juvenile delinquents," incessantly termed a "horde" or a "pestilence" by New York's tabloid newspapers and local news broadcasts, became so common it was abbreviated to "JDs." The city's vocational schools were outdated, disconnected from new technologies and patterns of hiring and training. Jobs were scarce for young people. City budgets allocated not a cent for new schools, parks, or other community improvements in East New York in the whole decade after 1958. Public services—sanitation, street repair, emergency responders—all dwindled. The transformation of East New York was rapid. In 1960, 85 percent of its 100,000 people were white. Just six years later, 80 percent were Black or Puerto Rican.

Dave and Sarah were not demographers. They did not study the numbers in the federal census or the city's neighborhood surveys. During my youth in East New York, from the end of World War II to 1962 (when I left for college), New York City's newspapers paid little attention to the area. For the moment, Dave and Sarah remained comfortable on Bradford Street. They were little alarmed by the changes in their neighborhood. Their daily lives were largely unchanged. The YM & YWHA—the "Y"—was still flourishing. The streets like Bradford, east of Pennsylvania Avenue, were filled with well-kept two- and six-family houses, only thirty or thirty-five years old and fully occupied. No one would dare imagine their being demolished and replaced by towers. Granddaughter Ilene began elementary school in 1962 in the same building Beverly and I had attended. The city had shored up the racial balance, so to speak, of East New York by constructing two middle-income housing developments for predominantly white families on the land south of Linden Boulevard. Many of my junior high school classmates lived in these safe and well-managed buildings.

Still, there were danger signs. In the fall of 1962, the city's Commission on Human Rights began to investigate blockbusting in East New York, a practice in which realtors persuaded homeowners to sell quickly and cheaply, warning them that an imminent "invasion" of their streets by Black families would depress housing values, and then reselling these homes to nonwhite people at enormously inflated prices. Perhaps Dave and Sarah were in denial. In a sense, they relied upon racial discrimination to keep their neighborhood stable. How could Black families get approved for mortgages to buy one of the houses on Bradford Street? Although my elementary school classmates and I dutifully deposited one dollar each Thursday in a passbook account at the East New York Savings Bank, that institution refused to offer mortgages in its own neighborhood. East New York had long been redlined by bankers. The bank preferred to finance the construction and sale of houses on Long Island.

Beverly recalls that the first sign of change in her parents' attitude came when she broached the idea of buying a weekend house at Montauk, on the eastern tip of Long Island. Dad instead encouraged her to invest in a new full-time home outside the city. He had an inkling that Brooklyn would soon become less safe, less desirable, for a family with two young children. By 1964, she had moved to a new housing development in Spring Valley, in Rockland County. Not long after, a robber broke into the back rooms of the Bradford Street house one evening while Sarah and Dave were out. Only Bubbe's watch and an old ring were stolen, but the thief was never caught. Without evidence, the police and my parents assumed that the robbery had something to do with the "changing racial situation" on these streets.

When I was leaving my high school girlfriend's home in the Crown Heights neighborhood, I would wait in her hallway as she watched for the approaching B10 bus going back to East New York. Seeing the bus, she would rush to warn me, and I would race to the bus stop across the street. Standing alone and vulnerable on a dark Brooklyn street was unwise on a fall or winter evening. Whites and Blacks, Jews and Puerto Ricans, had carved out side-by-side spaces, parallel tracks, in and through East New York. Though the schools were technically integrated, as far as their total population was concerned, junior and senior high school classes were usually composed of one group or the other. The honors program at Thomas Jefferson High School, which most of my childhood friends attended, was still almost exclusively a Jewish domain in the early 1960s.

Every summer, television images of riots, as close as Harlem in 1964 and as far away as Watts, Los Angeles, in 1965, generated more fear in East New York. In the summer of 1964, a street battle between Italian and Black youths broke out only a mile from the house. Two years later, on the evening of July 21, 1966, an eleven-year-old Black child was shot and killed during a fracas at the same corner. In the ensuing days, Mayor John Lindsay walked the East New York streets, appealing for calm, and the police presence in the neighborhood was intensified. The mayor was jeered by white residents. In the next two or three years, almost the entire Italian population north of New Lots Avenue abandoned East New York. That came as a shock. Legend had it that "Italian-Americans would always hold onto their streets." They had done so on Albert Avenue in the Bronx and in Bay Ridge and Bensonhurst in Brooklyn. Leaving East New York sent a message to the remaining Jews nearby. Slowly, subtly, Jews began to define themselves as white, having more in common with Italian and Polish Catholics than with other minorities.

Would East New York be the next tinderbox of urban unrest? Some of the stores on New Lots Avenue went out of business. Others, like the pharmacies, built prisonlike enclosures around their service counters. The selection of foods in the groceries began to reflect the tastes of Black and Hispanic residents. Even so, Dave and Sarah were not "panic-merchants," in the argot of the day. They learned to take precautions. Dave stopped shopping for clothes on Pitkin Avenue. He and Sarah stopped patronizing their favorite Chinese restaurant on Sutter Avenue, the one Dave used always to celebrate as "a great place—every time I come in I find money on the tables." Around 1958, a new modern supermarket opened on Linden Boulevard, four blocks from our house, so Sarah could avoid the signs of distress on New Lots.

The shifting demography of East New York felt to Sarah and Dave, and to their neighbors, like a natural event, akin to the rising sea levels or summertime high temperatures before anyone had coined the phrase "climate change." It happened "in the course of things." No one could do anything about it. That was, in fact, anything but true. Greed and corruption, stupid and short-sighted public policy all played a part. But Bradford Street's fear and passivity also contributed to the loss of their community.

Capitalizing on the fear generated by news coverage of urban riots, underscored by stories of violence in their own neighborhood, East New Yorkers in the mid-1960s were inundated by the blockbusting campaign. John, our long-serving postman, complained that his mailbag was weighed down with postcards urgently inviting owners to have their homes assessed for potential sale. These gave way to repeated phone calls—first at dinnertime, then (more ominously) at ten or eleven o'clock at night. At first they were friendly suggestions about cashing in on the value of these houses and putting the savings away for retirement. And then came the warnings: "You don't want to be the last one on your block!" "How would you feel to live on a street where every other house was occupied by *schvartzes* [the derogatory Yiddish term for Blacks]?" (Among non-Jewish residents, the N-word served a similar purpose.) Property values would collapse, our neighbors were told. It was a sociological truism, though probably easily disproved, that mixing races would lead to declining real estate values.

All this might have played out over the course of a decade. The real key to awakening the sleepy housing market in East New York was, in fact, an audacious conspiracy of corruption, masterminded by a crafty mortgage broker named Harry Bernstein of Eastern Service Corporation. Bernstein knew that the Federal Housing Administration would provide government guarantees for mortgages issued to minority purchasers under certain conditions. If you were able to inflate the value of the house for sale, and also inflate the credit-worthiness of the prospective buyer, an FHA guarantee would provide Bernstein and other speculators with enormous profits. Simple bribery did the trick. Here's how it worked. Bernstein would reward a local FHA inspector handsomely for appraising a house at twice its market value (say to $20,000). Similarly, a fat envelope of cash could "persuade" a Dun & Bradstreet auditor to certify that a plumber's assistant in Bedford-Stuyvesant (earning, say, $100 a week) was really earning $10,000 a year as an auto mechanic. Now, on Bernstein's mortgage application at least, this "entirely credit-worthy" purchaser could meet the FHA income requirement, which was one-half of the purchase price. Eastern Service would then charge a closing fee often ten or fifteen times the legal allowance of one percent. Lastly, Bernstein would offload the mortgage onto the federal Fannie Mae and Ginnie Mae housing-loan underwriters. When the plumber's helper failed to make the mortgage payments, the government was stuck with the foreclosed property.

As the scheme progressed, the harmony of our once tightly knit band of householders on Bradford Street dissolved. In June 1967, the Bradford Street dominoes began to fall. One by one, the neighbors stole away, often with scarcely a goodbye. In less than a year, the block had completely turned over. Harry Bernstein's Eastern Service Corporation bought houses to our left and to our right. Sarah and Dave Rabinowitz were among the last Jewish home-owners on the block, selling their house in March 1968 to James Walker, an African American machinist at the New York City Transit Authority, who was still living there twenty years later. But many of Mr. Walker's new neighbors could not handle the mortgage debt, and turnover in the surrounding streets was even higher. In the end, many Black and Puerto Rican families, purchasers and tenants, lost their homes and their life savings to the scandal. The illegal schemes of Bernstein and associates also eviscerated many of Brooklyn's white and mixed ethnic neighborhoods, displacing thousands of families and abandoning over sixteen hundred Brooklyn houses to federal receivership and ultimate ruin. Ten firms and forty people were indicted in what the federal attorneys called a "monumental scandal." Harry Bernstein, his wife, and the chief underwriter of the local FHA office were convicted of fraud, though Dun & Bradstreet escaped punishment. The federal government lost $250 million in the scheme, equal to about $1.8 billion in 2020 terms.

The Bradford Street neighbors did little to resist the destruction of their community. They did not help organize a block association to keep one another informed and to prepare a common resistance to blockbusting. They did not join the Council for a Better East New York, a coalition of community organizations striving to protect the mixed-class composition of East New York. Even when Sarah's friend Sylvia Gilbert, a doctor's wife and also a leader of the women's committee at the local Y, became president of the CBENY in 1962, Sarah never joined her at a meeting. East New York had other strong supporters of racial integration, who formed the United Community Centers in 1954. But none of the Bradford Street neighbors, even those who shared a leftist inclination toward social welfare, joined the UCC's work. By the middle of the 1960s, the leadership of these groups was fragmented and ineffective. No one discussed the UCC over mah-jongg games in the Bradford Street houses.

The Bradford Street neighbors dispersed to high-rise co-ops on the edges of the city, in Coney Island, the Rockaways, or the southeast Bronx. One or two went to live near married children in New Jersey or Long Island. What happened to our neighborhood is often described as "white flight." But this term seems inadequate and simplistic. These were not young householders eager to send their children to safer, whiter suburban schools. They were not dissatisfied with the housing they occupied. They did not dream of gardens, patios, or sparkling new kitchens. No one on Bradford Street was ready to retire. Politically, their generation of Jews cared deeply about equal opportunity in education, housing, and employment. They did not feel that Black and Brown families had been well treated, or that they undeservedly took advantage of government supports. Quite the opposite. Many of them would have backed greater public help for minority families, even if it meant higher taxes. Having grown up feeling themselves marginalized in a city and country still dominated by a Christian public culture—in political language, music, and holiday celebrations, for example—they did not feel so comfortable talking about themselves as "white" people.

Why did they fold their cards and flee so readily? Though they were homeowners, in their hearts they never stopped being transients. Like their immigrant parents, their end goals would be reached not within their own lifetimes, but within those of their children. (And there were few school-age children left on the block by the mid-1960s.) They would sacrifice almost any attachment, other than to their family, in order to survive. As small, independent businessmen, members of the petty bourgeoisie, they had no centuries-old organizations or foundations to mobilize in their defense. This was not their ancestral land. No one had a long history here. I never heard anyone express an ounce of pride in being an East New Yorker. Their synagogues had no experience in the public sphere, nor any inclination to resist change. The women of East New York had worked together successfully for community improvement, but they had no models for resisting assaults by outsiders. Conflict terrified Jewish families, as speculators and bankers well knew. To the historian in me, my community resembled most the shtetl Jews of Ukraine and Poland overrun by the Soviet Union in 1939–1941, with each family abandoning the local *kehillah,* or Jewish leadership council, and fending for itself.

In the event, as Black families moved in, Sarah tried to be receptive and positive. I believe that my parents would have actually welcomed a few stereotypically "sober and hard-working" Black families as neighbors, but they were fearful of being "surrounded" and isolated. Sarah felt that the young Black children in her neighborhood were at least as polite as her kids and our friends had been, and probably more so. She felt betrayed by her closest friends, who sold their houses without even a word. The hurt was deep. It meant the loss of all that they had collectively worked for—building the East New York YM & YWHA, getting funding out of Albany for a new junior high school and a handsome new branch library.

The social capital amassed by these local activist mothers had been cashed in by the municipal authorities and the banks for their own purposes. The "Y" was sold or given to the city. In the 1970s, the Boulevard Houses and the Linden Houses, across Linden Boulevard from Bradford Street, suffered rapid disinvestment from the New York City Housing Authority. They soon became frightening, crime-ridden places. The families of my schoolmates who lived there fled. Repeated foreclosures on Bradford Street and surrounding blocks led to destabilization of the neighborhood, with many of these properties sold again and again. The storefront businesses on New Lots Avenue shut down and sold out, quickly leaving the neighborhood a food desert. This area, the 75th Precinct overseen by the New York Police Department, became the "murder capital" of the city, with over a hundred slayings each year in the 1970s and 1980s.

The displacement of the established Jewish and Italian communities in East New York signaled the failure of the hierarchical politics of the city's Democratic Party "machine." Bradford Street's loyalty to the ward heelers, district leaders, and county committee members was not reciprocated. The failure in housing was part of a larger pattern of failure in city government. Just at this moment, Black and Latino parents were growing increasingly restive about the slow pace of school integration. Civic groups and alliances across racial lines consistently reported the failure of New York's Board of Education to relieve the isolation of minority students in low-performing schools. Slowly the demand for "community control" began to emerge—most explosively in terms of local schools but also in terms of other aspects of municipal life—housing, parks and recreation, sanitation, transit, and so on. Decentralization became a mantra in New York and across the country. Just after Dave and Sarah had left Bradford Street in the fall of 1968, the plan to create an experimental, community-controlled school district in nearby Ocean Hill–Brownsville, with local authority over hiring and curriculum, was ferociously contested by the predominantly white (and largely Jewish) United Federation of Teachers. After three teachers' strikes, the union's position on job security was solidified.

But the drive for citizen participation in community planning continued to strengthen in East New York. Despite the daunting challenges of poverty, the Black community slowly rallied in the 1970s and after, as the Jews had not during the 1960s. By 1975, the existing community boards, composed of volunteer members, were provided with district managers and given a role in the review of land use proposals, including changes in zoning. The energized members of Rev. Johnny Ray Youngblood's Saint Paul Community Baptist Church, just four blocks from Bradford Street, modeled the process for other churches, renewing the physical and social environment of my old neighborhood. Founded in 1979, East Brooklyn Congregations, rooted in the neighborhood's churches, has used innovative combinations of public, private, and philanthropic funds to build over 5,000 new housing units modeled on the low-rise 1920s scale of areas like Bradford Street rather than the high-rise public housing of the 1960s. The group has invested in new schools, renewed park facilities, and dozens of other neighborhood improvements. United Community Centers, a long-established and now revived organization, has initiated new health-care programs, created a farm on disused land, and established a farmers' market to improve the nutritional health of residents. It has been a tireless advocate for preserving the community against the threats of commercial mega-development. Severe problems persist in the neighborhood, but the contrast between the failures of the community in the 1960s and the energetic response of the past forty years is instructive.

After twenty years, with the mortgage paid, the Rabinowitz house at 742 Bradford Street had appreciated in value only minimally, from $13,500 to $18,000. (It might have sold in 2020 for $500,000.) Sarah and Dave moved to an apartment at Dayton Towers West, on 102nd Street in Rockaway, in 1968. Their housing was brand new, and its appliances were sparkling, but the place was not larger or more commodious than the house in East New York. There was no similar community in Rockaway, no "Y" in which to gather, no civic causes to fight for. On the third floor of a twelve-story building of a hundred apartments, all that connected Sarah and Dave to fellow residents were the corridors and elevators. The neighbors were friendly, but they were often decades younger, and many of them were not Jewish. They missed the point of Dave's jokes and had never heard, for example, of the kidnapping of the Lindbergh baby. After twenty years, Sarah and Dave were once again without peers.

The move undid Sarah's self-esteem as a housekeeper. Nothing could have been more hurtful. She now relied entirely on Dave to drive her to and from shopping. Her cherished daily routine was shattered. Instead of filling the Union Supply Company orders in their own basement, intermittently, she now had to accompany Dave for the whole business day at a rented storefront in Ozone Park, Queens. Instead of a homecooked meal, served on their own table, Sarah had to prepare a lunch for reheating on an electric hot plate, as if they were squatters or vagabonds. Every time she spooned Maxim freeze-dried coffee into water boiled on the hot plate, she sighed with regret. While Dave was out taking orders from customers or filling them at the storefront, Sarah was on her own most of every day, waiting for the possibility that a trucker would deliver a dozen cartons of Bromo Seltzer or Royal Crown hair pomade. She was terribly lonely. In her memory, the only tolerable days at the storefront came when a grandchild was left with her for overnight or longer visits. Even the nicest Italian-American neighbors at the storefront in Queens were not her kind of folks. After a year or two, the landlord refused to renew their lease. Then Dave had to relocate all the shelving and all the merchandise once again. Sarah lost the pleasures of her own space. She had much less time to herself, and though Dave was a bit less stormy, she could never entirely set her protective raincoat aside.

Even at home she was frustrated. Sarah did not love living near the beach in Rockaway. From childhood she was a devout people-watcher, but observing beachgoers often made her nauseated. Naturally a modest person, she was not at all tolerant of the obesity she witnessed among walkers along the boardwalk. She hated seeing people eat junk food. Her favorite word in Yinglish soon became *hallucious,* something revolting or atrocious (derived from *a chaloshes,* to faint). She would hold her stomach, as if to prevent herself from regurgitating the scene. Dave could sit for hours on the apartment balcony, called the "terrace," but Sarah felt almost immediately uncomfortable, endlessly assaulted by sand carried on the persistent offshore winds.

Where were Beverly and I while all this was happening?

Beverly's move to the suburbs proved to be a terrible trap. In 1962 and 1963, she had explored a lot of options around the city, even including the Upper West Side (Manhattan) Urban Renewal Area. But city life was a little too far a stretch. Beverly set her goal on a place in the Five Towns on Long Island's South Shore, but her husband insisted on living near several easily accessible and affordable golf courses. He preferred the newly developing Rockland County courses to the well-established, high-ticket ones on Long Island. While in Brooklyn, Beverly had begun to take night courses at Brooklyn College in history, anthropology, and English literature. As long as it wasn't a full-time responsibility, Mom had pitched in to babysit. Beverly loved her studies and did well. But moving to the suburbs put an end to Beverly's college adventure. Rockland Community College did not have what she could find at Brooklyn. In a matter of months, as the family settled in, she began to feel stifled. Thankfully, her parents assumed the role of super grandparents and mechanics, appearing every other weekend with a station wagon full of bagels and lox, cookie tins, and hand tools to install lighting fixtures. As Beverly's husband spent more and more time on the links, Dad quipped to me, without smiling, that "your brother-in-law plays golf three income brackets above himself."

I was engrossed in college and graduate school, studying American history and literature (but not the culture and experience of my own American people) and producing plays at college and during my summers. All through the mid-1960s, personal transformations absorbed so much of my energy—forming and breaking relationships, surviving a dangerous cancer scare, worrying and strategizing over the military draft, starting a career in museum work. And, of course, it was also a tumultuous time for my nation, with the struggle over the civil rights crusade, the war in Vietnam, and the emergence of a countercultural resistance to established power in the state, the economy, and educational institutions. Cambridge, Massachusetts, in the 1960s hardly left me the brain space to think about my parents' lives in Brooklyn. I believed that I had absorbed what I could from their loving nurturance, and I was now on my own. What they had given me could be safely deposited in my memory, perhaps one day to be extracted and examined—but not much and not then.

Was this my "assimilation" in its purest form? With a Harvard degree, my entrée to a distinct new culture was secure. It was wrapped in a theatrical veneer of Anglo-conformity—the Georgian architecture of our dorms, talk of "house masters," "common rooms," and "senior tutors," and the requirement that we wear coats and ties to all meals. But the experiential heart of the culture for me was not this obeisance to Oxbridge traditions, but rather the permission to think deeply and share my curiosity without embarrassment. I lived among minds worth treasuring, and I learned as much from my roommates' courses as from my own. We all knew, of course, that there was another, more exclusive Harvard, with many legacy admissions, final clubs (Harvard's version of fraternities), and a rumored demi-monde of rowdiness. In eight years of undergraduate and graduate school, I almost never crossed into that world. Our fun came in biting wit, vicious satire, and silly self-deprecation. My studies and my subsequent museum work did not require that I forgo my New York Jewish identity. I brought the whole package along with me: my street smarts verging on an intensity often daunting to others, a self-confidence verging on arrogance, and a collection of social and intellectual skills useful for both collaboration and antagonism.

But it is true that Harvard made its peculiar, elite culture seem normal and authoritative. In those days before identity politics, we could be what we wanted to be on the inside, as long as we respected the "normality" of Harvard's veneer. We could come with distinctive backgrounds and experiences, but at the tutorials and in the seminar room we spoke only a common academic language. The American history and literature I studied, for example, tended to focus most on what had happened, what had been written, and what had been studied by the Puritans and their offspring in New England. I'm sure that I would have had a different and more difficult time if I had insisted on observing kashrut and Shabbat. For nonwhite students and scholars, for my female classmates, for those who were gay, even for those who were the first in their families to go to college, as I was, but who hadn't had the lucky experience of my high school amid New York's life and culture—for all of them Harvard paid little respect, made little provision, and was mostly deaf to their gifts. Still, for all that, I did not become another person. I did not for a moment consider turning Rabinowitz into Roberts or Raven, as all my father's brothers had done, and I insistently sprinkled bits of Yiddish into my proper conversation and writing.

My scholarly and professional work, oddly enough, focused on lessons that I could not apply to the world I knew best, back in Brooklyn. In a chapter of my senior thesis, I explained that Herman Melville had, over the course of his writing career, redefined the concept of memory. In his earliest books, he portrayed memory as a static depository, a "bank vault." By his later books, remembering had become a dynamic, up-thrusting disturbance in one's conscious mind, a "fountain." And yet, as I've said, I could not see that my parents' words and actions would not rest in some quiet, unmoving corner of my mind but, instead, would rush forward from time to time, and like a fountain, explode into my thought and action. I knew the concept, but I acted as if it were irrelevant to my own case.

I went to work at Old Sturbridge Village, an outdoor museum of nineteenth-century rural New England life, where I tried to interpret the balancing act of Yankee farmers between a fierce independence and self-reliance ("Good fences make good neighbors"), on the one hand, and a strict adherence to communal norms ("Best not do that, mistah!"), on the other. And yet, I could make no connection between this and the dilemma my parents were confronting two hundred miles to the south, in feeling that their deep communal attachments were being betrayed by the isolating, egotistical behavior of their most treasured friends and neighbors.

I realize now that I was substituting metaphors—"vault," "fountain," "balance," "fences"—for the real objects of ordinary life. I could no longer touch the daily materiality of Sarah's and Dave's lives. I didn't witness firsthand the stuff they moved from Brooklyn to Rockaway, and which familiar touchstones of my childhood they tossed away. The dinette table on which we all ate and where I did homework for a dozen years, the stand under the telephone I used to ask my girlfriends for dates, the office desk, with its fold-down drawer for a typewriter, that Dad bought for five dollars when I finally got my own bedroom, the linoleum flooring in the kitchen on which I mastered the spinning of tops, the vanity on which my mother's army of perfume bottles were arrayed—all gone. I didn't observe these losses, and I didn't spend time mourning them. My business now was more to make sense and less to use my own senses, to write about cultural preoccupations and not employment occupations. Whether I was costumed to portray a New England country lawyer to the visitors at Old Sturbridge Village or hunched over a Harvard library table to read eighteenth-century sermons, I was a detached interpreter.

Many years later, Mom and Dad expressed their disappointment that I "had shut them out." To be sure, this separation had begun years earlier, during my secretive, supercilious, and pubescent "secession" from the household's focus on making and spending money. How could I explain, especially during their terrible crisis months of 1967–1968, why I was inattentive to their problems? I don't think I was cruel. My ears were full, listening to President Johnson remove himself from a candidacy for re-election, rallying for Gene McCarthy and then Bobby Kennedy in a crusade against the Vietnam War and for social justice. My emotions were drained, time and again, by the headline news: the assassinations of Martin Luther King and Bobby Kennedy, the rioting that followed King's death, the violence at the Democratic National Convention, the protests at the Olympics, and the dreadful political campaign. And, *mitten drinnen* (in the midst of all that), as one might say in Yiddish, my own March 1968 was taken up with a whirlwind romance that led to a wedding and a child.

Far away from my self-absorption, my parents went on with their adjustment to life in a high-rise apartment building. Sarah's peer group was now spread over the littoral edge of Brooklyn. Arranging weekend get-togethers was harder. They were less informal, more like planned reunions. Former neighbors could not just "drop by," or come in for a cup of coffee and a piece of cake. They had to drive over, find parking spaces (a challenge in summer, when they were competing with beachgoers), and bring along store-bought chocolates or cookies instead of leftovers direct from their own kitchens. Those summer evenings on the shared front porches were entirely gone. The jokes sounded stale, the atmosphere felt forced, the pain of the betrayal still stung.

Coincidentally, Dave's Union Supply Company business also began to founder. The routine was increasingly exhausting—unpacking shipments from manufacturers and distributors, loading up the red ten-ton truck every morning, and driving the truck to small groceries along the backstreets of towns in Queens and Long Island. It was a long day and not as easy at age fifty-five as it had been at forty. So Dave adapted. He decided on another plan: pick up an order, return to the rented storage space in Ozone Park, fill the order, and deliver it to the customers in a smaller Ford Econoline van. That was less physically demanding, but the to-and-fro trips to each store also implied servicing fewer customers. Of such decisions were headaches made.

Dave could never figure out how to hire someone to help with deliveries or phone orders. In any case, he soon found himself under pressure from competitors. Into the market marched companies like Hudson Distributing, operating a dozen step vans from a central warehouse with several dozen employees. They began to poach Dave's customers. Hudson offered promotional and quantity discounts that Dave could not match. His frustration grew and grew, and the pressure on Sarah became almost intolerable.

The expulsion from Bradford Street had knocked the props out of Sarah's and Dave's lives. There they had integrated their work and social lives, their civic life, and their personal identities. Now they needed to scramble in order to reconnect these broken pieces. That effort undermined their always-fragile confidence. Eventually, it was all too much, and they began in 1974 to dissolve the business—selling off the stock, getting rid of the delivery van, mulling over their future. Once again, as twenty years earlier, Dave and Sarah were in limbo. They were only sixty and fifty-eight years old. They decided to leave Rockaway and anchor themselves near Beverly, in Spring Valley. They lived in a small rental apartment at Blueberry Hill, not far from a market to which Sarah could walk, and a ten-minute drive from Beverly's house.

Dissolving the supply business in 1974 was the third major moment of economic crisis in Dave's adult life. In early married life, he had barely sustained his livelihood as a peddler. In the 1950s, he had wandered for years amid the ruins of his jewelry business. Now he was again "out on his bum," as he would say. Dave still ached to be a breadwinner, but he did not have the energy to start a new business or find one to revive. Instead, he began applying for jobs. He discovered that the job market had changed a great deal since the 1930s and 1940s. He had no experience matching his talents to someone else's business. He had never learned to type or to operate the business machines that filled local offices. He worked for a few months for a producer of file labels, but when the company closed he was out of a job. His son-in-law tried to interest him in several businesses, like making custom kitchen cabinets, but both Sarah and Dave were wary of losing their nest egg in such ventures. And Spring Valley was even more barren than Rockaway. It was a wearying trip into the city, undertaken less and less often. Making new friends in this complex of garden apartments was difficult. Their granddaughters were increasingly busy with their own lives, and the older one, Ilene, soon went off to college. Sarah and Dave felt empty, or rather emptied, of significance. Without a job, Dave constantly disrupted Sarah's housekeeping. He was always in the way.

Although Beverly had a much closer relationship with Mom than I did, she could never honestly disclose how frustrated she was becoming in her marriage. In retrospect, Beverly's path looks like a coherent, but hidden and difficult, plan to reinvent herself. It started soon after moving to the suburbs. Reviving her lifelong interest in design, Beverly began to scout out the antique shops north of the city. Then she enrolled in a two-year-long interior design course in Manhattan. Finally, she went to work selling furniture and advising on interiors at an Ethan Allen furniture store in Stamford, Connecticut, which gave her valuable experience in marketing. At a critical juncture, she also realized that the social life she and her husband had built around country-club friendships was vapid. Beverly and Harvey had little to do with each other. He dismissed her creative efforts. A break came with the closure of his employer, an automobile import company. Without telling her, he invested all of his $2,500 severance payment in country club dues. It was a breaking point. Many years later, Beverly could say that her ex-husband had "chosen golf over God," that is, over membership in a local synagogue and an attachment to a more thoughtful community than what came with three rounds of eighteen holes and half a dozen gin-and-tonics.

In 1976, she made the decision to separate from him and move to California with her younger daughter, Sharon. Ilene was already enrolled at the University of California at Santa Barbara. Beverly was 39, restarting her life after twenty years of marriage. In her handbag she carried the slender proceeds of the sale of the Spring Valley house—her only financial assets. She was eager to try out the skills she had kept under wraps since her twelfth year. Mom was devastated. Beverly was finally snapping the emotional tether to her mother. This seemed to Mom an impossible and suicidal decision. Dad, however, was more supportive. He could feel the excitement of Beverly's ambitions. Like him, she was a born salesperson, with a persuasive manner, an elegant appearance, and solid business sense.

Unlike him, she knew that she would have to cultivate strong contacts to pave the way to success.

As Beverly was deciding to move west, I was going in the opposite direction. My yearlong experiment with academic life, teaching at Scripps College in Claremont, California, had failed, and I missed the edginess of East Coast conversations. I found campus interactions stultifying, and suburban life in the heat and smog of southern California dreary. I missed the professional companionship of artists, artisans, and architects, and the relationships I had cultivated with innovative classroom teachers in my early museum career. When my wife was offered a good job in Boston, I quit my college teaching position. We drove slowly eastward, vowing to avoid interstate highways as much as possible, stopping at town halls and senior centers in one small town after another to learn about the country I was dedicated to interpreting as a historian. We arrived at Spring Valley just in time to wish Beverly well on her move west, and continued on to Boston. We bought a box spring, a mattress, and a cheap Sony television, and we settled in to watch the 1976 election returns.

Dad helped Beverly pack her belongings for her great escape while Mom sulked at their nearby apartment. When they drove Beverly and Sharon to the airport, Sarah was in tears. She insisted on boarding the plane, where Beverly was already seated. (In those days, airport security was not so strict.) Weeping uncontrollably, she embraced her daughter and granddaughter, crying, "Mamela, I won't ever see you again!" A few days earlier, as soon as the moving van had driven out of Beverly's driveway, Dave had resolved to leave the New York area, his lifelong home. Once Beverly was gone, he packed several suitcases filled with all the lightweight clothing they owned, some boxes of pots and pans, and their vital documents. He piled everything into his car and told Sarah to get in. They took off on a long drive to Florida. They would spend ten or twelve weeks reconnecting with the old Brooklyn crowd, many of whom had joined the exodus to the South, and then reconnoitering a new place to settle. The sixteen years since the Kennedy election had broken Sarah's dream of a family home. But after all the *tsuris* of the intervening years, 1976 ended with all of us starting life a thousand miles apart from one another, in new and happier places. Sarah's dream of an intact household, safe from intruders, would now never be fully realized. Dave's role as a provider for all would be only a memory.

Fed up with having to wind it, Dad took the clock to a local shop to remove the gedeyrem (the innards). The clock weights were gone, and in their place a nine-volt battery had been installed. It was now a clock that worked without its works.

11

Dave Never Has to Rewind the Clock

About a half-century after my mother, Sarah Rabinowitz, née Schwartz, purchased a bottle opener for her mother, I set out on a rainy Thanksgiving morning with my fourteen-year-old son, Jonathan, to visit my parents in Deerfield Beach, Florida. Dialing one car service after another, I wasted a good hour searching for a ride to the airport, until I reached Chatarra Cars of Brooklyn, a low-rent alternative. Our driver arrived, unshaven and unkempt. His vehicle looked equally unpromising. As we piled our travel bags into the trunk, which lacked a lock, our "chauffeur" confessed that he did not know the route to La Guardia. More disturbing, he asked if I wanted to drive. Worried but desperate, I assured him that I could direct him on this route. We got about a mile along, near the busy intersection of Flatbush and Tillary Streets, when the jalopy broke down completely, in the middle of the right-turn lane. We escaped the wreck, pulled our bags out, and stood in the rain, pitifully unprotected, the blameworthy target of a hundred horn-honking New Yorkers, until a yellow cab came to our rescue. He drove us to the Delta terminal, just in time to board.

The flight was uneventful. At Fort Lauderdale, we slid into our designated rental car and headed north on I-95. As only an occasional driver I excitedly drank in the challenge of expressway traffic, soon to discover that I was (a) stuck behind an elderly couple steaming along at 40 miles per hour in the left lane, and (b) surrounded left and right by a convoy of huge pickup trucks, each carrying an arsenal of rifles in their cargo beds.

We exited on Hillsborough Boulevard and came to the entry gate for Century Village. We waited for five or ten minutes, stalled behind a line of refrigerator-repair trucks, sheriff's deputies, airport shuttle buses, and other applicants for admission to the community. Given the multitude, I pondered how much security could actually be provided. At the guard desk, we offered the name and apartment number of my parents. A scratchy recording of my mother's voice came back, "Richard Rabinowitz is coming in." The guard pressed a button, the orange arm lifted, and we were "in."

Century Village East in Deerfield Beach (there are two others) consists of 254 buildings with about 8,500 apartments, arranged around a golf course. The landscape, with grass mowed to an inch of its life, was dotted with artificial ponds (their wetland edges hosting real live egrets), swimming pools (with showers and restrooms), and some tennis courts. At its center was the "Million-Dollar Clubhouse" (in 1970s dollars), which included a fitness center, indoor pool, crafts studios, classrooms, and a theater seating 1,600. Nothing in the design was indigenous to Florida. No trace of the land's history or former inhabitants remained. In fact, the design partook only of a modern landscape architect's catalog of reusable elements, the developer's vision of "an active lifestyle" for seniors, and the modest financial resources of its target population. The twenty-one areas were named, in the faux-English manner often ironically favored by legatees of the American Revolution, Ashby, Berkshire, Cambridge, Durham, and so on down the alphabet. But the buildings themselves looked nothing like British manor houses or the interwar urban apartment buildings many residents knew from youth. Instead the developers had adapted the design of the early postwar California garden apartment complex. Each building, of two or four stories, arranged a line of a dozen or so apartments along a covered walkway. Each floor was accessible by an outdoor staircase with open risers. The taller, four-story buildings, called "deluxe" or "luxury," were equipped with elevators. The buildings were constructed of pressed concrete forms, prefabricated and hoisted into place. Everything was painted toothpaste white, except that the doors of each building were painted in exactly the same distinctive color. The six buildings of Richmond all had blue front doors. The floors were a concrete slab, the windows of aluminum, the walls bare of baseboards or cornices. Plain, simple, unadorned, inexpensive to build and easy to keep clean.

Jonathan and I found our way to Richmond F, and we were careful to locate the parking space signposted "Guest." On an earlier trip, I had for a while occupied a space next to my dad's "346," in order to unload my suitcases. This intrusion on the assigned space of a neighbor, apparently, threatened to undermine the social harmony of the whole building, and I had to scurry down to move my car before I was indicted for trespassing and deported to New York. We took the elevator to the third floor. Mom was standing in the walkway, half in tears, as though we had sailed around the world in a little boat to reach her. We embraced. Jonathan got the usual comments about how manly he now looked. Dad noticed that I had sprouted grey hairs, closing the age difference between us. He pulled each of us to his chest in an emphatic bear hug, with a long, deep "ooh" for emphasis.

We put our bags inside the apartment and immediately faced Mom's welcoming interrogation, "What can I get you? Are you hungry? When did you eat? Was the traffic bad? How was the trip?"

Exactly in the reverse order of what was logical. "Go wash yourself up," she suggested, and we each made our way to the bathroom. By the time we returned to the dinette table, a dish of chopped liver, a plate of tomatoes, a tray of rye bread, and a bowl of homemade cole-slaw had appeared, along with an irregular assortment of knives, forks, napkins, and repeated invitations to "try this . . . tell me if it's good." Dad hovered nearby—he had evidently already eaten—and he supplied his assessment questions, "so how's the *Geschäft* [business)? And "now tell me, no fooling, Jonathan, are you doing well in school?" With Mom's delicious food filling our mouths, we didn't need to provide detailed responses.

Perhaps an hour and a half intervened between this welcoming snack and the proper Thanksgiving dinner. (I was glad that I had brought Jonathan on this trip, as his appetite masked the embarrassing modesty of the portions I was consuming.) Everyone sated, Mom finally taking a few nibbles of her own food—"not bad, not bad, if I say so myself"—the company split up. Dad and Jonathan adjourned to the sitting room, where they watched the NFL on television, my son providing sage comments on the coach's strategies and Dad denouncing the ineptitude of the defensive secondary and others. "Bunch of bums."

I helped Mom with the dishes, against her will, and then the two of us sat in the living room. She didn't ask, and probably didn't want to know, about the progress of my romantic life, which was a relief. We never were comfortable talking about relationships. Thankfully she didn't worry aloud about the effect of a divorce on Jonathan. He was perfect in her eyes. In any case, she was done with parenting, at least in my case. (She and Beverly had a more continuous dialogue, with advice passing in both directions.) We seemed to find a more convivial subject in "the way things are, nowadays." Mom would detail something she'd observed at the supermarket, or at the swimming pool. "Let me tell you something," she would always begin, as if she was slowly savoring a thought that had been cooking on her stove for days and days. "People now don't . . . the way we did *in di alt teg* (in the old days)." I felt as though she had been saving up these choice bits just for me. I was then called upon to mount this tiny gem in its properly jeweled setting. "Here's what I think is going on," I would start, summoning up the appropriate context in changing social mores, economic trends, technological advances, or consumer tastes. I was genuinely delighted by her sharp-eyed witnessing of everyday life, as acute as it had been in the shtetl, apparently, or in the East New York of my childhood. In turn, she was happy to have a historian for a son, or maybe just someone to listen to her so intently.

Unlike many of the interviewees with whom I had done oral histories, Mom avoided consolatory phrases. She never said things like "it will all work out," "it was all for the best," "you'll be fine," or "it was meant to happen." As I learned more about her early life, I noticed that she always conveyed a painful, unresolved undercurrent to her stories. Anti-Semitic pogroms, the stigma of being a newcomer, poverty, unemployment, helplessness in the face of illness—all of these were always close to the surface. When she complained that young people today have such a hard time making ends meet, the strain of her own household in East New York in 1937 was obviously on her mind. Even stories that should have been tinged with triumph could have a sad lining. Late in life, to give one example, she recounted a story from her earliest days in America.

When Papa took us to our first apartment in Brooklyn, we lived on the middle floor of a three-story building. The grandmother's room was on the top floor and her daughter and granddaughters lived down at street level. Each afternoon when

I got home from school, I would say hello to the old lady. She looked so lonely up there. I would go upstairs to read "Little Orphan Annie" aloud to her, practicing my English. She got such a kick out of the stories. And, you know, I wondered, why wouldn't her own grandchildren go up there and do that? She was so lonely.

Mom was the Empress of Empathy, but she wielded her authority with equal doses of anger and moralism.

In the evening, after a helping of applesauce and mandelbrot, the television again dominated. And once again, Jonathan's presence and his ability to laugh at sitcoms occupied Mom and Dad and allowed me to hide out with a book in the living room. Without Jonathan, I would have been inevitably drawn back to the dilemmas of my own fourteen-year-old self, when I found it hard to reject, courteously, my father's request to spend the evening with him in watching the boob tube. But instead of reading I mused about my parents' lives in Florida: What was important for them? How did they mark the passing of time? How did retirement alter their relationship?

There was no lingering around the breakfast table on the following morning. Before we got to digest the final spoonful of oatmeal or Cheerios and bananas, the real business of the day was announced: a shopping expedition. As she had all of her married life, Mom had plotted out (all in her mind) her sequence of meals for the next week and scribbled down her shopping lists. Some spaces were left in case she found that the necessary ingredients (especially fish and meat) were available on sale, or not available at all. Jonathan and I were given an out. "Relax, read the paper, you could use the rest-up," but we had already consumed the sports scores, the only valuable news in the local paper, and we wouldn't miss this hunting-and-gathering expedition for the world.

Dad brought out the granny cart to load into the car's trunk. He did not trust me to drive, so Jonathan and I piled into the back seat. The trip was well planned. Dad would drop Mom off at the Publix supermarket in the nearby shopping center and complete his banking business next door. Jonathan and I would check out the Sports Authority shop for bargain-rate sneakers, swimsuits, and other paraphernalia too expensive in gentrifying Brooklyn. After Mom was done and we had loaded her purchases into the car, we would all go to Pop's fish market, to J. J.'s fruit-and-vegetable stand, and home. Because we were visiting, Mom and Dad didn't expand this adventure beyond Hillsborough Boulevard. Their kosher butcher shop was up in Boynton Beach, about twenty miles away. They also enjoyed zipping over to the giant flea market in Pompano Beach, just four miles south, where they could look over the cut-rate handbags, housewares (Mom still a sucker for gadgets), and hardware supplies, and indulge in a rare treat, a store-bought cup of coffee. And, in fact, except for a few summertime jaunts to the beautiful ocean beach, the landmarks on their personal geography were all commercial establishments. The big shopping mall at Town Center in Boca Raton, the big box stores like Ross and Home Depot, the bargain outlets and dollar stores in the smaller shopping centers all registered on Mom and Dad's mental maps, each one known by its precise location along various interchanges of Interstate 95. Century Village was a tightly fenced, limited-access community sitting in a maximum-access landscape—family, community, and religion on one side of the fence, commerce on the other.

Shopping had become central to the Rabinowitzes in Florida. Their long-term focus on financial stability, on "getting and spending," was now confined to "spending." Dad was no longer earning an income by his work. Early on in their move to Florida, he tried to hire on as a driver of the Century Village trams, which carried residents from every corner of the complex to the clubhouse without charge (from which they could board city buses to take them to sites around the county). But when he found that steering the open-sided vehicles was too nerve-wracking, he quit. He had been earning money since early in his childhood, during the presidential administration of Warren G. Harding. Through his whole life, he defined himself as a provider and now, at age sixty-four, he was done with that.

They were probably the most frugal, the most value-conscious people on the planet. Their first home at Century Village cost just $23,500 for a two-bedroom, two-bath garden apartment, purchased for cash. They paid a monthly maintenance charge and a small fee for the Village's amenities, all together less than $250. They had an occasional meal out, or a movie afternoon, and they joined or contributed to every event sponsored by Hadassah and the American Cancer Society, but they had little interest in big-ticket celebrations. It was impossible to take them out for birthday or anniversary dinners, especially at finer restaurants—"who knows what they put into the food?" When it came to household furniture and expenses, they were adamantly negative. Once they furnished and carpeted their apartment, they felt no need to upgrade its appearance. As Beverly became more successful in her Los Angeles design business, she tried to buy appliances or ornaments for the apartment, but Dad's response was invariably the same: "We don't need that!" One of the worst arguments I ever had with my mother came when my wife and I tried to buy a replacement mattress for the convertible sofabed in the sitting room. (We were both hobbling around with back pain from trying to sleep on it.) Dad had died a few years before, but Mom had revived and deployed his entire cache of condemnations. We were bawled out all morning and then chewed out all afternoon. A dark cloud even hung over our dinnertime. You would have thought that we were marauding Polish anti-Semites on an Eastertide pogrom, the way that ninety-five-year-old woman fulminated. Did she care for the old mattress? No, but she insisted fiercely that her ideals of frugality and decorum would rule the roost in her house.

They were frugal but not stingy. By the time I was out on my own, every birthday card contained a check, usually for $25. In the 1960s, they gave Beverly a lump sum of $2,500, to balance the amount they had invested in my college education—although Beverly had never complained. Dad lent me several thousand dollars in the early days of my consulting business, just to tide me over in difficult moments.

But spending no longer connected them to a social world, as it had along Livonia or New Lots Avenues in Brooklyn, or when they used family connections to save on big-ticket purchases. (Perhaps we would have won the guest room mattress argument if we could have claimed that the shop owner was a cousin of my wife's mother's uncle's boy Seymour.) Now they shopped at chain stores owned by large corporations and were served by employees whom they hardly recognized from one shopping trip to another, often recent immigrants working for Florida's very low minimum wage. Sarah made it a point, however, to greet the staff at Publix personally whenever possible.

Mom and Dad no longer talked much about money during their retirement. They had enough, just enough. Their income came from Social Security, from the modest investments in corporate bonds that Dad had made in the 1960s, and some savings from an insurance settlement. Dad long suspected the dangerous temptations of a credit card, and even when he got a card, he paid every cent owed within the no-fee period. For the first forty-odd years of their marriage, his urgencies had ruled the roost, set the agenda for each day, given the home its color and temperament, cheery or grumpy. "Making a living" was forever preeminent, more important than keeping house, and that was always the main concern of Dave's life. Even when he was having a hard time, during the 1930s and again in the mid-1950s, the income side of the ledger outshone the expense column in significance. He had perennially handled the rudder, she the oars that kept them moving forward methodically—healthy, warm, well fed. He was by no means a tyrant, but everything bent to his will. Until these years in Florida.

Beverly and I wondered how he could survive without working. The answer was, splendidly. He had, after all, seldom taken much pleasure from his business itself. He had never taken particular pride in the job well done or the service he provided. Cash was his only real gratification, even when he was younger. When he had enough money to live, he could shed his identity as breadwinner with no regrets. Like the wartime heroes who had walked quietly away from the cockpit or the helm in Dave's favorite novels, he walked off and never looked back. After a couple of years in Florida, he learned (or Mom taught him) to stay out of her way while she organized the housework or the cooking. He was available to make the small repairs, manage the supply closet, change the batteries and light bulbs, and take care of the car. And he always kept the checkbook and paid the bills.

Food shopping remained Sarah's domain, and hence she became the commander-in-chief, Dave her loyal lieutenant. For all their frugality, they never stinted on food purchases. Mom bought the nicest cuts of meat, always kosher, the freshest piece of fish, and the tastiest fruits and vegetables in season. She never made hamburger except from steak she ground herself. They continued to save, dreading the possibility that they could become dependent on their children in a medical emergency or for long-term care. Mom never retired. The pace of her work barely slackened even as she aged. She maintained her housekeeping regimen decade after decade, getting as much pleasure as ever from cooking and requiring only half a day every other week from a cleaning woman. For a little more than seven years after Dave's death, until she passed away, she stayed on in her own apartment, grateful that she could avoid what she disparagingly called "assistant living," as if it were an inferior mode of existence. By the time of Mom's final illness, she still had enough to pay for round-the-clock care.

Without the scaffolding of work, Dave evolved into a different person. For years and years, he had not been attached to anything outside his family. He despised political talk. When Sarah's brother Isaac and his wife Luba arrived for a visit, and inevitably for a heavy dose of politics—Isaac and Luba remained attached to Soviet Communism long after almost everyone in the Soviet Union—Dave left the room. "I'm not interested." And then, in 1972, he and Mom took a trip to Israel. The highlight of the tour was Mom's reunion with a cousin who had left Wysokie Mazowieckie in the mid-1920s, as well as this cousin's children. Forty-five years of separation melted away. Stories of living in barbaric rooftop shacks in pre-independence Haifa were swapped for tales of the tenement lives of Sarah's family in Brooklyn. But the oddest effect of the trip was on Dad. He came home full of curiosity about Israel. Suddenly he started reading about labor practices, immigration laws, military vulnerabilities—anything and everything. His reading was not systematic or critical. He did not check out the nonfiction section of the local library to read analyses or historical accounts of the Palestinian conflict.

But he did become a news junkie. As soon as we returned from our shopping trip and put away the purchases, Dad retreated to the back porch room, which had louvered windows that allowed outside breezes to enter in temperate seasons. In hotter seasons, the windows closed completely, and the porch served as an additional sitting room. Here Dad did his desk work, read every line of the daily *Sun-Sentinel,* and watched his sports shows in the evening. He sternly silenced the conversation around him whenever Walter Cronkite came on the air. Equally important, he became deeply invested in causes. He'd always been a sports spectator, but now he became a fierce partisan of the Miami Heat basketball team, watching almost every game, calling out fouls on the opposing players and expressing nasty opinions about coaching mistakes. He'd never been on a tennis court in his life, but the success of Pete Sampras and Andy Roddick in tournaments suddenly assumed vital importance. And now he was an ardent Democrat, quick to label Ronald Reagan a "schmuck" at least three times every five minutes.

After lunch, Jonathan and I set out with Dad for the clubhouse to obtain a guest registration that would allow us to enter the Village more easily and to use all the recreational and entertainment facilities. Dad had to vouch for us, testifying that we were not felons and that he would, as a certified resident, be responsible for any damages we inflicted on the property. We each obtained a photo ID. That allowed us to check out the equipment for the upcoming multigenerational contests in shuffleboard and pool. As a testament to his misspent youth (or his underemployed twenties spent at the "Yeshiva" pool hall on Alabama Avenue), Dad wiped out both his son and grandson at both sports. As we left the clubhouse, we checked out the activities and classes—yoga, Yiddish language and literature, Mideast politics, lapidary, batik—and picked up the schedule of free afternoon movies. On my first trip to Century Village in 1977, I had enjoyed a chance to see Woody Allen's *Annie Hall* once again, in the company of many elderly residents. It was great fun until I realized that I was the only person laughing.

Dad pointed out the roster of stage shows offered in the evenings. For two or three dollars a seat, Mom and Dad could treat themselves to a parade of Borscht Belt veterans—Jewish comedians and Italian-American singers, mostly. Dad could laugh at some of the same jokes he had tried at Ida Schlachtman's wedding, where he had met Mom, more than half a century before. Often he had used his next phone call with me to pass along a quip by old-timers like Pat Cooper or Myron Cohen, and his mirth was augmented by knowing that it was familiar shtick. Other posters on the clubhouse wall invited residents to evenings of dancing—ballroom in the early years, but increasingly line dancing ("the stroll," "the hora") as the population of widows swelled.

Over time, Dad gradually gave up visiting the clubhouse. He had no patience for listening to other people in a class or book club and no interest in competing with possible cronies at cards or billiards. He played paddleball twice a week for many years with a batch of other *alte kakers* (old farts) at a local schoolyard, all through his eighties. And in all that time, he never shared a cup of coffee with any of them. I went with him once, just to watch. The fellows came together, they drew cards to form teams, they played, and they departed. Dad came home with no stories, no jokes, no health warnings, and no inside dope on local goings-on. His social life apart from Mom was nil. His wallet was devoid of any membership cards, other than the Century Village ID, but he had a special stash of senior discount coupons. Left to his own initiative, he would have spoken only to his family or to his television. Dave eventually found his own peace and quiet. The tumult around him dissolved, and the tumult in his head quieted.

When Dad, Jonathan, and I returned home from the clubhouse, we discovered Mom working at the dinette table. Year after year she conducted a greeting-card business on behalf of Hadassah, sending cards to celebrate grandchildren's birthdays, children's anniversaries or professional achievements, or the passing away of cousins and neighbors from up north. Each card earned a premium for Hadassah's good work in Israel. Sarah's phone rang off the hook in graduation season. Dave obligingly carried a box of cards, envelopes, and postage stamps to set up Sarah's table at every Hadassah meeting. For thirty years, she soldiered on, even as the membership rolls thinned and the phone calls grew more infrequent.

Sarah had become the couple's prime connector to the outside world. The once publicly self-effacing "greenhorn" embarrassed by her lack of an American education, the young woman who nearly broke down after her own mother's death, became a social genius at Century Village. She hunted down the folks from East New York who had moved to nearby developments in Florida, and she brought them together for coffee and chats, anything but the "early bird dinners" she disdained. It was Sarah who would invite Dave's oldest friend, Al Berlin, over for coffee or arrange for Dave to join her at a charity benefit. She introduced herself to other women, which led to their making new friends. Most shared exactly the same background, though some came from Montreal, Philadelphia, or even Buenos Aires—traces of the Eastern European Jewish Diaspora in the first third of the twentieth century. The arrival and departure of the Canadian "snowbirds," who needed to return home regularly to renew their national health insurance coverage, were the best markers of seasonal change. But there was more caution in Sarah's sociability these days. She had been badly hurt by the betrayal of her Bradford Street neighbors, abandoning the street without giving her a moment's warning.

Like their roles, their use of space had been reversed. Dave had always been the outside man, the adventurer. Now he stayed close to home most of the time. Sarah was the joiner. She was out and about every day, slowly evolving into the community sage that Shenka, her mother, had been in the shtetl and the tenement. While inclined to kindness, she also began to take on her mother's more austere character. By her eighties and nineties, diminutive Sarah became a regal presence around the Richmond swimming pool. Always nicely dressed, her face and hair made up, she sat for an hour or two in the shaded side of the pool. Around her gathered a coterie of other ladies, some in swimsuits and cover-ups and others in housedresses. After being introduced to her companions, I hovered around the outside of the group. I loved eavesdropping on their conversations. Mom lent an attentive ear to stories of disarray and divorce among the children of residents, boasts of the admission of grandchildren to Ivy League colleges, sad tales of medical misadventures in a local hospital—offering a sigh here, a warm congratulation there, and for sad stories a matching tale of *tsuris* overcome. She drew the line, firmly, at racism. No one could speak of her Haitian or Jamaican aide as a "girl," and the Yiddish slur-word for Black, *schvarzer,* was banned when she was around. More observant Jews arrived at Century Village after 2000, and many of them fell into blaming African Americans for the crime that beset New York City, the degradation of the American media, or other troubles in the United States. Sarah Rabinowitz had respected Eleanor Roosevelt and her husband. She admired Golda Meir and Shimon Peres. But she absolutely idolized Barack and Michelle Obama. Provoked by a racist comment about the Obamas, or even by some *frum* (observant) matron's complaint about Obamacare, Sarah would explode, "Who do you think you are? Here's a man educated at Columbia and Harvard, a fine person, with a lovely family . . . and you, who are you to make such comments?" The water in the Richmond pool would reach 212° Fahrenheit, and the assembled klatch would vaporize.

In a more sober vein, Sarah stood watch over the mortality of her neighbors, of her old friends, and of her cousins. She outlived almost everyone she knew from her pre-Florida life. Sociable to the end, she never replaced these close friendships. In her youth, she had spoken of people "dying," but now they were simply "also gone." She never wept for their passing, but only for their suffering. The stock of sympathy cards in her bedroom closet would dwindle, and she would have to call New York for refills.

Mom put away her Hadassah work and began to prepare our supper. There was no helping her. She had it all ready for reheating and serving. The menu flowed from her lips like the most well-practiced waiter. "Would you like soup?" "I have some steamed brussels sprouts, OK?" "Then we can have the chicken with the potatoes." "How does that sound?" I don't recall ever having actually made a choice. It was all so good. Meanwhile, I noticed that she was beginning to *bentsch licht,* to light the Friday night candles, as she did every week. She would also buy a ticket and spend an hour or so at High Holy Day services, sometimes with and sometimes without Dave. And aside from keeping kosher, separating meat and dairy dishes and utensils for the first twenty-odd years of her Florida domicile—the Shabbos candles were almost the sole remaining ritual of Sarah's Judaism.

Over dinner, Dad pressed us to acknowledge the excellence of their lives at Century Village. They were obviously so happy there, so we could not find anything less than perfect. And we said so. Dad was sensitive to Century Village's reputation as déclassé among some Jewish New Yorkers. There were many fancier and more expensive places along Florida's Gold Coast, ranging from the hotels in Palm Beach to single-family houses in Boca Raton to high-rise apartments in Fort Lauderdale, Miami, or Miami Beach. And even at Century Village, some wealthier residents came only for the winter and migrated at Passover to the homes they had retained in the North. Dave scorned all of these alternatives as wasteful pretension, evidence of moral weakness. "What have they got at (name your site) that we don't have here? You just can't beat this place!" I noticed that Dad's pride in the place became even more aggressive over time. What began in 1977 as a pleasant surprise—"it's really working out well!"—became by 1990 a smug, if defensive, satisfaction—"For us this is perfect!"—and then in his last years a profound pronunciamento—"In the whole of Florida, you wouldn't find something as good as this!" Although Dave was no longer primarily a breadwinner, he took pride in having made exactly the right decision as to how they might live well in retirement.

It was true. As a historian of American communities, I was impressed with Century Village. Since the founding of the Plymouth colony in 1620, Americans had established one utopian community, one perfect location for "God's New Israel," after another— Shaker villages, Mormon Nauvoo and Deseret, New Harmony, Oneida, and 1960s countercultural communes. Many of these "intentional communities" entangled social ideals with heterodox notions about sexuality—free love, celibacy, polygamy, polyamory. Some, like Oneida and Amana, aimed to create alternatives to capitalist industrialism. Most of the labor at Century Village—landscaping, building maintenance, caretaking—was performed by African Americans and nonwhite immigrants. Century Village had no policy on sex, so far as I could tell. But it did limit residence to those fifty-five and older, and as its population aged, the husbands tended to pass away before their wives, so widows came to predominate. Everyone chuckled, with a suggestive tone, at the story of ladies lined up outside the relatively rare apartments of widowers, pot roasts in hand. The occasional hint of sexual scandal notwithstanding, probably few purpose-built communities in the United States had ever worked so efficiently as these Florida retirement estates. Century Village was a perfect amalgam—one-third suburban gated community, one-third a low-cost Grossinger's Catskill Resort, and one-third an earnest Henry Street Settlement. The first aimed for security, the second for activity, the third for self-improvement. These places were advertised as "the Fountain of Youth," where older Americans could keep always active and ever young. Indeed, about a dozen tennis players hit the courts on every cooler morning, and one would pass an equal number of joggers in an hour's walk around the perimeter. But an even larger number enrolled in the clubhouse classes. And gossiping around the swimming pool was, in all likelihood, the most popular recreational exercise.

For Depression-era youth like Sarah and Dave, it was perfect sufficiency that the place provided—enough time, space, and stuff to live without strain. Century Village banished the scarcities that had encumbered the lives of its residents in the years before they retired—not enough money, not enough health, and disharmony with neighbors and family members. The community thus offered its denizens the chance to shed the complications of their earlier lives. Along with winter coats and checks on the car's antifreeze, they could let go of the unplanned interruptions that marked all the years of their youth and early adulthood—unpleasant news from children and neighbors, strangers appearing in their midst, and inconvenient breakdowns in the systems of traffic and commerce. Instead, health crises became the common coin of talk around the swimming pool. After a few years, almost every resident was so well-informed on hospital procedures that she could have qualified for board certification.

An emblem of this Florida life at my parents' apartment was a beautiful nineteenth-century French wall clock, ornamented with porcelain tiles for the hours, that Beverly had given Mom and Dad.

It had to be wound weekly. The chimes had been disabled so that they no longer tolled the hours, but the clock ticked away the minutes softly and accurately. Until one day, when Beverly was visiting and noticed that it had stopped. Unable to find the winding key, she took it down from the wall and looked within. The weights were gone, and in their place a nine-volt battery had been installed. Fed up with the responsibility of winding it, Dad had taken it to a local shop to have the *gedeyrem,* the *kishkes* (the guts, the innards), removed. It was now a clock that worked without its works, at least until it required a new battery. Mom and Dad's life in Florida had become a smoothly running machine. Easier. Requiring less maintenance. A well-earned peace after a lifetime of struggle and stress.

As I sat up late that night, after everyone had gone to sleep, I anxiously reflected on how much my life had diverged from that of my parents. I was frankly weary of these two days of having to learn the rules by which Mom and Dad had organized their lives—planned their meals, plotted their schedules, gathered provisions and information, and discarded what was used up. I saw the utility of every single gesture and how much it satisfied them to have devised a solution to every problem. Visiting them was, in some ways, like proceeding page by page through an instruction manual. My own life had left me strangely ill-equipped to intuit how to behave. No doubt this had much to do with the very different way I had organized my adult life. Back in Brooklyn I had left bookmarks in a dozen books I was in the "middle" of reading, sometimes for months or years. Magazines were covered with sticky notes, reminders and suggestions for future perusal. My refrigerator contained cheeses turning all shades of green and blue. A stack of letters (and later an inbox of emails) waited, sometimes forever, to be answered. If Mom and Dad occupied a place with clear boundaries, I knew that I was to be found somewhere in the middle of everything.

I loved city life. I loved walking out of my house and passing the jumble of homes and shops and offices and eateries, as well as a library and a hospital. Most of all, I loved the flow of people crossing my path from all over the world. I made a practice in my trips to Manhattan to exit the subway a stop or two before my exact destination so that I could walk a bit and see the changing city for myself. I did as little shopping as possible in supermarkets, preferring the specialty stores that sold the best fish or cheese or bagels or coffee or chocolate, closer to Shenka's and Sarah's kind of shopping in the 1930s (but at a much higher price) than to Mom's in Florida. I loved not knowing beforehand what I would find or what I would bring home. I hungered for uncertainty, for the slow process of discovery, for improvisation and misdirection.

In the 1980s, I was in the most hectic phase of creating a career: defining a distinctive professional approach to the development of new history museums in every corner of the United States, building and sustaining a new consulting practice, publishing a book about New England religious life. And I was creating a new personal life: getting divorced and remarried, being a single parent most of the year, moving to New York and joining a fine community of friends. During my days and nights in Florida, I could barely avoid thinking about all of that. I was too self-absorbed to understand then how much my parents' placid patterns of life proceeded from and represented a triumph over their own stormy pasts.

I found it impossible to explain to Mom and Dad what I actually did for a living. It sounded something like producing television shows, and that led my parents to think that the museum galleries I was designing would eventually yield pots of gold. As they would have said, they did not "know from nonprofits." On one trip to Florida, I discovered Dad reading a barely disguised novel about the behind-the-scenes shenanigans at a broadcast company like CBS, featuring lots of sex, drugs, and backstabbing. "What low-lives these people are!" Later in the same trip, he once again urged me to "get out of the museum business. Go into television."

"But," I reminded him, "you told me how disgusting the people are."

"Yeah," he fired back, "but think of the fortune they're making." For twenty-eight years, Dad and I had a regular Sunday routine. On the phone he would ask me, "So, how is the *Geschäft* (the business)?"

And I would reassure him, "just fine, going great, got a new job in Cincinnati (or Phoenix or Seattle)," and he would cluck approvingly. That was the extent of our conversation. I calculated that I thus lied to him 1,400 Sundays in a row.

But once, just once, he captured it perfectly. I talked about how we were planning to involve oral historians and local artists in creating a citywide history "museum without walls," and he injected, "I get it. You're making jewels for paupers. That makes no sense to me, but as long as you're doing what you like, that's fine." If he ever knew something of the more complicated truth, he did not want to taint our mutual affection with questions, questions, and more questions. But I had a hard time accepting his witty snap judgment as a real, if bitter, truth about my work.

Mom made it a fundamental principle never to boast to neighbors and friends, or even to reveal much, about her children or grandchildren. She reflexively averted the *ahora,* or evil eye, a rare remnant of her Polish childhood. In Yiddish folklore, to become the object of envy was to invite a curse, and so Mom often ended her sentences by murmuring *"kinehora"* ("no evil eye"). Success or failure, it's nobody's business, she announced. But this reticence also conveyed, probably unintentionally, that all the fussy details of our professional lives were less important than the basic fact: we were loved as her offspring, no matter what we accomplished in the eyes of the world. Occasionally I would see signs of pride. I discovered a picture of me with President George H. W. Bush, taken by an official photographer at the moment of our dedicating a project in Lower Manhattan in 1989, hung unframed in the sitting room. A copy of my first book, a scholarly study of New England religion, rested on the coffee table in the living room, seldom touched.

These physical reminders were unusual in Mom and Dad's Florida apartment. The furnishings could have been anyone's—a heavy breakfront, a coffee table, a dining table and four armchairs, all of a matching dark walnut; a side table with a glass case on its top, filled with pieces of cut glass and other ornaments, a comfortable sofa and side chairs of no special style, a secretary with drawers holding important papers, a painting of a seaside scene. Nothing in the room spoke of the lives of my parents. There were no souvenirs, no objects that invited questions like, "Where did you get that?" They did have one wall of family photos—mostly from weddings and bar mitzvahs—and an enlarged picture of themselves in Jerusalem, but nothing that registered the years spent in Poland or New York. You could never have guessed who lived there.

My house in Brooklyn could not have been more different. It was filled with traces of my life. I dwelled in a memory palace. I could tell a story about each book, where it had been acquired and with what (often unfulfilled) intention I had wanted to read or consult it. Many shelves and corners were filled with tchotchkes and other reminders of my travels or my projects. Almost every wall not covered with books had antique maps of places I loved—Italy, the Hebrides, Brooklyn, the South Sea islands visited by young Herman Melville. Every piece of art had been acquired in a conversation with its artist, at a time and place I could vividly recall. Above all else, I knew myself as a collector of stories. And my house was an enormous anthology of the stories of my own life.

And not just at home. I traveled around the country looking for objects that told stories, that revealed the rich complexity of human life in America, that could become the centerpieces of museum exhibitions that have widened the public's understanding of the past: a salmon-butchering machine that would replace immigrant Chinese skilled workers in the Puget Sound canneries; a Swedish-English dictionary designed to help housemaids decode the orders given by the mistresses of the great Minnesota houses in which they served; a cast-iron "pilau" pot in which West Africans could cook the rice stews they remembered from days before the Middle Passage and their enslavement in South Carolina.

In retirement, my parents had ceased investing objects with new meanings. They themselves were the only remnants of the tenement world of their youth. Full of personal history, they needed no reminders to jog their memory of what life had been like in Poland or New York. For them, as for many Americans, the Sunbelt (and most especially Florida) was a clean, well-lighted place, safe from the coercions of the past. Nor did they cultivate traces of their new lives in Florida. The only Florida-branded object in their house was a spoon rest on Mom's stove top, a souvenir of their trip in 1976 to scout out possible places to relocate. Sarah and Dave could share stories with fellow refugees from the eras of the Depression or World War II, but they didn't need to be surrounded by souvenirs of that time. When they came to Brooklyn for the first time after I moved into my townhouse, they brought along their winter coats, scarves, hats, and boots, and left them in my cellar when they went back to Florida—for safekeeping should they ever have to return for a visit in the colder months.

In a curious way, storytelling had replaced the struggles of everyday life for Dave and Sarah. Their stories, told artfully, embellished with the characterizations of long-deceased acquaintances and family members, became their most prized artifacts, the most important keepsakes in their apartment. Dave had had lots of practice as a young stage performer. He loved reminiscing about that time, working over the "material" of such stories. Mom was, as I've said, more of a moralist, attributing her unquestionable wisdom to people and places she had left behind years before. A well-told story proved that one had truly overcome the disadvantages of immigration, poverty, and the lack of opportunity for education and advancement.

On one of their trips north, we drove into Manhattan to see the work I was doing at the Lower East Side Tenement Museum and the historic Eldridge Street Synagogue. Mom and Dad reveled in the tales they could tell of life in the tenement, of selling newspapers and hiding under the seats of nickelodeons. Every anecdote about their past emphasized its distance from their present. Florida, they insisted, freed them to separate themselves from the impoverished creatures they had been. Early in their lives, during the 1930s, they had located that detachment from poverty at the movies, but only for two or three hours at a stretch. Now it was a sanctuary for the rest of their lives. It was incomprehensible to Sarah that her brothers, still living in Brooklyn, could not understand this. Each week she implored them to join her in Florida, to reunite as a trio again, to melt decades of painful struggle in the warmth of the Sunshine State.

For a few years this worried me. Would the comforts of Florida take off their edge and curtail their reflectiveness altogether? Would they want to forget who they had been? I needn't have troubled myself. The stories flowed on and on. At the last lunch of my visit with Jonathan, my father brought out a rare treat, a big bottle of beer, to accompany our chicken salad sandwiches and leftover coleslaw. As I've said, though he liked beer, he treated himself to a glass very seldom. "I thought this would make a nice send-off," he said. I went to the kitchen drawer to get something to remove the bottle cap. And in the middle kitchen drawer, near the potato-masher and the Rubbermaid spatulas, I found the old wooden-handled bottle opener, its green paint mostly worn away. I remembered it from my childhood. "Mom," I asked, "this has been here forever. Where did you get it?"

She described buying it at an outdoor pushcart market in Brooklyn a half-century before, as she was coming home from work in the Garment District. She was about seventeen or eighteen at the time. It was a present, she said, for her mother, my bubbe, on the occasion of a Shabbos dinner at the family's apartment on Williams Avenue in East New York. "She had such a hard life," Mom said of her mother. "She worked so hard."

That anecdote rested in my memory for another thirty-odd years. The green-handled bottle opener was one of the only family items to survive their early days in America. And thus, when Mom passed away, I found it in her Century Village kitchen drawers—an opener not for bottles and cans any longer, but rather for memory-stories of a long and loving life. Its last service, dear reader, was to break the seal on the stories that have filled the book you hold in your hands.

On another Friday night in Brooklyn, at another Shabbos dinner, eighty-seven years after Sarah brought the bottle opener to her mother, Lynda and I gather with two couples, close friends. This is the first time we have all met in person after the terrible pandemic year. We have been in close touch on Zoom throughout the year, but there is still plenty of news to share—book contracts, new jobs for children, school disruptions for grandchildren.

Our band of six is both more and less religiously observant than the Schwartzes who gathered in 1934. *Less,* in that we start with a toast of Prosecco, and for some a shot of Oban single-malt whisky—definitely not on the menu of the immigrant household. But also *more,* because we all full-throatedly sing the Shabbos Kiddish, ending with the prayer over the wine "Blessed are you, Adonai, Ruler of the Universe, who creates the fruit of the vine." Then we all join in the prayer over the home-baked challahs (slightly salted, recognizing the tearfulness of our world, or as a remembrance of the ancient Temple sacrifice): "Blessed are you, Adonai, Ruler of the Universe, who brings forth bread from the earth."

As the conversation proceeds, interweaving politics and art and literature with reflections on this painful year of isolation and this forthcoming year of hoped-for communion, I find myself thinking again of my mother and of my fundamental question: *What was Sarah Rabinowitz for herself?* As the youngest child in my family, I'm used to following two conversations at once—one with my companions and one in my own head. I ask myself, *What do we actually mean when we say that "God created" the wine and bread?* When Sarah was a young child in Poland, she knew where these Sabbath-eve holy foods came from—the wheat and the grapes from fields and vineyards of men named Jankowski and Barycki, the processing by Szmul the taverner and Chaim the baker. When she came to America, of course, and traded her child's local knowledge for an understanding of the commercial market, she became aware of a great and ever-increasing number of intermediaries between the produce of the terrain and the Sabbath table. As a person passionately devoted to the kitchen, she acquired in daily and weekly shopping expeditions—her eighty-year-long American education—knowledge of a web of relationships among people connecting her to the food she prepared: shopkeepers, suppliers, processors, giant agricultural producers, and all those who worked for them. Her brother Isaac had been right all along: her food consumption was irremediably influenced by capitalist profit-seeking, government oversight, and global trade policy. The shopping basket is shaped by Monsanto, General Mills, and JP Morgan Chase—not to mention the US Food and Drug Administration, the US Trade Representative, publishers of diet books, newspaper columnists, cookbook writers, advertisers, and thousands of other parties, all of whom also "create the wine and the bread." And now we know that a changing climate is enormously important, for which everyone and no one is singularly responsible. Even if her day was consumed by daily tasks, Sarah knew that she was enmeshed in this larger world.

As I've said, the elderly Sarah would occasionally ruminate on the wondrous complexity of the world and ponder what role divinity played in its creation and order. Her God was not an Enlightenment clockmaker, who set the world on automatic pilot and went away. Nor was the Divine One her personal problem solver. She never asked, "What Would Moses Do?" As to the Jewish law, the *halacha*, she could take it or leave it, according to the moment. Always skeptical of rabbis, she was not easily swayed by the established authorities in any domain.

But one thing was certain about my mother, and it came to me as our evening's conversation was drawing to a close. After our long separation, my friends and I all dearly wanted to say the *shehecheyanu* prayer, recited at the beginning of every holiday and many important occasions, including seeing a friend for the first time in a month (or more). "Blessed are you, Adonai, Ruler of the Universe, who has granted us life, sustained us, and allowed us to arrive at this time." It is the prayer of belonging and renewal. Even when the teachings of the holy Jewish books failed Sarah, when the ethics of the Fathers seemed too remote, when nothing quite fit correctly, she was nevertheless deeply loyal and attached to "her people." She departed this life as she had entered it, as a Jew. Everything flowed from that.

FURTHER READING

ACKNOWLEDGMENTS

Further Reading

Note: Although stories retrieved from my memory and that of other family members provide most of the historical evidence recounted in this book, I have learned *a lot* by comparing and contextualizing my family's stories with those presented by other scholars, observers, and memoirists. Here are some suggestions for pursuing these subjects further.

On Materiality and Work

In recent years, many historians and other students of culture have expanded their gaze beyond written documents, employing a wide variety of methods to explore the role of objects and spaces as containers and expressions of historical meaning. Among the most provocative are Glenn Adamson, *Fewer, Better Things: The Hidden Wisdom of Objects* (New York, 2018); Laura Arnold Leibman, *The Art of the Jewish Family: A History of Women in Early New York in Five Objects* (New York, 2020); David Seamon and Robert Mugerauer, eds., *Dwelling, Place and Environment: Towards a Phenomenology of Person and World* (Dordrecht, 1985); and Laurel Thatcher Ulrich et al., *Tangible Things: Making History through Objects* (New York, 2015). My own approach is described most fully in Richard Rabinowitz, "A Reader's Reflections," in *Curating America: Journeys through the Storyscapes of the American Past* (Chapel Hill, NC, 2016), 337–360.

I have insisted on the complexity of thinking behind the day-to-day labors of my family members. Other explorations of the mental exercise of the manual worker include Matthew B. Crawford, *Shop Class as Soulcraft: An Inquiry into the Value of Work* (New York, 2009); and Mike Rose, *The Mind at Work: Valuing the Intelligence of the American Worker* (New York, 2004).

On the history of specific objects, I've consulted Andrew S. Dolkart, *Biography of a Tenement House in New York City: An Architectural History of 97 Orchard Street,* 2nd ed., Center for American Places, Chicago (Charlottesville, VA, 2012); Carol Herselle Krinsky, *Rockefeller Center* (New York, 1978); Charles Lockwood, *Bricks and Brownstones: The New York Rowhouse, 1783–1929* (New York, 1972); Anne Cooper Funderburg, *Chocolate, Strawberry, and Vanilla: A History of American Ice Cream* (Bowling Green, OH, 1995); Geoffrey Jones, *Beauty Imagined: A History of the Global Beauty Industry* (Oxford, 2010); Daniel Okrent, *Great Fortune: the Epic of Rockefeller Center* (New York, 2003); James M. Rock and Brian W. Peckham, "Recession, Depression, and War: The Wisconsin Aluminum Cookware Industry, 1920–1941," *Wisconsin Magazine of History* 73 (1990), 202–233.

Life in the Shtetl

Two masterly online databases detail Jewish history in Poland before the Holocaust: *The YIVO Encyclopedia of Jews in Eastern Europe* (http://www.yivoencyclopedia.org/default.aspx); and Polin Museum of the History of Polish Jews, *Virtual Shtetl,* s.v. "Wysokie Mazowieckie" (http://www.sztetl.org.pl/en/city/wysokie-mazowieckie/).

The best source on the history of the Jews of Wysokie Mazowieckie is entitled *Sefer Zikaron: The Memorial Book of Wysokie Mazowiecki,* ed. I. Rubin, originally published in Tel Aviv in 1975, and now available at http://zchor.org/wysokie/zikaron.htm.

There are hundreds of such memorial books. In the United States, the most important repository is the YIVO Institute for Jewish Research, housed in the Center for Jewish History in Manhattan. Among histories of particular *shtetln,* two of the finest are Theo Richmond, *Konin: A Quest* (London, 1995); and Eva Hoffman, *Shtetl: The Life and Death of a Small Town and the World of Polish Jews* (Boston, 1997). Diane K. Roskies and David G. Roskies, *The Shtetl Book: An Introduction to East European Jewish Life and Lore,* 2nd ed. (New York, 1979) is full of rich material. On the recent historiography of Jewish life in pre-Holocaust Poland, see Steven Katz, ed., *The Shtetl: New Evaluations* (New York, 2007).

In addition to her work as a curator and filmmaker, the publications of Barbara Kirshenblatt-Gimblett have been critical for my research. See "Objects of

Memory: Material Culture as Life Review," in *Folk Groups and Folklore Genres: A Reader,* ed. Elliott Oring (Logan, UT, 1989), 329–338, and "Food and Drink" in the *YIVO Encyclopedia.* Kirshenblatt-Gimblett, with her father, Mayer Kirshenblatt, produced an exhibition and catalog of his paintings from memory of growing up in a shtetl much like my mother's; see *They Called Me Mayer July: Painted Memories of a Jewish Childhood in Poland Before the Holocaust* (Berkeley, CA, 2007).

Polish History

My account of the Polish context of Sarah's childhood starts with Ezra Mendelsohn, *The Jews of East Central Europe Between the World Wars* (Bloomington, IN, 1983). On the social history, see Georges Castillan, "Remarks on the Social Structure of the Jewish Community in Poland Between the Two World Wars," in *Jews and Non-Jews in Eastern Europe,* ed. Bela Vargo and George L. Mosse (New York, 1974), 187–201; and David Engel, "What's in a Pogrom? European Jews in the Age of Violence," in *Anti-Jewish Violence: Rethinking the Pogrom in East European History,* ed. J. Dekel-Chan et al. (Bloomington, IN, 2011), 19–37.

World War I in Eastern Europe is rendered in *The Forgotten Front: The Eastern Theater of World War I, 1914–1915,* ed. Gerhard P. Gross (Lexington, KY, 2018); and Mark Levene, "Frontiers of Genocide: Jews in the Eastern War Zones, 1914–1920 and 1941," in *Minorities in Wartime: National and Racial Groupings in Europe, North America and Australia during the Two World Wars,* ed. Panikos Panayi (Oxford, 1993), 83–117.

On the pandemic of 1918–19, I depended on Marek L. Grabowski et al., "The Lethal Spanish Influenza Pandemic in Poland," *Medical Science Monitor* 23 (2017): 4880–4884, at https://www.ncbi.nlm.nih.gov/pmc/articles/PMC5649514/.

On the post–Great War conflicts, see Piotr S. Wandycz, *Soviet-Polish Relations, 1917–1921* (Cambridge, MA, 1969); Norman Davies, *White Eagle, Red Star: The Polish Soviet War, 1919–20* (London, 1972); Jeffrey Veidlinger, *In the Midst of Civilized Europe: The Pogroms of 1918–1921 and the Onset of the Holocaust* (New York, 2021); Richard M. Watt, *Bitter Glory: Poland and Its Fate, 1918–1939* (New York: Simon and Schuster, 1979).

My rendering of Polish life in this period is influenced by two works of reportage and fiction: Isaac Babel's *Red Cavalry,* trans. Peter Constantine (1926; New York, 2003); and Vasily Grossman, "In the Town of Berdichev," in *The Road,* trans. and ed. Robert Chandler (New York, 2010).

Eastern European Jews in America

The literature on this subject is enormous. A small sampling would include: Charlotte Baum, Paula Hyman, and Sonya Michel, *The Jewish Woman in America* (New York, 1975); Stephan F. Brumberg, *Going to America, Going to School: The Jewish Immigrant Public School Encounter in Turn-of-the-Century New York City* (New York, 1986); Neil M. Cowan and Ruth Schwartz Cowan, *Our Parents' Lives: The Americanization of Eastern European Jews* (New York, 1989); Hasia R. Diner, *Roads Taken: The Great Jewish Migrations to the New World and the Peddlers Who Forged the Way* (New Haven, 2015); Susan A. Glenn, *Daughters of the Shtetl: Life and Labor in the Immigrant Generation* (Ithaca, NY, 1990); Blu Greenberg, *How to Run a Traditional Jewish Household* (New York, 1983); Jeffrey S. Gurock, *Jews in Gotham: New York Jews in a Changing City, 1920–2010* (New York, 2012); Gurock, "The Orthodox Synagogue," in *The American Synagogue: A Sanctuary Transformed,* ed. Jack Wertheimer (Cambridge, MA, 1987), 37–84.

Jenna Weissman Joselit, *A Perfect Fit: Clothes, Character, and the Promise of America* (New York, 2002); Joselit, *The Wonders of America: Reinventing Jewish Culture, 1880–1950* (New York, 2002); Joselit and Susan L. Braunstein, eds., *Getting Comfortable in New York: The American Jewish Home, 1880–1950* (New York, 1990).

Eli Lederhendler, *New York Jews and the Decline of Urban Ethnicity, 1950–1970* (Syracuse, NY, 2001); Tony Michels, *A Fire in Their Hearts: Yiddish Socialists in New York* (Cambridge, MA, 2005); Deborah Dash Moore, *At Home in America: Second Generation Jews in New York* (New York, 1981); Annie Polland and Daniel Soyer, *Emerging Metropolis: New York Jews in the Age of Immigration, 1840–1920* (New York, 2012); Riv-Ellen Prell, *Fighting to Become Americans: Jews, Gender, and the Anxiety of Assimilation* (Boston, 1999); Ellen M. Umansky, "Finding God: Women in the Jewish Tradition," *CrossCurrents* 41 (Winter 1991–92): 521–537; Beth S. Wenger, *New York Jews and the Great Depression: Uncertain Promise* (New Haven, 1996); Sydney Stahl Weinberg, *The World of Our Mothers: The Lives of Jewish Immigrant Women* (Chapel Hill, NC, 1988); Weinberg, "Longing to Learn: The Education of Jewish Immigrant Women in New York City, 1900–1934," *Journal of American Ethnic History* 8 (Spring 1989): 108–126.

Barbara Myerhoff, *Number Our Days* (New York, 1978), deserves special notice as a brilliant ethnography of American Jews and Judaism. Other studies of "lived religion" among non-Jews in the United States include David D. Hall, ed., *Lived Religion in America: Toward a History of Practice* (Princeton, 1997); Robert M. Orsi, *The Madonna of 115th Street: Faith and Community in Italian*

Harlem, 1850–1950 (New Haven, 1985); and Richard Rabinowitz, *The Spiritual Self in Everyday Life: The Transformation of Personal Religious Experience in Nineteenth-Century New England* (Boston, 1989).

The Lower East Side

Memory also has a history. The Lower East Side of Manhattan is itself a historical artifact explored in the following works: Hasia R. Diner, *Lower East Side Memories: A Jewish Place in America* (Princeton, 2000); Diner, Jeffrey Shandler, and Beth S. Wenger, eds., *Remembering the Lower East Side: American Jewish Reflections* (Bloomington, IN, 2000); Irving Howe, *World of Our Fathers* (New York, 1976); Suzanne R. Wasserman, "The Good Old Days of Poverty: The Battle over the Fate of New York City's Lower East Side During the Depression" (PhD diss., New York University, 1990); Moses Rischin, *The Promised City: New York's Jews, 1870–1914* (Cambridge, MA, 1977).

Studies of Assimilation

Immigrant, ethnic, assimilation, adaptation—these words change their meanings over time. I found the following helpful: Russell A. Kazal, "Revisiting Assimilation: The Rise, Fall, and Reappraisal of a Concept in American Ethnic History," *American Historical Review* 100 (April 1995): 437–471; Susan Wierzbicki, *Beyond the Immigrant Enclave: Network Change and Assimilation* (New York, 2004); William L. Yancey, Eugene P. Erickson, and Richard N. Juliani, "Emergent Ethnicity: A Review with Reformulation," *American Sociological Review* 41 (June 1976): 391–403.

Mothers and Daughters

The landmark study is Nancy Chodorow, *The Reproduction of Mothering: Psychoanalysis and the Sociology of Gender* (Berkeley, 1978); also see Jane Flax, "Conflict between Nurturance and Autonomy," *Feminist Studies* 4, no. 1 (Feb. 1978): 171–189; Flax, "Mother-Daughter Relationships," in *The Future of Difference,* ed. Hester Eisenstein and Alice Jardine (Boston, 1980); Randy D. McBee, *Dance Hall Days: Intimacy and Leisure among Working-Class Immigrants in the United States* (New York, 2000); and Mudita Rastogi and Karen S. Wampler, "Adult Daughters' Perceptions of the Mother-Daughter Relationship: A Cross-Cultural Comparison," *Family Relations* 48 (July 1999): 327–336.

Masculinity

George E. Vaillant's pioneering psychiatric scholarship has helped illuminate masculine development for me. See these works: *Adaptation to Life* (Boston, 1977); *The Wisdom of the Ego* (Cambridge, MA, 1993); and "Ego Mechanisms of Defense and Personality," *Journal of Abnormal Psychology* 103, no. 1 (1994): 44–50. Other important studies include Harry Brod, ed., *A Mensch Among Men: Explorations in Jewish Masculinity* (Freedom, CA, 1988); and Sarah Imhoff, *Masculinity and the Making of American Judaism* (Bloomington, IN, 2017).

On boys in popular culture, see Ryan K. Anderson, *Frank Merriwell and the Fiction of All-American Boyhood: The Progressive Era Creation of the Schoolboy Sports Story* (Fayetteville, AR, 2015).

Personal and Family Narratives

Among the many examples, I have found most useful the following: Billy Crystal, *700 Sundays* (electronic resource, New York, 2005); Samuel G. Freedman, *Who She Was: My Search for My Mother's Life* (New York, 2005); Chaim Grade, *My Mother's Sabbath Days: A Memoir,* trans. Channa Kleinerman Goldstein and Inna Hecker Grade (New York, 1986); Irving Howe, *A Margin of Hope: An Intellectual Autobiography* (San Diego, 1982); Alfred Kazin, *A Walker in the City* (New York, 1951); David Laskin, *The Family: Three Journeys into the Heart of the Twentieth Century* (New York, 2013); Roger Rosenblatt, *The Boy Detective: A New York Childhood* (New York, 2013); Richard White, *Remembering Ahanagran: Storytelling in a Family's Past* (New York, 1998).

Memory and Narrative

The diverse writings of Jerome Bruner have long been guideposts for my thinking about learning, memory, and storytelling. For this project, I have treasured his contribution, "The Remembered Self," in *The Remembering Self: Construction and Accuracy in the Self-Narrative,* ed. Ulric Neisser and Robyn Fivush (Cambridge, England, 1994), 41–54; Patricia Hampl and Elaine Tyler May, eds., *Tell Me True: Memoir, History, and Writing a Life* (St. Paul, MN, 2009); Steven Hoelscher and Derek H. Alderman, "Memory and Place: Geographies of a Critical Relationship," *Social & Cultural Geography* 5 (Sept. 2004): 347–355; Alan Parry and Robert E. Doan, *Story Re-Visions: Narrative Therapy in the Postmodern World* (New York, 1994); William Zinsser, ed., *Inventing the Truth: The Art and Craft of Memoir* (Boston, 1998).

Further Reading

Fiction and Film

Some of the most probing assessments of Jewish family life in the early and middle twentieth century are in works of fiction. Examples include Sholem Asch, *The Mother,* trans. Nathan Ausübel (1930; rpt. New York, 1970); Will Eisner, *A Contract with God and Other Tenement Stories* (New York, 2006); Mike Gold, *Jews Without Money* (New York, 1930); Gerald Green, *The Last Angry Man* (New York, 1956); *The Last Angry Man,* dir. Daniel Mann (Columbia Pictures, 1959), film; Bernard Malamud, *The Assistant,* "The Grocery Store," and "The Magic Barrel," in *Novels and Stories of the 1940s and 50s* (New York, 2013); Isaac Rosenfeld, *Passage from Home* (New York, 1946); and Jo Sinclair, *Wasteland* (1946; rpt. Philadelphia, 1987).

Typical of the Frank Merriwell stories is Gilbert Patten (Burt L. Standish, pseud.), "Frank Merriwell's Life Struggle; or, A Bluff That Did Not Work," *Tip Top Weekly: An Ideal Publication for the American Youth,* no. 252 (New York, February 9, 1901).

New York City History

Tyler Anbinder, *City of Dreams: The 400-Year Epic History of Immigrant New York* (Boston, 2016); Nicholas Dagen Bloom and Matthew Gordon Lasner, eds., *Affordable Housing in New York: The People, Places, and Policies That Transformed a City* (Princeton, 2016); Amanda Dargan and Steven Zeitlin, *City Play* (New Brunswick, NJ, 1990); Joshua B. Freeman, *Working-Class New York: Life and Labor Since World War II* (New York, 2000); Thomas Kessner, *Fiorello H. La Guardia and the Making of Modern New York* (New York, 1989).

David Nasaw, *Children of the City: At Work and At Play* (Garden City, NY, 1985); Nasaw, *Going Out: The Rise and Fall of Public Amusements* (New York, 1993); Robert Parmet, *The Master of Seventh Avenue: David Dubinsky and the American Labor Movement* (New York, 2005); Richard Plunz, *A History of Housing in New York City* (New York, 1990); Luc Sante, *Low Life: Lures and Snares of Old New York* (New York, 1991); David Ward and Olivier Zunz, eds., *The Landscape of Modernity: Essays on New York City, 1900–1940* (New York, 1992).

Brooklyn and East New York

The diversity of East New York history in the twentieth century is best explored in the East New York Oral History Project, compiled by Sarita Daftary-Steel. Available at https://oralhistory.brooklynhistory.org/collections/sarita

-daftary-steel-collection-of-east-new-york-oral-histories/. My own oral history is included in this series.

Other valuable works include Carole Bell Ford, *The Girls: Jewish Women of Brownsville, Brooklyn, 1940–1995* (Albany, NY, 2000); Samuel G. Freedman, *Upon This Rock: The Miracles of a Black Church* (New York, 1993); Alter F. Landesman, *Brownsville: The Birth, Development and Passing of a Jewish Community in New York,* 2nd ed. (New York, 1971); Wendell Pritchett, *Brownsville, Brooklyn: Blacks, Jews, and the Changing Face of the Ghetto* (Chicago, 2002); Jonathan Rieder, *Canarsie: Jews and Italians of Brooklyn against Liberalism* (Cambridge, MA, 1985); Gerald Sorin, *The Nurturing Neighborhood: The Brownsville Boys Club and Jewish Community in Urban America, 1940–1990* (New York, 1990); Walter Thabit, *How East New York Became a Ghetto* (New York, 2003); and Craig Steven Wilder, *A Covenant with Color: Race and Social Power in Brooklyn* (New York, 2000).

World War II in New York City

These two studies provided hard-to-find data on this subject: John R. Stobo, "The BNY [Brooklyn Navy Yard] in the Interwar Period: Labor History" (2004–05), http://www.columbia.edu/~jrs9/BNY-Hist-Prep-War-3.html# Unclassified; http://www.columbia.edu/~jrs9/BNY-Hist-Prep-War-4.html# Unclassified; "An Introduction to the Labor History of Navy Yards" (2005–08), http://www.columbia.edu/~jrs9/Navy-Yard-views.html; Carla J. Dubose-Simons, "The 'Silent Arrival': The Second Wave of the Great Migration and Its Effects on Black New York, 1940–1950" (PhD diss., City University of New York, 2013).

Social History and Consumer Culture after World War II

Increasingly, the America to which members of my family assimilated was a consumer society rather than a political one. The lineaments of that culture are described in these works: Lizabeth Cohen, "The Class Experience of Mass Consumption: Workers as Consumers in Interwar America," in *The Power of Culture: Critical Essays in American History,* ed. Richard Wightman Fox and T. J. Jackson Lears (Chicago, 1993), 135–160; Cohen, *A Consumers' Republic: The Politics of Mass Consumption in Postwar America* (New York, 2003); Glen H. Elder, Jr., *Children of the Great Depression: Social Change in Life Experience,* 25th Anniversary edition (Boulder, CO, 1999); Stuart Ewen, *Captains of Conscious-*

ness: Advertising and the Social Roots of the Consumer Culture (New York, 1976);
Neil Harris, "The Drama of Consumer Desire," in *Yankee Enterprise: The Rise
of the American System of Manufactures,* ed. Otto Mayr and Robert C. Post (Washington, DC, 1981), 189–216.

Daniel Horowitz, *The Morality of Spending: Attitudes Toward the Consumer Society in America, 1875–1940* (Baltimore, 1985); Grant McCracken, *Culture and Consumption: New Approaches to the Character of Consumer Goods and Activities* (Bloomington, IN, 1988); Ulrike Malmendier and Stefan Nagel, "Depression Babies: Do Macroeconomic Experiences Affect Risk-Taking?" (August 2007), http://www.econ.yale.edu/~shiller/behmacro/2007-11/malmendier.pdf; Roland Marchand, *Advertising the American Dream: Making Way for Modernity, 1920–1940* (Berkeley, 1985); Elaine Tyler May, *Homeward Bound: American Families in the Cold War Era* (New York: Basic Books, 1988); Richard Rothstein, *The Color of Law: A Forgotten History of How Our Government Segregated America* (New York, 2017); Susan Strasser, *Never Done: A History of American Housework* (New York, 1982); Frank Trentmann, *Empire of Things: How We Became a World of Consumers, from the Fifteenth Century to the Twenty-First* (New York, 2006).

Domestic Space, Kitchen Equipment, Culinary Practices

Primary Sources

Two periodicals were essential to my investigation: *Forward,* newspaper, New York (1897–1979), https://www.nli.org.il/en/newspapers/frw; *House Furnishing Journal,* vols. 1–12, 14–16 (1916–30), New York Public Library.

Other sources include George Filipetti, *The Wholesale Markets in New York and Its Environs: Present Trends and Probable Future Developments* (New York, 1925); Mabel Hyde Kittredge, *Housekeeping Notes: How to Furnish and Keep House in a Tenement Flat* (Boston, 1911); and United States Bureau of the Census, *Fifteenth Census of the United States: Census of Distribution, Retail Distribution. Retail Chains* (Washington, DC, 1933).

The Edlund bottle opener was perhaps included in an exhibition at the Museum of Modern Art. See the master checklist of Exhibition 80: "Useful Household Objects under $5.00" (Sept. 28–Oct. 28, 1938), ms., https://www.moma.org/calendar/exhibitions/2745. Succeeding exhibitions of this genre, 1939–42, are also available on the MOMA website.

Further Reading

Secondary Works

Sarah Archer, *The Midcentury Kitchen: America's Favorite Room: From Workspace to Dreamscape, 1940s–1970s* (New York, 2019); Ruth Schwartz Cowan, *More Work for Mother: The Ironies of Household Technology from the Open Hearth to the Microwave* (New York, 1983); Hasia R. Diner, *Hungering for America: Italian, Irish, and Jewish Foodways in the Age of Migration* (Cambridge, MA, 2001); June Freeman, *The Making of the Modern Kitchen: A Cultural History* (Oxford, 2004); Linda Campbell Franklin, *From Hearth to Cookstove: America in the Kitchen: An American Domestic History of Gadgets and Utensils Made or Used in America from 1700 to 1930. A Guide for Collectors,* 2nd ed. (Orlando, FL, 1978).

Barbara Kirschenblatt-Gimblett, "Making Sense of Food in Performance: The Table and the Stage," in *The Senses in Performance,* ed. Sally Banes and Andre Lepecki (New York, 2007), 71–90; Alan Kraut, "The Butcher, the Baker," *Journal of American Culture* 6 (1983): 71–83; Kraut, "Ethnic Foodways," *Journal of American Culture* 2 (1979): 409–420; Harvey A. Levenstein, *Revolution at the Table: The Transformation of the American Diet* (New York, 1988); Levenstein, *Paradox of Plenty: A Social History of Eating in Modern America* (Berkeley, 2003); Earl Lifshey, *The Housewares Story: A History of the American Housewares Industry* (Chicago, 1973); Shelley Nickles, "'Preserving Women': Refrigerator Design as Social Process in the 1930s," *Technology and Culture* 43 (2002): 693–727; Ronald C. Tobey, *Technology as Freedom: The New Deal and the Electrical Modernization of the American Home* (Berkeley, 1996); Kathleen Leonard Turner, *How the Other Half Ate: A History of Working-Class Meals at the Turn of the Century* (Berkeley, 2014); Jane Ziegelman, *97 Orchard: An Edible History of Five Immigrant Families in One New York Tenement* (New York, 2010).

Documenting and Contextualizing My Family's Life

I have explored the Rabinowitzes and the Schwartzes through all the rabbit-holes of Ancestry.com and discovered excellent documentation.

There is much useful information in the Brooklyn Residential "white page" and Classified "yellow page" directories for the New York Telephone Company, available through the Brooklyn Public Library, for example, https://archive.org/details/brooklynnewyorkc1941newy. The New York Public Library has "reverse" Brooklyn telephone directories (listed by address) for several years, on microfilm.

Further Reading

The voyages of my family members as immigrants in the 1920s are beautifully illustrated in a catalogue for an exhibition in Antwerp: Red Star Line Museum, *Red Star Line, 1873–1934* (Antwerp, Belgium, 2013).

I was aided in understanding my father's economic niche by James C. Scott, "Two Cheers for the Petty Bourgeoisie," in *Two Cheers for Anarchism: Six Easy Pieces on Autonomy, Dignity, and Meaningful Work and Play* (Princeton, 2012), 84–100.

Acknowledgments

One doesn't begin a family history. We are born into it. It's hard to know when this book project began. As I add the final details, I'm sure I don't know where it ends.

The book emerged out of wonderful conversations with the *chaverim* in our Park Slope Second Shabbat group, including Lisa Altshuler, David Blight, Jane Dorlester, Miriam and David Fleischmann, Leon Goldstein, Aron Halberstam, Florence Hutner, Adina Kalet, Neil Kuttner, Ardele Lister, David and Tori Rosen, Mark Schwartz, Alvin and Deena Steinfeld, and Helen Zelon, and over coffees and dinners with friends like Edward Ball, Ian Callaghan, Charlie Cannon, Ruth Cowan, Hasia Diner, David and Christine Jenkins Gauthier, Philip Gura, the late Lois Horton, Cynthia and Sandy Levinson, Leonard Majzlin, Andrea Most, Meg Ostrum, and Holly Sidford.

My probes of family relationships and personal development benefited greatly from conversations with several professional psychologists, especially Barbara George, Dr. Stephen Green, the late Dr. Sherman Pazner, and Deena Steinfeld.

Daniel Soyer, Samuel Norich, and Anita Norich helped with translations from Yiddish. Andrew Gustafson, Andrew Dolkart, and Ron Shiffman assisted my understanding of New York's urban development.

I was heartened, occasionally chastened, and saved from many blunders by the careful readings of the evolving manuscript by Rick Beard, Avi Decter, Richard Franke, Roberta Brandes Gratz, Stephen Green, Leonard Majzlin, Suzi Moore, Eric Rabkin, David Rosen, Lawrence Schwartz, Richard White, Allan Winkler, and Helen Zelon.

Richard Hoyen, who provided illustrations for this book, as well as the map of "Sarah's Brooklyn," is the visualizing genius every writer needs. His intuitive grasp of the dimensionality of my ideas is their first and best test. I cannot imagine writing a book without him.

Malcolm Swanston of Axiom Maps designed the map of "Sarah's Poland."

In 2016, Dale and Ted Rosengarten kindly included me on their teaching tour of Holocaust sites in Ukraine, Poland, and Germany— along with twenty-two lively undergraduates. Dale accompanied me on a visit to Wysokie Mazowieckie, where my grandparents married and my mother was born. I am indebted to Dale and Ted for this companionship.

I received valuable comments about an early version of this book at a 2018 meeting of the Writing History Seminar in New York City. Nancy Beiles arranged a talk about kitchen implements as clues to family history at the Museum at Eldridge Street, also in 2018.

Thanks to William Kelly, Melanie Locay, and their staff members at the 42nd Street Library of the New York Public Library, I've enjoyed the privilege of a seat in the Wertheim research study. Since I first sneaked into the library as a high school junior in 1960, this has been my truest home in my hometown.

The members of my extended family, blessedly, treated this as a sort of reunion, a testament to a beloved aunt and grandmother.

I'm grateful to my cousins Jeanne Schwartz, Carl Schwartz, Jeffrey Schwartz, Lawrence Schwartz, and Bari Roberts Harris. My niece, Ilene Weingard, devoted a career's worth of expertise to painstakingly restore our family photos. My son Jonathan Rabinowitz remembered a lot about his grandparents that I never knew. And, of course, every page of this book is enriched by the amazing memory of my sister, Beverly Haas, who lived this narrative alongside me. We never have had so much fun and shared so many tears. I highly recommend working together on the creation of a family narrative as the remedy for all outstanding family issues.

At a critical moment, the enthusiasm of my agent, Christopher Rogers, carried me through the middle innings of this contest with the past. Equally important, the literary companionship of my editor at Harvard University Press, Kathleen McDermott, has perfectly performed the role of the late-innings closer. I've loved my professional collaboration with the Press staff, including Kate Brick, Tim Jones, Annamarie McMahon Why, and Kimberly Giambattisto of Westchester Publishing Services, in readying this book for print. The anonymous readers recruited by the Press made many useful suggestions and a couple of important corrections.

A special thanks is due Sherry Kafka Wagner, the most brilliant storyteller I have ever known, who has inspired me to plumb my family stories since we started staying up late swapping tales fifty years ago.

Lynda B. Kaplan, my wife, has been an essential partner in every aspect of this project. Over the years, she witnessed and remembered much that went right past me. A keen student of drama, she helped me distinguish the revealing moments in my story from the tide of ordinary events around it. Always encouraging though careful in her praise, she's listened to every word of this book read aloud, at least a dozen times, and has been my best guide for what will make most sense to its readers. Lynda's loving bond with her own mother, who passed away during the writing of this book, confirmed for me the special love between mothers and daughters that I have tried to evoke here. The memory of Betty Kaplan is a blessing for us.